# THIS FISH IS FOWL

AMERICAN LIVES    Series editor: Tobias Wolff

# THIS FISH

# IS FOWL

## ESSAYS OF BEING

# XU XI

UNIVERSITY OF NEBRASKA PRESS    LINCOLN AND LONDON

Acknowledgments for previously published
material appear on pages xi–xii, which constitute
an extension of the copyright page.

"I Enjoy Being a Girl" copyright © 1958 by Richard
Rodgers and Oscar Hammerstein II. Copyright renewed.
Williamson Music Co. owner of publication and allied
rights throughout the world. International copyright
secured. All rights reserved. Used by permission.

Publication of this volume was made possible
in part by the generous support of the H. Lee
and Carol Gendler Charitable Fund.

Library of Congress Control Number: 2018035066

Set in Garamond Premier by E. Cuddy.
Designed by N. Putens.

for Agnes Lam

# CONTENTS

# ILLUSTRATIONS

## ACKNOWLEDGMENTS

As one who came belatedly to the writing of literary nonfiction, I would like to acknowledge two writers who have been most influential in my appreciation of and development as a writer in this genre, Robin Hemley and Sue William Silverman. Their work served as models for my earliest attempts at the personal essay, and for their support, conversation, encouragement and friendship over the years, I will be forever grateful.

Earlier versions of these essays were published as follows:

"To Be American": *Fourth Genre* 13, no. 1 (Spring 2011).

"Why I Stopped Being Chinese": *The Iowa Review* 45, no. 1 (Spring 2015), http://www.iowareview.org/issue/volume-45-issue-1-spring-2015.

"BG: The Significant Years": *Hotel Amerika* 8, no. 2 (Spring 2010); *The Near and the Far: New Stories from the Asia-Pacific Region*, ed. David Carlin and Francesca Rendle-Short (Melbourne: Scribe, 2016) (republication).

"Default Home": *Platte Valley Review* 32, no. 1 (Fall 2011).

"Letter from America": *Muse*, May 2009.

"Winter Moon": *Still* (responses to the photographs by Roelof Bakker), ed. Nicholas Royle and Ros Sales (London: Negative Press, 2012).

"The Summers of My Discontent": *Far Eastern Economic Review*, "Authors' Corner," October 7, 2009, http://www.feer.com/authors-corner/2009/october53/The-Summer-of-My-Discontent.

"The Crying City": *Bellingham Review*, Spring 2016.

"Maternity Leave": *Wasafiri*, no. 61 (March 2010).

"My Mother's Story: The Fiction and Fact": *Ploughshares* 38, nos. 2–3 (Fall 2012).

"Precarious Precision": *Toad Suck Review*, no. 3 (January–February 2013).

"Journeys through Past Times: A Norwich Narrative": *The Norwich Commissions* (Worlds 2011 conference publication), Fall 2011.

"Home Base": *Kweli Journal*, December 22, 2014, http://www.kwelijournal .org/prose/2014/12/22/home-base-by-xu-xi.

"And Then, Filial Time": *Asian American Literary Review* 6, no. 1 (Spring 2015), http://aalr.binghamton.edu/spring-2015-trading-futures-toc/.

"Off Season with Snake": *Your Impossible Voice*, no. 7 (Spring 2015), http:// www.yourimpossiblevoice.com/off-season-with-snake/.

"The English of My Story": *Lake Effect* 18 (Spring 2015); selected for the notable essays and literary nonfiction list in *The Best American Essays 2016*, ed. Jonathan Franzen and Robert Atwan (Boston: Houghton Mifflin Harcourt, 2016).

"Ambition Game": *Arts and Letters*, no. 26 (Spring 2012).

"The Book That Saved My Writing Life": *First City*, June 2009.

"This Door Is Close": *First Things First*, The Script Road—Macau Literary Festival Series (Macau: PraiaGrande, 2013) (also in Chinese translation).

THIS FISH IS FOWL

# ON BEING

# TO BE AMERICAN

To make a prairie, it takes a clover and one bee,
One clover, and a bee.
And revery.
The revery alone will do,
If bees are few.

EMILY DICKINSON (1755)

To be American, you must take yourself seriously. Very, very seriously. I did not understand this when I first set foot on these here shores. It was hard to hear "these here" seriously, although that is, I would eventually discover, serious diction if uttered unsmilingly. So I came, listened, and departed three years later, at the not-so-tender age of twenty, having absorbed a tiny bit of America: Dickinson, for instance, who was serious and whom I liked despite her occasional frivolity, as when she fluttered over feathers or prairies and bees. Must I care about prairies and inter-species copulation, this latter act requiring a ridiculous position, at least according to one American? Dickinson, unlike Whitman, who not only took himself seriously but expected everyone else to do likewise, was not concerned about serious life because what mattered to her was death.

*See-RYE-ous*, says my friend Jenny in syllabic Chinglish (this here is Chinese English to you, my American friend). Jenny arrived in the middle West, got her degree, and fled, horrified, never to return except for brief forays to Manhattan to eat-drink-shop on Fifth Avenue, which is at least fun if not serious. In Hong Kong Jenny surrounds herself with drinking friends like me who have some acquaintance with America and who appreciate that *see-RYE-ous* can be the correct intonation of a word that translates as "stern weight"—*yihm juhng-chung*—if you elide the tone, and if you don't take the business of translating Cantonese into English seriously, that is.

To be American you must at some point acquaint yourself with the nation's history, this nation that, at two-hundred-plus years, takes its own history quite seriously. I finally did acquaint myself enough to pass a citizenship test, though I could not readily name the second senator in New York State at the time. Was it not enough to have memorized Dorothy Parker's Algonquin quips or e. e. cummings's mud-luscious lines? Surely this proved an acquaintance that, if not *auld*, since two hundred years is easily forgot, counted for something? At the time, the national voter turnout was hovering below 60 percent, which meant many Americans probably could not name their state's second senator. What flummoxed me more than the test, however, was why no one took world history seriously. I recall one Cincinnati acquaintance loudly protesting the lack of world historical knowledge among the young, he being middle aged and belatedly recognizing that his time spent in such knowledge acquisition now impressed no one save himself; his idea of world history began with the Roman Empire and ended in England, as all other history was presumably negligible. But about Cincinnati, Mark Twain did say he would stop there only when the world ended because everything arrived there twenty years too late, including, no doubt, its inhabitants. I paraphrase Twain, but that is not of "rigid importance," another almost-translation of *serious* from Chinese, since the quote is only attributed to him but not fully verified. Why anyone feels the need for verification is perhaps another reason why acquaintance with this or any nation's history is such a rigidly important and weighty affair. America creates such a lot of history in a mere two-hundred-plus years, what with its presidential musical chairs—not to mention ambassadorial, judicial, senatorial, congressional ones—that it is downright impossible to keep up with its history or even its present. *Downright.* Now there's another case of misconstrued diction that was more serious than I realized, even in the academy. Twain didn't quite make it into the academy, though, at least not the ones I attended, yet no one would deny he was American, even if he is absent from the memory of a goodly number of Americans and even from the canon at some academies.

To be American you must prove you can laugh at yourself in ironic self-deprecation if you are young or wish to be hip and preternaturally young. Irony has nothing to do with laughter, of course, just as self-deprecation does not, but then to be young and American is all about taking yourself deathly seriously while pretending not to. Having departed this country young and returned after a spell, I was surprised to find that America had moved on, that laugh-out-loud laughter (silently now, L-O-L) was no longer the best medicine unless you only read *Reader's Digest*, which the rest of the world swallows as real American. *To swallow* is to be fooled in American, damaging the esophagus undoubtedly, because I swallowed the idea of being American as if allegiance and residence and good standing with the IRS would make me American. It wasn't as simple as taking patriotic duty seriously because in some circumstances that will get you killed, which seems downright unpatriotic: to be all you can be one day and blown up in Iraq the next because some historical figure playing presidential musical chairs decides to declare war. Do you laugh at yourself if you are

American about the fact of starting a war? My friends in Hong Kong excuse me when they loudly protest the war because in their eyes I am not a real American. How could I be since I wasn't born "over there," despite the fact that I spell and punctuate American, which these days even some British editors will allow. Will swallow. Have I fooled them all as well as my friends in America because I have become American, which is not quite the same as being American? After all, I can name the president now, along with the second senator of New York State, although her name dances on the tip of my tongue and then disappears, thanks to the fast-moving chair dance and my arrival at middle age, or so the neurologist says. He, the doctor, will not take my desire for early Alzheimer's detection seriously because I am too healthy, too mentally alert, too readily able to name the president, the state he came from and its subsequent history of shame, and even the vice president, although he slipped off my tongue for a moment but returned, and I did recall his senatorial state of origin. I, on the other hand, must take this doctor seriously because he made it into medical school, a *see-RYE-ous* accomplishment, spent years practicing his specialty and, now that he has arrived, denounces the state of medical care in these here United States as too drug happy, just as he declares that most people, meaning Americans, would not do as well as I did on his memory and knowledge test, one that was a far, far more difficult thing than crossing the borders into citizenship. That I might be genetically predisposed to Alzheimer's is probable but difficult to prove. He, the doctor, is the man who laughs a little at me, kindly I think, unlike Victor Hugo's tragic hero whose deformity freezes his face into perpetual laughter. The French gave America Liberty and the cul de sac, which is reason enough to recall some Frenchman's words, even if the history of the world no longer makes us laugh.

To be American you must at some stage of your life take medicare (lowercase) seriously, by which I mean medical care and not the semisocialist welfare state senior citizenship brings. It is difficult to take American-trained doctors seriously in Hong Kong. For one thing, British medical standards and practices dominate, and everyone knows real health care is all about balancing *yin* and *yang*, for which the Chinese herbalist will prescribe the right concoction if you are too much one or the other. I did, however, take American-trained dentists seriously because American teeth are healthier than Hong Kong teeth, and there is reason to floss whether or not you're American, a practice the rest of the world, and certainly China, still hasn't learned, although the young are catching up. It is advantageous being young in a global era because like my friend Jenny, the young will go to Manhattan to eat and drink and shop and witness American teeth, feeling them up as their tongues slide under, over, and around that dental gleam some hormonal night in the wild west of Chelsea, where the young go to party and play now that the East Village is so yesterday. Today is already yesterday in New York City, where history piles upon itself as rapidly as excrement reappeared on sidewalks once the pooper-scooper mayor stepped down. But medical care is serious business because it spawns profitable television dramas, these days down the path of the willingly nip-tucked or verbally abused coupled with their salacious seductions, all of which makes you contemplate the grave with a modicum of desire well before the onset of Alzheimer's, longevity past its use-by date, or some debilitating, incurable disease.

To be American you must be perpetually exhausted and feel bad about it because no one in the world works as hard as Americans, especially in corporate America, where to desire time off is almost criminal or mortally sinful, but who insisted it had to be so? It is hard for the world to understand why being American presumes the right to desire ungodly amounts of wealth and possessions because you wish some recompense for a twenty-four-seven work life that is all for the sake of profit in this here capitalist economy. Capitalism. Now there is a truly American dream, which loans a home to every family until the subprime earthquake takes it away, not unlike Daddy and his T-Bird. Milton Friedman, a not-so-quiet American (from Brooklyn and a Leo no less) was mightily impressed by Hong Kong's brand of laissez-faire capitalism, which he says created our postwar prosperity (consequently, Friedman is kindly regarded on these here shores). As a part-time resident and native daughter of the city of Hong Kong, I have always appreciated our low taxes and entrepreneurship, which permit the birth and death of businesses to mimic the life cycle of a fruit fly. (A female fruit fly can only be considered virgin for twelve hours after emerging as an adult.) But I am not sure how correct this American economist was in naming our economic miracle "capitalism," especially the laissez-faire governmental nonintervention. Intervention abounds to control the price (upward) of real estate, to purchase shares of the largest bank in response to an economic crisis, to regulate life in this highly efficient city with an extraordinarily well-paid civil service (so civil, in fact, that an Independent Commission Against Corruption had to be formed to stanch the graft that bled from the ranks of the service, drowning the public's trust), to peg a "freely convertible" currency rigidly to the greenback. As well, intervention minimizes democratic representation and perpetuates a class structure favoring an elite that reflects and genuflects to the overlord in power. Nonintervention simply means the government smiles a lot but doesn't give a flying fuck about you, not really.

Not to give a flying fuck. Now there's a truly American outlook on life. I am reminded of a pair of flying-while-fornicating vultures, a decal image I would press onto T-shirts for a summer job during my college years, under which read the words: "Fly United." For such memorable souvenirs would vacationing Americans (and a few Canadians) part with their greenbacks. That was life then in these here United States, where

Americans and Canadians comingled funds in an upstate New York resort while temperatures soared and the living was easy.

But to return to Jenny, which is where I began, because to be American means I must split myself in two, being American over here (or is it there?), where I am not with the likes of Jenny, and being something else when I am with her and others in my life who are not Americans. It would perhaps be simpler to be expatriated, a highly American condition abroad where you can either be lost in translation or, in a quaint echo of your colonial forebears, go native. It is so either-or, being American I mean, because to be, for example, Hong-Kong-ian (or Hong-Kong-ese, we are not fussy about nomenclature), you can also be Canadian or Australian or some national of European persuasion and speak Japanese or Spanish in your spare or full time as suits your temperament. For that matter you can even be an astronaut, which many Hong Kong people are, having split their lives between Vancouver and their home city (or London or Toronto or even the Republic of Singapore, which is both city and state, a splittist condition of modern postcolonialism), landing at one or the other as the stars decree. Why is it that to be American you must be first and foremost American and may not pledge allegiance to another nation unless you are born accidentally weird or if in fact you happen to be a traitor? Life is surely not so either-or, although to be American I have found that it is usually best to be clear and straightforward about things, living in one place at one postal address, for instance, as opposed to having several domiciles as I have. Which is why I only accept mail at one post office box on a rural route, which is as sweet as home can be, this singular post office being the reason why I, like Eudora Welty, also choose to Live at the P.O. The rest of the world embraces poste restante, but being American, it struck me as preferable, even desirable, to live at this box, where my mail can pile up for weeks at a stretch (and even months) without anyone making too loud a fuss. This is far more restful than poste restante; believe me, as one who made use of said service during a long-ish stint in Greece, you feel pressured to check daily in case your mail goes astray, which it was often known to do but which in the case of my American post office, it rarely ever does. So here I am, American, even though the sea right now is not shining because yet another typhoon has hit Hong Kong. I gaze across the harbor from my rooftop in Kowloon and ponder an American contribution to the city's skyline, the tower with chopsticks as spires (erected by I. M. Pei, an American whose name still sounds foreign to many American ears), which is the Bank of China. So now I return full-circle—which is rather un-American I might add, not succumbing to a linear narrative—and recognize my condition as a sort of Chinese who is sort of American while squatting in a sort of home in Hong Kong. It is enough to make you shudder, this neither-fish-nor-fowl existence. Although every time the fish-fowl dilemma rears its curious head, I instantly see the graphic art of M. C. Escher, who is most avowedly *not* American, although he too was someone who left the land of his birth for the foreign shores of Italy for quite a spell, and for other lands as well, though he did eventually die back home in the Netherlands. Which is finally getting me back to where I really want to be, considering death as Dickinson did, this American whose sensibility was quite Japanese, or so some Japanese think. At this point, I am stumbling over an impossible architecture à la Escher in this reverie on being American. But the point, I suspect, was all about my early American encounter with Dickinson's prairie. It was so impossible, that prairie poem, I disliked it so intensely when I was eighteen because at eighteen it is still possible to have intense feelings about something as insignificant to the world you came from as a poem by an exceptionally quiet American of whom no one you knew in Hong Kong had ever heard. I disliked it because I had fallen so much in love with Emily's alabaster chambers and buzzing flies at the moment of demise that I could not accept this same imagination would fritter away time on clovers and bees. There was no one to tell me then, *just hang on a spell, you'll see, she's got something there*. And so I rabbit on (English fashion, the English countryside being littered with rabbits the way the Northeast is not) about being American when what I really want to know, when all I really care about is to know what to take *see-RYE-ously* before death. Before he kindly stops for me because I too, like Emily, will not stop for him, I ask if in fact "the revery alone will do."

To have chosen to become American, because it was a choice and not foisted upon me by war, parental design, or the need to escape a seriously oppressive regime (unless you consider the stern weight of four thousand years of tangled Chinese history a form of oppression), has led me to Dickinson's busy-bee life among the clover. Trying to make prairies, per-haps, or more accurately, seeking the prairie that might one day be home. There was precious little time for "revery" with all this fuckin' flying and flying while fucking around with life. But I hung on a spell, not knowing what else to do with being American, this thing I had acquired somewhere along my life, and if Monsieur Death would kindly leave me alone for a spell, this reverie might end with a modicum of hope, if not feathers. At least about being an American of this ilk, which, come to think of it, ain't the worst thing I could be. Ain't. Now that's the sweetness of the prairie.

# WHY I STOPPED
# BEING CHINESE

The HOW is impossible. Chinese blood and hair, clichéd almond eyes. You do not escape physiognomy or the interlocked outer and inner miens. The WHY is not about the HOW, and this is not some how-to manual of shame. Instead, let's zero in on the WHO, WHAT, and WHERE in this rhetoric of HOW and WHY.

The WHO should be brief. Chinese Indonesian, former Indonesian citizen, native of Hong Kong, domiciled in the world. The world is impossible. You cannot really live in three places at once, even though you have pretended you do so via cyberscape. Instead, let us converse with the dead in the tried and true Chinese tradition of ancestor worship, and the starting point is paternal Grandpop, tyrant and philanderer, that cultured world wanderer on someone else's dime, or so Mum accused.

The problem. Grandpop was ancient, and both your parents were already a tad too old to be having you and the younger ones. Thirty-three to be having me, the first child, in 1954, was likely painful for Mum. Dad was twenty-nine. The problem is that this parental WHO should have happened in the early twenty-first century (or at least the late twentieth), which would have made us, the children, TCKs. That's the easier WHO, being third-culture kids. They need reflect far, far less on which skin colors, which languages, which countries demand or deserve allegiance. A passport is a mere carrying card for border crossings, and the idea is to fit in everywhere and nowhere as awesomely possible. Alas, born too un-awesomely soon.

I am being peevish. I am tipping over to the almost-elderly side of middle age and still wondering, *why Chinese?*

Another problem. Grandpop was very Chinese, even though all but one of the five children from the former mistress and younger second wife (half his age, my mother's age) speak nary a word of the language. My father did, as do his real-not-half brothers, but his Mandarin was the wrong Chinese for my moment of birth. When you, Dad, are surrounded by southern babblers of Cantonese in 1949, the year of China's rebirth under Mao, because you've fled Shanghai for Hong Kong (as he did that year), you no longer know what kind of Chinese you are. It was likely easier back in Chinese school in Tegal, a village in Central Java, where Grandpop was Honorable Father to whom you bowed, Confucian style, your forehead knocking repeatedly against the ground. When all you had to do was grovel. But then you grew up, left home, learned English because it was the thing to do, and before you knew it the world turned and there you were, in British colonial Hong Kong and married, and the next thing you know, the little ones are babbling in English and, *dammit, man, I say*, in Cantonese, that coarse, guttural, sewer cycle of atonality, offending your musical ear. Poor Dad. Here was this violinist tenor schooled in Italian opera and European classical music with a smattering of international pop. His ear (unlike that of the Confucian gentleman at age sixty) was not "attuned" to the voices of the Chinese world around him, 六十耳 (不) 順, disturbing the universe of the sage.

I like Cantonese, still do, and sound more fluent than I really am, but at sixty, this really shouldn't be a problem anymore, should it?

The maternal problem: Mum was too pure of blood. Five generations in Central Java did not eradicate the racism, the superior attitude of fair-skinned Chinese against the dark-skinned Indonesian natives. This is the history of the world, and my mother's family was no different, even while they inbred into madness, lost the language, and abandoned the culture in favor of the comfort of the sarong and the rich, heady, tropical spices and fruits of the natives, which was the far, far better thing to do.

Which is why I grew up in Cantonese Hong Kong without Cantonese food or the language at home. I can, however, eat spicy, spicy, *laat, laat,* so *laat*, this déja-taste of my mother's tongue, although her language was lost to the tongue of our British colonial masters.

The WHO has been less brief than desired.

The WHAT is a Nation, a four-thousand-plus-year History with too many emperors to recall, a Culture and Language that shape-shift as you traverse the world, infused as these now are with the rest of humanity. *There are Chinese everywhere*, say my country folk with pride.

Yet is that pride or sorrow? The *wah kiu* or *hua qiao* scattered around the globe have pined for their home village since the Tang Dynasty when Li Po penned his homesickness ode (床前明月光—*from my bedside moon is bright*, etc.). Too many men without women landed on foreign shores, as my paternal ancestors did. In our genealogical chart, the earliest *arrivistes* married unnamed "Indonesian women." It was not till three generations later that named Chinese wives appear in our doctored family history. Who were these anonymous women, those natives who said yes to my horny ancestors? Were they shunned by their own communities, seen as whores? Were they whores? After all, what respectable Javanese girl would fuck these yellow-skinned barbarians who landed on their shores? To my great-to-the-power-of-seven Indonesian Great great-grandmama, thanks for my skin that does not burn, even under a tropical sun.

And yet. Is that "gratitude" actually pride or merely foolishness, pretentiousness, an inferiority complex, racism, fear? All of this and more, no doubt, in the sea change of human consciousness after the migration tsunami subsides.

The Nation, though, is more complicated. The Chinese language loves this term "complicated," 複雜—*fuk jaahp* (Cantonese) or *fu za* (Mandarin)—its etymology suggests a doubling, repetitive, overlapping effect, a complexity combined with an assortment that is both numerous and petty. Life as a Chinese in the world is *fuk jaahp*, which seems to be the default position for anything too difficult to contemplate, at least in the Chinese Hong Kong (or, as some still say, Hong Kong Chinese) society I find myself located more often than not.

For one thing, there is corruption. While Hong Kong has its I C A C, the Independent Commission Against Corruption, China simply executes the corrupt official or businessman who is too blatant, or who the people protest against vociferously enough (especially if death, destruction, and other evidence of callous indifference to humanity is involved) that even the central government can no longer ignore it. But you can't execute all the corrupt people all of the time. This is simply no way to run a country.

For another, there is the possibility of being incarcerated for saying the wrong thing. Now I know there are those who say that political dissidents deserve what they get in a one-party, unabashedly authoritarian state, but doesn't that make you wonder why you should elect Chinese nationality? There are two ways a Hong Kong–born citizen like myself can enter the motherland, on a "return to your home-village certificate," 回鄉證, which is relatively inexpensive and which my Hong Kong Chinese friends, even those with foreign passports, have obtained, or on a visa with my U.S. passport, which is much more expensive. The latter does, however, offer consular protection, while the former ensures that if you cross the wrong official or say the wrong thing and offend the authorities, you might end up in jail.

I like my freedoms, still do, and prefer to pay for these if I must, even though China rises and rises, inviting her people back to her bosom, tempting us with the one-armed *ka-ching(!)* of her economic miracle, promising a better, brighter future under a sun that these days is no longer red, just invisible due to pollution.

But were you ever Chinese enough?

Once, back in the eighties, not long after I'd moved to New York, I encountered an ethnic Chinese woman from Taiwan in one of those self-improvement business courses for advancing your career. She had lived in the United States for more than twenty years, while I was not yet even a citizen, having entered the country on a student's visa for grad school and married an American, which was reason to remain in the country. I had lived and worked in Hong Kong as an adult for around seven years and was still fairly current on contemporary Hong Kong life. Her Taiwan was enshrined in a Kuomintang past, and she and her family were rooted in New Jersey. Yet all it took was for her was to hear me speak English like an American to say I was not a "real Chinese," while she presumably was since she lived "more Chinese" in America than me and spoke English with a pronounced accent. I hesitated to point out Taiwan's "non-China" political status, even in America's eyes.

She was unusually shrill, scornful of my easy integration into American society. Yet my life has been in many ways "more Chinese" than hers, insofar as *where* my life has been lived, significantly around a Chinese world in Hong Kong and Asia. Hers has been in suburban America. She probably only visits the ancestral home on self-improvement vacations. Yet her attitude was not uncommon. All my life I've encountered ethnic Chinese who deny me the right to be Chinese because of my language, demeanor, blood. Even the Hong Kong Government does not fully recognize me as Chinese because I do not have a parent born on Chinese soil (legally in my birth city I am and always have been classified as "foreign," albeit with a permanent right of abode). It does not matter that I often encounter "real Chinese" who look at me blankly when I say, *you know, Chinese literature,* Journey to the West *or* Dreams of Red Chambers *or Mo Yan, you know, the second Chinese guy to win the Nobel for Literature?* Or even when I order a Chiu Chow meal for Cantonese friends who gaze at me, mystified, and ask, *how do you know this,* as if another region close to their own should be so entirely foreign.

The WHAT is 複雜 beyond words. To be American you just have to pledge allegiance and pay taxes on worldwide income.

The WHERE is the red dust of the Great Chinese Novel, *Journey to the West*, in which *Dreams of Red Chambers* is embedded. Gao Xingjian, the first Chinese writer to win the Nobel for Literature, is not Chinese enough for China. Neither is Ha Jin because he left China, writes in English, and won the National Book Award in the United States. As the mongrel writer I am, should I take solace in all that? Yet do we not write into that red dust, that mystery, that common Chinese uncertainty if Chinese blood courses through our veins? After all, did I not study Mandarin as an MFA fiction student in search of roots or authenticity, for something beyond Aristotle's dictum, thus almost losing my fellowship for my digressive trespass? Was not my most important writing of self that Chinese language "偶記"—an "occasional journal" titled 我是不是中國人？—essaying on whether I was or was not a Chinese person? *The study of Chinese does not meet the MFA requirements for a fiction writer in America,* or so I was more or less told. Admittedly, they had a point. After all, I'd already met my language requirement with French. Oh, my dear Muse of American English fiction, *voulez-vous coucher avec moi, ce soir?*

Aristotle's dictum: *dictum de omni et nullo*—the dictum of all or none. Once again, my very existence proves him wrong. Such "reversals of fortune"—even for the man who first articulated that dramatic *idée*—should have a universal appeal, *n'est-ce pas?*

WHERE is the content and context for literary expression in a globalized, cosmopolitan world. Are you a traitor or patriot to write in that *lingua franca* English for an international reading public about the lives of the contemporary Chinese? And who or what do you betray and to whom or what should you be loyal? Since when was being a writer about being or not being "Chinese," whatever that is? Doesn't literature succeed and endure because it's "universal"? Or is that some Western myth of artistic expression that vanishes into Anglo-American banana-white dust?

So finally we arrive at the WHY, which suddenly seems immensely simple. Here is the moment of surrender: I must stop being Chinese.

As you can see for yourself, it is just too complicated.

# CITIZENSHIP

In the autumn of 1995, I lost my American passport. It was shortly before a trip to Myanmar, so I was frantic about not having a travel document. Having recently moved back to Hong Kong after living in Singapore for a year, no place felt like home. Which was why I had been carrying my passport with me, along with my Hong Kong identity card and U.S. driver's license, both also lost in the same wallet when I got out of a taxi late one night after getting royally drunk with a client.

I realized my wallet was missing as soon as I reached home, which required a short uphill walk to my flat. Taxis simply refused to drive up the narrow path, and I had stopped arguing the point. I ran down to the foot of the hill, but the taxi was gone and there was nothing on the ground. It was past midnight. No one was around. I must have dropped it, but if so, why had it already disappeared? Visions of my reconstituted passport, my photo replaced by a stranger's, swarmed through my brain, and I knew I needed to report it missing to the consulate as soon as possible. I cursed the state of nations that did not allow dual citizenship—if only I still had my Indonesian passport then there'd be no panic about my upcoming trip! But Indonesia disallows dual nationalities, and I surrendered that citizenship when I naturalized, and the United States only permits dual citizenship under specific conditions for which I did not qualify.

To date, I've traveled on eight passports of two nations and held a ninth of a notion in the form of a World Passport, unused, acquired in my early teens. It still astonishes me, even though it shouldn't, that there are millions of people around the world who have never been issued (and likely never will be) even a single passport.

Each evening after the local news on Hong Kong television, Earth goes *live*. For about three minutes, cities of the world grace the screen in real time. Here is Budapest's morning traffic. In Dubai the afternoon temperature is blistering. The city of Los Angeles slumbers but its highways never sleep. It's a crap shoot because you never know which corner of the world will illuminate your home. On one of our weekly Skype calls, I told my guy in New York of this daily visual interlude, which both startled and intrigued him. In recent years, "Earth Live" has been my passport to world citizenship, solace for having to live in Hong Kong, apart from my life partner.

To be a citizen of any country, all you have to do is acquire that nation's passport. Right now, in 2017, nation-states are veering precariously toward a new idea of citizenship, one that defies globalization, one that retreats to borders with walls, real or imagined, one that believes citizenship is a birthright only of those who *belong*, which increasingly seems narrowed to mean a cleansed ethnicity or believers of the "true" religion or those with the "correct" sociopolitical-cultural, even gender-biased vision of what life in that country must be. Yet right now, in 2017, there are likely many passports, real or imagined, crossing national borders at a rate unprecedented in history.

There is an obsolete meaning of passport that is, in effect, a license to beg. In sixteenth-century England, military patients discharged from a hospital were given a permit to head to their destination and ask for alms along the way. Such a practice would relieve a person's temporary misfortune. The alarming refugee crises circumnavigating the globe might be well served by a similar form of passport. To be a child tossed around on an open sea, your citizenship pinned in clear plastic to your chest until the waves swallow it and your parents—what could be more horrifying? Or to almost suffocate inside a truck, padlocked from the outside, in your journey toward a hoped-for new citizenship—what could be less humane? The very nature of passport suggests a rule of law, this document "issued by a *competent* officer (as a secretary of state) of a country," according to *Merriam-Webster's Unabridged.* The OED doesn't demand competence, but both dictionaries more or less agree that it is a country's government that issues passports, and one that, we trust, is competent, even though the history of the world evidences how often this is not the case.

Citizenship is more broadly defined, as lack of a passport does not necessarily prevent you from being a citizen of a particular country, thus giving you the right to live there. In most nation-states, it would be difficult to strip an individual of citizenship so as to deny the right of abode, unless, perhaps, the person were an immigrant. Even so, what if the immigrant's country of origin no longer exists? To where would they be banished? A stateless person without passport can not necessarily enter any other country. Purgatory, it should be noted, is not yet a nation-state.

You are born in [fill in the blank] nation, and in most instances this means you become a citizen of that state, unless the circumstance of your birth does not meet the requirements that make you one. Citizenship really is that simple and that complicated.

My various citizenships have umbilical ties to my rights of abode. A post-war birth in the British colony of Hong Kong granted me a "permanent" right of abode as a Hong Kong "belonger," although how this is defined has evolved over time. This entitled me to a Hong Kong British passport that did *not* grant me the right of abode in Britain, presumably because it was issued by a colony and not the nation-state. However, given that I could claim at least partial Chinese ancestry, the People's Republic of China, which was then Hong Kong's geographical reality and former sovereign ruler, would not recognize me as British.

Meanwhile, as my Indonesian-national parents' firstborn, I simply had to travel back to Indonesia, where I was *not* born, to be shown off to adoring relatives. My parents had each ended up in Hong Kong after the war. Then, the city welcomed new arrivals of Chinese ancestry, and borders were porous enough for Asian nationals in search of better lives who knew English, which they both did. Their Indonesian passports proved no barrier to obtaining either the rights of abode or to work, and their citizenship ensured they could always return to live and work in Indonesia. This is not at all true today for Indonesians or other nationals who arrive in my populated-to-bursting-point city. Postwar, Hong Kong needed people and readily granted citizenship to the city in the form of right of abode. Today, it cannot afford its ever-increasing citizenry and may even regret the admission of mongrels like my family.

So there I was, a minor on my mother's passport. If during that trip of my infancy I had been orphaned or abandoned—my parents lost in a sea of oblivion, say—I would likely have had a right of abode in Indonesia. Of course, had I been born a few years earlier in Hong Kong when it was still under Japanese occupation, who knows what my options might have been?

Meanwhile, the city of Hong Kong had its own ideas of ethnicity. This took the concept of citizenship, which can be defined as belonging to a community, to a whole other level. Despite my obvious Chinese ancestry, albeit mixed with Indonesian blood, I am not officially considered Chinese by the government of Hong Kong. There are two reasons for this state of being. First of all, my parents did not register a Chinese name on my birth certificate, even though my father gave me one as he did all my siblings, and both my parents do have Chinese names. More significantly,

I elected to take an Indonesian passport shortly after I turned sixteen, about a year before my departure for college in the United States, which meant I "belonged" to Indonesia rather than British Hong Kong. In fact, to ensure I could return home after graduation, it was necessary to obtain a stamp from the director of immigration certifying my right to remain "unconditionally" and that no visa be required for reentry to the land of my birth. Such was the state of unconditional love by my colonial *mater*, the bureaucratic answer for a modest fee payable to the Shroff.

This did not become a problem until I began traveling on my second passport book, issued in 1977, because I was unable to obtain a new book in 1979 when I had finally run out of pages. The latter problem is not unique among frequent business travelers of many nations. In my case, it was less the professional need to travel and more the desire I harbored to be a citizen of the world. The World Passport I obtained as a teenager was real, issued by the World Government of World Citizens established in Paris in 1948 by Sol Gareth "Garry" Davis, an internationalist and peace activist. Davis was an American who renounced his U.S. citizenship. His dream was to become a "free human being without benefit of any national credentials," who could travel the world without passport. He lived a long life, and before his death in 2013 at the age of ninety-one had registered more than 950,000 people as world citizens. This is a larger population than in any of the thirty least populated nation-states in the world today, the largest being French Polynesia at fewer than 280,000.

However, back in 1979, my concern was as much practical as it was philosophical.

The Indonesian consulate told me they had run out of passport books. I was working for an airline and took advantage of the free and discounted tickets to travel as much as possible. This was in addition to my job that required me to travel to most of the online and a few offline locations of the company at least twice each year. The forty-eight pages of my passport were filled with visa and entry stamps. How, I demanded, was it possible for a nation to run out of passport books? As my late aunt would have said, the consulate was simply *useless!* She worked at the consulate as a secretary and was my passport to navigating its bureaucratic muddle.

The solution other nations, the United States included, used was to affix additional blank pages to the back of your book. By the time the consulate finally had new books to replace mine, it was 1983, and my passport had transformed into a motley collage of not one but two sets of added pages, glued to the back of the book and further extended, accordion-like, by scotch tape. It looked fake.

It also meant Hong Kong Immigration could never find that stamp, the one declaring my right to land in Hong Kong without a visa, because it was buried on the back page and hidden by the extra pages, which have long since come unglued from the spine. Unconditional love had become a thing of the past, lost to a memory of a stamp in my first, youthful

**1.** My "fake" Indonesian passport with its forty-eight accordion foldout pages added in 1979. Photo courtesy of the author.

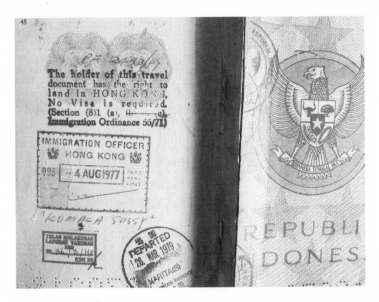

2. The stamp in my 1977 Indonesian passport showing my right to land without a visa in my birth city. Photo courtesy of the author.

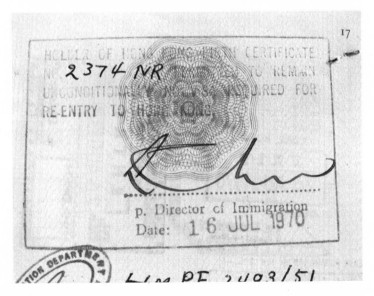

3. The stamp in my 1970 Indonesian passport showing my right to remain "unconditionally" without a visa in my place of birth. Photo courtesy of the author.

passport book of 1970. The current stamp only allowed visa-free entry, and my right of abode in my birth city could therefore be interpreted as conditional. Often, I had to wait while immigration officers checked with supervisors about this, the situation made all the more precarious by the seemingly impermanent nature of my passport.

In the twenty-first century, technology has improved citizenship. Today, I zip into Hong Kong with only my permanent identity card, one with a chip and a metallic arrow to direct its insertion into a reader. My thumbprint assures my identity and voilà, the gate pops open into Customs. Today, I look Hong Kong Chinese enough for Hong Kong Immigration, but fortunately not mainland Chinese, because Customs invariably waves me through the green channel while mainlanders with too much luggage get stopped and searched.

Officially, however, I am still not Chinese in Hong Kong because my card lacks the three stars designation. Since Hong Kong's return to Chinese sovereignty, I require a visa to enter the People's Republic, while other Hong Kong belongers privileged by three stars on their ID card can enter with a permit or 回鄉証 to "return to one's village." I long ago gave up on that bureaucratic ethnic claim and pay an immodest fee once every three years to the Chinese government's travel bureau for a multiple-entry visa to my country of origin. During Obama's presidency, the United States and China negotiated a reciprocal agreement that extended ten-year multiple-entry visas to qualified citizens for crossing each nation's borders, but the announcement came right after I had just renewed mine for three. The next time I renew, who knows if the rules will have changed yet again or whether or not I'll even qualify.

When I became a U.S. citizen in 1987, it was easier to be an American than an Indonesian. For a start, I did speak English and had lived in the country a total of nine nonconsecutive years, four on the F-1 foreign student visa and the remaining five on the infamous green card held by legal aliens. An alien's ethnicity (or class, religion, or gender identity) is not really an issue, especially not if citizenship is obtained through a real marriage, as mine was. However, friends of various persuasions who had acquired citizenship by other means were not treated differently. This, I decided, was the meaning of democracy, where legal aliens were equal in the eyes of the government, regardless of ethnicity, class, religion, or gender identity.

As an Indonesian born outside that country, I was a kind of alien, although not officially so. I did not speak Indonesian except for the language of food or irritation (*babi, kambing, soto, satay, gado gado, ayam*, etc., or *ah doo!*). I had never lived in Indonesia. My only claim to citizenship was the ability to sing the national anthem. Recently, at a Balinese dance performance in Jakarta when the anthem was played, I stood beside my Indonesian hosts and sang "Indonesia Raya" with them, surprised that the lyrics could be recalled from a childhood of August 17 celebrations, the commemorative day of the country's independence from Dutch colonial rule. Of course, I can still also sing the Dutch children's songs my Indonesian aunt used to sing to me, the same aunt who dismissed the consulate as perpetually, eternally, undeniably *hopeless*. Musical memory, it appears, crosses national borders at will.

In the early eighties, I once had to go to the Indonesian consulate in New York City to renew my passport. Indonesia is not nearly as trusting as the United States, and passports are only renewed for two years at a time, while Americans are given ten before having to worry about renewal. It was the first time I had done this without my aunt's assistance, and I was nervous. I entered the consulate, passport in hand, and mumbled something about renewal. The man at reception immediately began speaking to me in Indonesian. *Tida besa Indonesian*, I said, a truncated sentence construction to indicate my inability to speak, adding in English, *I was born and raised in Hong Kong*—hoping to justify my ignorance—*and only besa Kina*, meaning I only could speak Chinese as my Asian language. The dark-skinned, ethnic Indonesian looked me up and down and said in fluent English, *are you sure you're an Indonesian?* He was half-joking, teasing me in the way I recognized my Indonesian Chinese family would when they tried to make me be more Indonesian. But I also heard in his voice the nationalist critique of my citizenship: ethnicity was not the issue, but language and culture clearly were.

The day I pledged allegiance to the American flag in New York, I was surrounded by people of multiple ethnicities. The pledge I needed to learn, along with the lyrics to "The Star-Spangled Banner," as neither were part of my upbringing. I applied for my first blue book that same day, the passport I later lost, the travel document I coveted for so long that would ease travel and life. In 1991 I flew internationally for the first time as a U.S. citizen from New York to Hong Kong and China. This was a decade after my second entry to the United States on the F-1 visa with a right of abode but no right to work except at my university, as long as I remained a full-time graduate student. My reentry to the city of my birth was extremely swift and uncomplicated, and it was only for the trip to China that I needed a visa. It was also the first time I could visit the Chinese mainland. Previously, when I was an Indonesian citizen, it was not possible. This has changed now that China welcomes visitors from all over the world. Both my uncles who ran travel agencies in Hong Kong did a huge business booking tours to China for Indonesian Chinese and ethnic Indonesian citizens.

Why did I not consider British citizenship? As a girl, the Hong Kong British passport did not feel real, which was why I chose Indonesian instead. My first husband was British, and I would have qualified as a spouse for a real British passport, one with a right of abode in the United

Kingdom. The marriage was short-lived, which was partly the reason I did not apply. But it is only now, essaying on citizenship, that this refusal to do so puzzles me into reflection.

It is strange to say I did not covet UK citizenship since I chose to marry a citizen. He was Scottish, and I did very much want to visit Scotland. At the time, I had never been to England or elsewhere in the British Isles. My now-ex, then-husband and I were living in a village in Hong Kong's New Territories, and we even considered moving to New Zealand, as rural life appealed to us, which British nationality would have facilitated for life in the Commonwealth. I had even elected to remain in Hong Kong to be with him instead of returning to the United States for graduate school. I had been accepted at the University of Utah to do a PhD in English but declined the offer. There were financial constraints, and I also wasn't entirely certain about an academic career. However, it was likely the question of American citizenship that was really at the heart of my decision.

In the summer of '74, shortly after graduating with my BA in English, my F-1 student visa was revoked, and I had to leave the United States voluntarily if I wished to return again. My American Indonesian Chinese Dutch uncle was frantic. *You'll be deported! You'll never be allowed back!* His American wife, one of my favorite aunts, tried to calm him. She was mostly concerned with problem solving, as in, *so what do we do now?* It is remarkable to recall how calm I was despite this rather drastic reversal of fortune.

In the early seventies, foreign students could apply for a permit to work during summer vacations. While F-1 students were allowed to stay in the country in between school semesters, the right to work during these times was not automatic. You could work on campus in, say, the cafeteria or at the library or as a lab research assistant, although the better-paid work-study jobs were reserved only for U.S. citizens. I worked on campus during the school year as a dorm resident assistant and in summers slung trays as a waitress and rang up sales at cash registers in a resort town along with other Chinese foreign students who had introduced me to those jobs. Without that income, I could not afford college. For the first two summers of my three undergraduate years, this passport to work during vacation was granted.

Once I graduated, however, I was supposed to leave the country unless I was headed to graduate school. I had received an acceptance to the University of Utah and, given my desire to remain in the United States, said yes to starting in the fall. As I had each year previously, I went to the Foreign Student Office and applied for a work permit for summer, intending to earn something toward the looming expense ahead. Then I headed back to the resort town for the jobs that awaited me, as the permit usually came through soon afterward. Unfortunately, 1974 was the year President Nixon revoked that right, and suddenly, foreign students all over the United States were unable to work off campus on the F-1 student visa. My right of abode was not revoked, as I could legally remain in the country on my visa for the summer before moving to Utah, as long as I did not work.

Looking at the Dreamers today, who, as of this writing, may see DACA revoked, I sympathize with their plight. What good is an abode you cannot afford? Even your employers regard you and say, *that's ridiculous, what do you mean you're not allowed to work, all students should earn their way through college!* The greater irony is when those same employers say, *I want you to work, you don't steal from the register like those other kids.* Those "other" white American kids at the resort town in upstate New York. The owner of the gift shop I had worked at for the past two summers asked me to keep an eye on new employees. It was not about ethnicity or passport, simply about who was a hard and honest worker and who wasn't. Who needed the money more. The American kids he regularly fired didn't seem to care whether or not they had the job, as being fired never seemed like a big deal to them. At twenty I was terrified of being fired and did all I possibly could to ensure I kept my job. Citizenship is odd; it really is that simple and that complicated.

Bureaucracy was my undoing. Despite the denial of a permit, the word from the government, at least according to my university, was that we all *probably* should stop working for the moment until their appeal decision came through. The haze around that denial enveloped us all with its lack of clarity. When I told my employers at the gift shop and restaurant—I always worked double shifts to make enough money—both the Jewish American shop owner and the Italian American restaurant manager said, *but do you want to work? Yes, of course*, I said, and they responded, *then come to work* because neither would ever tell. But a Hong Kong Chinese student from my college, one who had been picked up by Immigration, did tell. He gave Immigration all the names of the other Hong Kong students and told them where we worked. Later that summer I too was picked up by Immigration. The two officers were civil and actually rather apologetic. They had to remove the F-1 visa from my passport and told me to get it back in Albany at the end of summer so that I could stay on for graduate school. *You'll be fine*, they said, *it's no big deal. We just have to do this.* When I asked what I should tell my employers, they looked at each other and shrugged. *We don't really know. No one told us anything about that.* One of them finally decided, *you might as well keep on working and then go to Albany at the end of summer. That's all we can tell you for now.* As a fiction writer, I know you absolutely cannot make up real life, so you may as well not.

I imagine a dreamer today, someone who has known virtually no other life except one in America, being told they must return to Mexico or Guatemala or some other nation. They might not even speak the language well, likely have no relatives or friends they really know, and understand nothing about how to go to school, work, or live in that country. Would they even know which city or town or village to go to? Where would they live? Does the government in question even recognize their citizenship? At the end of that summer, I did as I was told and headed to Albany, and there I was shocked to be given eleven days to leave the country. *Can I appeal?* I asked. *Yes but you have to go to Buffalo.* I went. My appeal was denied, and the countdown to the deadline ticked ominously louder.

There appears to be nothing about this voluntary departure, which I did before the deadline, that besmirches my record. The University of Utah reissued an I-20 acceptance for the spring semester, which, if I had chosen to go, would have renewed my F-1 visa. In later years, I was able to apply for and receive tourist and business visas for travel to the United States, as well as a second F-1 student visa in 1981 when I was accepted for the MFA at the University of Massachusetts. I was initially denied that second F-1 by the American consulate in Hong Kong. The reasons the officer gave me were these: I was a divorced woman and therefore probably only going to the United States to try to get married, and secondly, she had never heard of the MFA degree in creative writing and doubted its veracity as a real academic discipline. So no, I could not become even a temporary citizen of America's academic community because my gender profile and career aspiration were questionable. Of course, had I been a sexy European model who was hired in New York, the way the current president's wife once was, why, then I might readily be granted a visa to enter the country where I could meet a rich American to marry and obtain citizenship. My appeal against that denial was successful, otherwise I might not be penning this essay today.

But in 1974, faced with the prospect of returning to the country that had asked me to leave, I decided to take my chances on Hong Kong and my Indonesian citizenship. In '79, my Indonesian green book passport got me into East Berlin through Checkpoint Charlie, which the American blue book would not have done. Two years later, I found my way to

Moscow because Indonesia was an ally of the Soviet Union. I was glad to have seen Russia pre-Glasnost and, more importantly, pre-Putin. These, these are the joys of citizenship in the right country at the right time.

Britain, however, did not seem like the right country at the time. The United Kingdom allows dual citizenship, and prior to Brexit, it would have been advantageous to hold both UK and U.S. passports. But the world around me was and is forever rife with irrational postcolonialisms. My Indonesian citizenship did not allow me visa-free entry to the Netherlands, not even for transit on board a train, which seemed ridiculous given how many Indonesians, including many of my relatives, had settled there. The Nepalese Gurkhas in Hong Kong, who had fought valiantly under the Union Jack, would be confronted with a cultural and political statelessness when the United Kingdom and Hong Kong denied them proper citizenship. Koreans in Japan cannot become "real" Japanese despite their former colonization. After the handover of Hong Kong to China, Britain offered a large number of "real" British passports to Hong Kong Chinese citizens, but few applied.

So there I was, a mixed-race Asian who was not considered British by the Chinese or Chinese by the British Hong Kong government or a real Indonesian by the country of my nationality. The future of our city's postcolonialism and the state of immigration laws were at best murky, given the evidence of both world and personal history. For all I knew, if I did become British British, as opposed to Hong Kong British, I might lose right of abode anywhere in the world if some future prime minister decided to change the rules for immigrants by marriage or the Hong Kong Government no longer welcomed "real" British citizens. I chose the path of least resistance. As a young married woman with little money to travel for the moment, what difference did it make which citizenship I held? As long as I could work and make a life, which I could in Hong Kong as a permanent resident, what more did I need?

For years, my U.S. citizenship has been a boon. If necessary, I can seek consular protection as a writer in China because I travel there on my U.S. passport. I am able to live and work in any American state or territory and can enter numerous countries without a visa. I can even travel to Israel, which I have done, and Jerusalem remains one of my more memorable global moments, astounded as I was to encounter the religious multitude

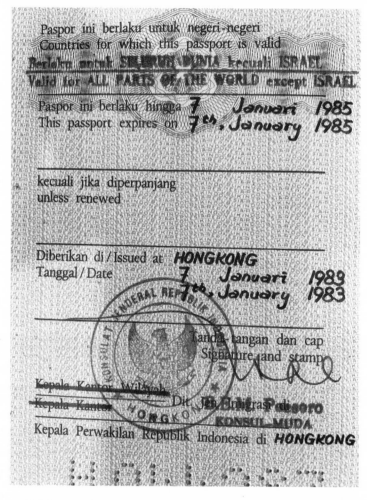

**4.** "Valid everywhere except Israel" stamp in my 1983 Indonesian passport. Photo courtesy of the author.

of its history. This was the one country I could never have entered as an Indonesian. At the Hong Kong International Airport prior to boarding my flight to Tel Aviv, I was pulled aside to answer questions about the Indonesian surname on my U.S. passport. *Was I Muslim? Did I live in Indonesia?* No, no, definitely not, but what I couldn't say was, *and what if I am or do?* El Al security were polite but clearly had a job to do.

Since 9/11 I have been vigilant about maintaining my Global Entry citizenship, this passport that eases reentry to the United States, this bureaucratic fast track for global Americans. You fill out a long form that proves a history of frequent international travel, subject yourself to an interview, and are fingerprinted like a criminal, after which you too, for a fairly hefty fee, may zip through U.S. Immigration by presenting your passport at a card reader instead of standing in line. It is convenient, yes, but more significantly, my registration ensures I will not as likely land on a watch list of suspected Islamic terrorists because of my surname.

Many years earlier, I once got into a debate with an advocate for Islam in Amherst, Massachusetts, where I was a graduate student. He was proselytizing; I was resisting. As an Indonesian Chinese, I said, my people had been victimized by nationalistic forces in Indonesia who were Muslim, so no, I did not have a desire to convert. He was undeterred, and it soon became evident he was flirting as well. He was handsome, this highly articulate brother. In other circumstances, the conversation would have continued over coffee. But what sticks in my memory is how unaware he was of the global nature of Islam, since he knew very little about Indonesia, the most populous Muslim nation. Yet now, when I am far less vehement than my youthful, religiously defiant self—I was raised Catholic, grew up among Buddhists, associate with Islamic, Jewish, Protestant, Taoist, Mormon, et al. folks, and am not held captive by any one religion—my citizenship cannot prevent the misperception of my possible religious leanings.

These days, China does occasionally grant real Chinese citizenship to non-Chinese businessmen who have made a lucrative life in Hong Kong and who choose to renounce their other nationalities. This gives me pause, given China's inward-looking history as the Middle Kingdom, as do the nationalistic, jingoistic declarations of the current American administration. It is painful to imagine the United States as a country in which deplorable citizens live in racial-, religious-, and gender-biased isolation, armed to the teeth, as if warring is the solution to living. I eschew this image because I haven't yet given up on the democratic evolution that underpins this nation's history. Citizenship is malleable and transformed by a citizenry, regardless of national borders. We can elect Schengen or Brexit, DACA or tightened borders, civility or cruelty, common sense or unreason. In the end, we are all citizens of this one world we inhabit. Till death, or heaven or hell, do us part.

# BG

The Significant Years

Before Google (hereinafter BG), there was no failure of the open page. The year, of course, was 2004, August 19, specifically; two days after Indonesia celebrates independence from the Dutch is my mnemonic, given my former nationality. That day was the birth of GOOG, its stock ticker symbol, which even now, in the midst of an economic crisis worse than 1997 or 1987 or even 1929, still tracks triple digits on the NASDAQ, while one-time giants like Citibank (which perhaps should become my former bank) have sunk to as low as a buck. (Meanwhile Madoff, a former NASDAQ chairman, has sunk even lower). Post-Google (hereinafter PG) began that day, to wit, PG 1. The calendar thereafter was easy to establish despite leap year, thanks to Microsoft Excel, and in keeping with some conventions, 1 BG began on what was formerly known as August 18, 2004. It should be noted that some historians argue the PG calendar really began in January 1996, when Larry Page was rooting around for a dissertation project. In fact, the TruGoogol Group still maintains an oppositional calendar (PG: Prior to Google and OG: Once we were Google), but its inelegant nomenclature and failure to identify a specific date doomed it from the start.[1] TruGoogol will likely be silenced in time, along with the diehards of the true millennium.

The Chinese have a similar calendar, or rather the Republic of China does, although these days we might say the "former" republic, as there is only "one China" according to China, and even according to the United States, which is at least consistent about the "one," although allegiances have shifted over time. The superpowers of any moment are the ones that count, in the moment that is, despite democracy and *vox pop*, since Taiwan is still Formosa to some and the Chinese Republic to others. So 1912 is a Chinese Year 1, if you track time from the founding of a republic and the end of dynastic rule. Google was, after all, formerly "googol," which, unlike its successor, did not achieve Proper Nounhood, but that is another history. But if you google[2] the Chinese calendar, it becomes instantly apparent that in the history of calendars, we still have no idea where in time we really are since a little whimsy and the moment dictate our notion of how to count, how to measure, how to perpetuate time, although in the era of PG you own all time in the form of the perpetual calendar. If I care at all about the Chinese alternative, it is only because of my former right to Chinese citizenship as one who belongs to that pecu-liar minority, the "overseas Chinese" or *wah kiu*,[3] a right now revoked, although I have the right of permanent abode in a tiny corner over which China has sovereignty, the SAR,[4] formerly, Hong Kong.

Which brings me, finally, to the significant years.

43 BG (circa AD 1961–62): I discovered world citizenship, not, as Wiki-pedia suggests, the philosophical or altruistic ideal, but the real deal, one with a passport. It was something I read about in one of the four Hong Kong English newspapers of the day (all but one now virtually obsolete) and, being a bored teen, wrote away immediately for further information. Perhaps a fortnight later (it's difficult to recall correctly the feeling of time BG), an airmail packet appeared in my family's mailbox. The papers, those mysterious, official documents, explained in plain language how I could obtain this passport that would allow me to travel freely worldwide. I

need belong to no nation and could speak what language I chose. There was, however, a caveat. This travel document was only recognized by a few nations, fewer, I noted, than even those that did not require visas of my Indonesian passport. Those papers are lost now, a matter of some regret, but space was at a premium in tiny Hong Kong, and other printed matter engaged me instead once I got over my adolescent disappointment.

It was Garry Davis who, sometime between B G 60 and 59, renounced his U.S. citizenship in Paris and founded World Government, the organization that issued the passport I sought. At the age of twenty-six, this former bomber pilot pursued a belief that nations and borders unnecessarily divided us. "I am eager to express to the young war veteran Davis my recognition," said Albert Einstein, "of the sacrifice he has made for the well being of humanity. . . . He has made of himself a 'displaced person' in order to fight for the natural rights of those who are the mute evidences of the low moral level of our time." Over the years, such luminaries as Yehudi Menuhin expressed support for Davis and his cause. In approximately B G 17, Richard Falk at the Center of International Studies, upon receiving Davis's materials, responded that he shared "the basic impulses that motivate your activity. It is ahead of its time, but embodies an outlook that needs to become accepted if our species is to endure and survive." Google has been kind to Davis. As recently as P G 2, Davis's website is still searchable and promoted his cause.

35 B G (circa the academic year 1970–71): The Institute of International Education (hereinafter I I E) on Hong Kong Island had a library. There were large volumes there, larger even than the *Encyclopedia Britannica* at home, that listed colleges and universities in America and the courses of study available. I knew about S AT s and had already applied to take them. But to which university to apply, other than one in the country across the Pacific, was something I knew nothing about.

My mother was frantic about our financial state (*destitute!*, which we were not, but melodrama was her strong suit), and my father was depressed, as he had been since his business had failed some five years earlier. Informed judgment was not their strong suit. My grades were nothing like those of my smart cousins who could apply for and get academic scholarships, even at the Ivies. There would be no scholarships for me, and even though I didn't know much, I knew enough to know that foreign students were expected to foot their own bill. I was also the eldest child, that tedious experiment, who must blaze trails without compass, map, or even the right baggage or footwear. Meanwhile, my parents argued about money, about life, about what education girls really needed, about how impossible it was to afford university abroad. Before I discovered the IIE, I scoured want ads for jobs that required only a secondary education, applied for and got a position in insurance sales. Upon presenting this accomplishment to my parents, there was a stunned silence and absence of argument. *No,* they both said, *you* will *go to university abroad. We will find the money.* Now that my future course was clear, all I had to do was find a university, something about which my parents remained surprisingly silent.

The first thing my research revealed was that all schools offered English as a degree. This was startling. Although I was presumably educated, Google had not yet opened the door to knowledge that was daunting across borders. It soon became apparent that I could read these reference volumes for years and still have no idea why one university was better than another. The concept of a university tour was more than foreign; it was unimaginable when even my plane fare would be hard enough to afford. In retrospect, I might have done better at insurance sales, much like Wallace Stevens did, although not having read much American literature, thanks to a dauntingly stunted British colonial literary education, Stevens's work was still a future book for my shelf.

My IIE research yielded an initial long list of schools I wrote to, and

I rejected any that addressed their reply to "Hong Kong, Japan," because even though I didn't know much, I wanted my university to know more than me, not less. In the absence of informed judgment, there is merely decision, and I did decide in favor of 1) a Catholic education, since mine was reasonably good and somewhat American under the Maryknoll order, and 2) a place to which I wished to go. Which translated to Xavier in Ohio and the University of Minnesota, the first being obvious and the second because Mary Tyler Moore, or rather her TV persona, was situated in Minneapolis. I applied to and was accepted at both. Of course, had I been a student in the PG era, there's no telling where I might have ended up. The University of Colorado, no doubt, because South Park is in that state.

Some years later, around BG 25, I did again open a book to practice for the GRE, an exam that was rather difficult to arrange for because I was in Greece and of no fixed abode. I sat it in a suburb of Paris, which is daunting in retrospect because I cannot for the life of me imagine how I found the information, how I arranged payment without a credit card, how the Greek postal system did not fail me given my lack of knowledge of Greek. Time must have been more elastic then because it seems I could wait and plan, well ahead of the moment of execution, to write away for knowledge, to transact an international money order, to haunt libraries and various information centers, long before the internet café was a fixture on city corners, in laundromats and bars. All I can swear to is that by BG 25, my judgment was better informed because I ended up in Amherst, Massachusetts, Emily Dickinson's home, which seemed as good a reason as any to be in a place.

27 BG (during my terrible twenties): Telex had entered my life, along with the electric typewriter, one that had two font balls and even memory in the form of cartridges, an astounding technology. It was also a profound moment to be working for the airlines, especially in Asia, where

the economies were not yet tigers and the Thai baht had not crashed and precipitated an economic crisis. Data could be processed by nerds on the mainframe, and my mission, not impossibly, was to collect this data and turn out a frequent flyer program, a grand new marketing thing that would put our company on the map. There was a typing pool and plenty of paper, even carbon paper for file copies. Burnt offerings now, I imagine, like the paper cars, homes, computers, cell phones that Chinese people burn for their dead today. Carbon copies, up in smoke, sacrificial lambs to the gods of small and smaller bytes.

But telex was grand. As an officer-grade employee in the company, I had my own airline telex address. All I needed was the corresponding address to any other airline personnel in the world, and I could write a message, hand it to the operator, and within a day or two, someone on the other side of the world could read a printout of my message in her or his inbox. Excellent for official communication, but even better for unofficial ones, like the messages I sent to the guy I was dating at Braniff, based in Honolulu. We created code, the standard being his reservation request for bookings at the Broadcast Hotel, a fictional locale, the name of the street where I lived. It was how he said he was coming to town.

By the late BG era, there were multiple email options and instant messaging, and by the time PG came to pass, even twittering on devices that marry phones and laptops. With all those myriad ways, means, addresses, how does anyone find you anymore?

20 BG (during the dog days of summer): At the Cincinnati Public Library, the census was a matter of record. I sat in the library for hours trying to comprehend the mass of reports about America's population. Specifically, I needed data on ethnic groupings because I had a research contract with a diversity consultant who did cross-cultural sensitivity training and wrote case studies for corporations about minority hires.

In that same library, I was later to pore over volumes of business directories, identifying companies likely to hire me. In a bid to move to New York City, I wrote two hundred letters on a box called an Apple, one that resembled a portable television, using a program called MacWrite, and watched the pages rattle out on my brand new dot matrix printer. It was a little tricky, aligning those holes to catch correctly on the print roll, but significantly faster than my old electric typewriter, which lasted about as long as eight-track tapes. I had my three-by-five-inch disk with the master letter that could be overwritten two hundred times. If I really wanted to, I could have saved all two hundred letters, but that would have taken up too much disk space, since memory en masse was still future shock. The purchase of this ancient setup required an abiding faith in my ability to pay off credit card debt.

Rereading the previous paragraph, I realize I ought to consider footnotes, especially for the idea of paying off debt. Such references might ultimately lose their original meaning in our PG era, if they are not already considered archaic, which only confirms my suspicion that time has changed, is changing even as I breathe.

But the census, fortunately, is still understandable. After weeks of research, I was able to compile a summary of the Asian population in America, which was my task. Asians comprised 1.97 percent, a shockingly low number, and that included Native Americans, Inuits, and Middle Easterners. Still a green-card alien then, I began to see my identity in a new light. Previously, as a foreign student, I had considered myself part of a worldwide populace of multiple ethnicities, some mixed race like myself. For the first time as an almost-American, I actually understood the meaning of *minority*.

By the PG era, the census felt more user-friendly because Asians had risen to just shy of 4 percent, exclusive of Middle Easterners this time, and some say the number could rise to as high as 10 percent by the time 42 PG rolls round.

18 BG (as autumn leaves drifted by my window): I pledged allegiance, to a flag, I mean. Fortunately, this was a choral endeavor, because I stumbled over the indivisibility of one nation. It was a time of the great divide because some sizable percentage of the nation's wealth was held by a tiny percentage of the populace. The stock market crashed, the economy tanked, and I was laid off from my job thanks to a merger and acquisition, Wall Street's grandest Ponzi, one in which I was not quite senior enough to benefit from the golden handshake of betrayal, this job that brought me to New York, the one that two hundred letters and three rounds of interviews finally yielded, interview rounds paid for by excessive corporate exuberance that flew and housed and wined and dined me in Kansas City and New York. Don't ask, don't tell was the name of the game.

But I did have my blue U.S. passport now (even though I couldn't afford to travel), and the right to vote (which fortunately was free), and even the right to sit in judgment of those who did not view the law as an abiding concern. What more could you want in Life BG? So I trudged along to the office of unemployment and took my place in line with my fellow Americans.

It was a profound experience. For once I wasn't a minority because the minority was the majority in that government office, doing the hustle toward redemption. One step forward, two steps back, side step, back step, side step, back step. Again and again and again. My fellow Americans were kind enough to teach me the dance and to them I am grateful, those anonymous citizens who were much less likely than I to be entrepreneurial, to quickly find freelance work, to send out resumes each day from a transition office my company provided, to network and interview with sympathetic souls, to learn the latest technologies of LANs and WANs and desktop publishing, the last an arcane term now but one that ensured my next full-time position in a Wall Street law firm some eighteen months later. They, unlike me, did not have former colleagues to take them to lunch or offer moral support, did not have books to turn to for solace, did not have degrees and keys and rooms of their own to shelter them in troubled times. Yet they taught me the dance, that joyless hustle, because I too was one of them, in line, battling the same bureaucracy in order to pay the rent, to eat, to hold me over until the next W-2. There are no minorities in a country that values the rights of all citizens, whoever they are, whatever their circumstances and means. Of all the offices of the government of the United States I was to visit that year, this was the most significant.

The years to follow, as the BG era approached its end, tested the nation's indivisibility. The borders between to have and to hold widened, became a chasm of national impossibility as debt mounted; irrational exuberance took hold as the worldwide web spun and spanned divides but on threads so tenuous they broke whenever we sighed.

Shall I leap or shall I stay? Or place hope in second life as real life crashes so painfully down, thanks to bombs and planes and the loss of faith in holding hands across humanity? Meanwhile the zealots' faith is reason to fight, reason to hate, reason to close down the borderless world of the web except to hackers and malcontents.

A failure of the open page. A blank.

And here the system crashed, as systems must in the BG world of planned obsolescence, destroying all records except these. In our PG era now, we recall the BG time with both affection and distaste, wishing for a less perpetual calendar in the history of the world, whether BG, AD, BC, CE, BCE or before and after the founding of the first Chinese Republic.

And I am merely a chronicler of fictions, histories, calendars, believing that this era too must be recorded, somehow, even if paper will go up in flames, even if the disappearance of carbon copies transforms the language of acronyms, even if memory is cheap, selling itself to the highest bidder like love for sale, even if what is remembered is selective, even if there is no way of knowing what the years ahead will bring except for the perpetual motion of calendars and time. Time feels different now. Already P G begins to feel old and the blank page adopts a new identity. The server unexpectedly drops connections, which sometimes occurs when servers are busy, but take heart, dear one, you may be able to open the page later, and later means the calendar, the era continues, that time has not ended, not yet.

At least the significant years survive.

## Notes

1. TruGoogol is an invention. This is a liberty of "creative" nonfiction.
2. The verb *google* is distinguished by its lowercase status.
3. Also *hua qiao* in Putonghua or Mandarin, a one-time political designation for Chinese overseas, particularly those of us in Southeast Asia. The ones patriotic enough to heed the call of "loving the nation" were sent to far-flung corners of the nation during the Cultural Revolution, resulting in the loss of any citizenship, as happened to some members of my family. *Wah kiu* is Cantonese. The term no longer carries its former political weight.
4. S A R: Special Administrative Region, although why a city composed of a bunch of mostly uninhabited islands should be a "region" is anybody's guess.

# DEFAULT HOME

You must live somewhere. So that is home for now, you say. Wherever you lay your head. Wherever an intimacy of persons, places, or possessions compels.

*Home sweet home*, if only for a few nights of a business trip or other command appearance (family; friends; fearless adventure; *f-f-f u* I don't care I *have* to be there, wherever *there* is come hell or high watermark, waterline, water being still a source of life). A contract to work and live as far away as you never anticipated from the place that used to be home. A war zone or Chinese economic miracle zone perhaps, or, less melodramatically, the city where Mother still lives and grows older, alone at home, and not even you, who are neither the most loving nor filial child, could deny a need so negatively culpable that the only course of action was to say, *yes, I'll "go home."* You are the flexible one, after all and the siblings, the only "we," agree. Those intimate persons of the spirit of home.

*To live "at home."* For now (or for as long as it takes because life is bracketed now, forcibly placed between two curvaceous pillars of an aside). There used to be a home you lived in on the other side of the Pacific across a vast and empty land. In the Adirondacks. The comfortable home with no mortgage that stores your lifetime's possessions, the house that is the wrong color (but not so obnoxiously wrong you couldn't wait a year or two to repaint. Or five or forever and then, *time to sell*, the market rises up after a long slump and you will not have lived there for, *oh[!]* maybe so long you set off the alarm because you accidentally punch the wrong code). The home that is becoming merely a house. For who knows how long now that the space called home is a comfortless, barren roof room in an upwardly cramped city?

*Not the space but home as life.* Is it imperative to call some space home, whether a cardboard box on a hospitable city street where a warm enough climate prevails or this raised ranch on an inhospitable but gorgeous country road where autumn is a season of mellow fruitfulness and the wardrobe changes for trees on project runway?

Blink and another year passes.

*So here, "at home" in Hong Kong when you thought you lived in New York.* The City. The State. Okay, both, but only a train ride or puddle jump apart. On TVB Pearl a giant panda puppet repeatedly squeaks "who is Benjameen?" in a Chinese English voice, this Zoo of Talking Pandas a brand image for a *National Treasure* TV program. Pandas are precious in our motherland-home, although there were no pandas in your Hong Kong childhood. Nor was there land occupied by persons, places, possessions where once there was only water in that deep, deep harbor Charles Elliot considered strategic and thus conquered this city for *England, my England*, when Colony was Queen (but today the repeatable squeak is *Content is King* for media content that is just believable or desirable enough to regularly consume despite the distraction of ursine speech or animated brands sauntering across the laptop, tablet, Blackberry, cell of whatever connection is the home that blinds).

*Is home "home" only by default, almost defunct?* You stare at the harbor from a treadmill at your gym, counting four-plus minutes for the ferry to traverse from Kowloon to the island. The journey used to take ten—a mile across—when Hong Kong really felt like home back in '66 (nineteen, not ten, as accidental history does not a home make despite our once-upon-a-British-time), and the harbor was your yard, the vista from a seventeenth-floor flat. When water was clean enough to buoy swimmers for an annual cross-harbor race. Who would swim the cesspool now of this disappearing sea? Would Charles Elliot cringe at this evolution or was this his vision too, that the barren rock would, like Monkey, burst into life, to become home for millions (seven and counting) stacked higher and higher on land stolen from the sea, raising Atlantis to the heavens for, *oh(!)* a blink of the eye, until we sink from the weight of too many persons, places, possessions, and return to our native home, a barren rock again?

# LETTER FROM AMERICA

April 2009

On one floor, electronic word-lights race along ten parallel tracks. I'm in New York at the Whitney, at American artist Jenny Holzer's *Protect Protect* exhibit. Elsewhere, her redaction paintings remind us the country is still at war. Using declassified government documents with sensitive material redacted, Holzer enlarged these into art-statements of protest. Autopsy reports, handprints of military personnel accused of war crimes, maps that Central Command used to delineate plans for invading Iraq. This artist builds word art around visual statements, her most famous being "protect me from what I want." The exhibit is both profoundly disturbing and stunningly gorgeous.

It's spring break, and I've fled the Midwest to head back east. From January to May, I'm a visiting writer at the University of Iowa. The year 2009 begins the longest continuous residence in my country of citizenship of recent years. In 2009 a mixed-race, dark-skinned man is president, one with connections to Indonesia, Africa, Hawaii, and Illinois, specifically Chicago. I ponder this while gazing at Holzer's running words, her pink, green, yellow, purple LED tracks that transport meaning to new planes, surprising you around corners, in arches, simultaneously assaulting and delighting the senses. Her parallel-track, ground-level display, "For Chicago," is perhaps a nod to the new president.

Later, when Hong Kong's daylight dawns, I am on the phone to our realtor about my family's rental flat. The thing he wants to know: *what's the mood like there?* We're closing in on 10 percent unemployment, I say, people are nervous, and New York's real estate has dipped a little but not a lot. He is reassured. It is the same in Hong Kong. The market advantages the buyer or renter, although *landlords who won't drop prices must afford to wait*. He's just doing his job, sales pitching to ensure we price for the market. When I ask about the mood, his reply: *there still are lines at yum cha*. But he sounds the same nervous note that vibrates in the voices of my American friends. No one quite believes things are all that bad, although everyone thinks things will only get worse before they get better.

In January, I drove into Iowa in a blizzard. My journey west was blessed by the weather gods. I encountered snow and cold but mostly clear skies during the three-day drive, although the radio portended storms. The last two hours were painstakingly slow as snow and wind whipped my small Subaru. I prayed GPS would carry me to my destination, a rental house for which I held the key.

The first night on the road was spent opposite the airport at Buffalo, New York, where I consumed buffalo wings in their birthplace. The second was in Mishawaka, Indiana, a Native American name, but I mis-said *Mishi-KA-wa*, which felt vaguely Japanese, rolling easily off my Asian tongue. When planning my road trip, I decided South Bend, Indiana, was a likely stopover. For one thing, I had heard of this midwestern city, which is also home to Notre Dame University. Its greater metropolitan area numbers more than three hundred thousand by the last census. Mishawaka was the hotel address, and I assumed it was some exurban South Bend overflow, where I'd be lucky to find a restaurant open. More likely, dinner would mean heading down some strip mall to junk food.

In Mishawaka, however, its newness felt like *The Truman Show*. This "twin city" to South Bend has a curiously postmodern face of suburban chic. At once *Desperate Housewives* and *American Pie*, its architecture recalls small-town America, with a nod to a twenty-first-century greening and clean design lines, beyond calico and frump. The hotel had a decent gym and was in better condition than the more expensive Buffalo one. The manager said they had opened about seven years ago and that the city was a ten-year-old reality.

But how late did restaurants stay open? Experience said nine at the latest. *Go to eat early*, my maxim in Middle America, except maybe Chicago, the only way to guarantee real food and not processed chemicals. The manager assured that nothing closed before ten, possibly eleven, and suggested Bonefish Grill. *They fly in their fish daily, or every other day*, he added, in response to my doubtful expression. Foolhardy perhaps, but I took my chances and was rewarded with an exquisite dish at this Florida-based establishment in what appears to be a popular branch. In the middle of nowhere during a recession, this relatively large space was almost full at well past the early American dinner hour. The patrons were maybe 35 percent African American, 10 percent Hispanic. I was *not* the only Asian face there, and the menu featured sushi. For the equivalent in Hong Kong or New York, my bill would have been twice as much. Middle America is still the land of good value.

Mine is not Alistair Cooke's *Letter from America*. In 2009 the country is more global and less American than the rest of the world imagines. By 2009 America has also seeped more fully into our global consciousness than we like to admit. At the recent G20 conference, the world was mad at Wall Street. This subprime mess, enhanced by derivatives and dubious financial instruments, has dumped us knee-deep into a worldwide quicksand. No one feels "comfortable" anymore—our global middle-class aspiration—given shrinking portfolios, a crumbling banking structure, and careening indexes. The Dow, Hang Seng, FTSE, et al. have suddenly become illogical mathematical problems, without predictably elegant curves to plot and explain. And here I am, a subway ride away from Wall Street, wondering why we are so mad, why we blame America for causing this crisis, and why, as China recently has demanded, that America fix things. Why, above all, do we think America *can* fix the mess? Isn't it our problem too?

Government stimulus packages, in the United States, Hong Kong, China, and elsewhere, might work. I am not an economist and have no crystal ball for such things. It's our cultural problem that engages me, this "value" that insists: BUT OF COURSE YOU MUST CONSUME! The world sells, and we *will* consume. Ringtones, apps, blogs, chatrooms, words that barely pass spell-check. And hardware too, often purchased virtually, for travel, restaurants, designer wear.

My Chelsea neighborhood in New York, which formerly housed the meat-packing industry, a transvestite hooker trade, and a working-class Hispanic population, has transformed completely in the last decade, the same period that transformed tiny Mishawaka. The longtime diner at the end of my block has been through two café-cum-bistro versions, serving the same breakfast and coffee of the old place for double the price and half the service. The new staff and clientele are young, beautiful, hip, indifferent. Meanwhile, Café Riazor, our favorite Spanish place on Sixteenth Street, dating back several decades, one that served tapas long before it was hip, now worries about quiet weekends. Good value, friendly service, and consistently excellent fare matter less than being new.

Galleries and clubs converge west toward the water. Designer shops line Fourteenth Street. Rents rise insanely for the same lousy tenements that once housed the poor, these dwellings that are now for the newly rich and "comfortably" aspiring. Old buildings are razed; new hotels, condominiums, offices rise up instead. Today, a shiny Frank Gehry graces the waterfront where dockworkers and sailors once roamed.

Our appetite is large and attention, deficit. We consume not because of need, as gigagazillion images, texts, ideas zip by, exhorting us to buy, to want, to aspire to rich and famous lives, consuming at godly heights. 衣食住行—clothing, food, home, transport—are the basics for life. But who insisted we "need" designer wear, gourmet fare, luxury flats, and Porsches instead of the bus? Did America? Perhaps Hollywood and the standard of living that evolved in post-Depression America led the way, but do we blame a culture because we too want more than we need? Beijing disappeared like an illusion and nip-tucked its face for the Olympics and beyond. Hong Kong is Prada-proud while devils steal away historic structures, open spaces, the city itself and perhaps even our soul, all for the sake of the marketplace.

Do we shoot the messenger or rewrite the message instead?

PROTECT US FROM WHAT WE WANT should be our global protest, echoing Holzer. Hundreds of jobless former Wall Streeters currently haunt New York's charities, heeding Obama's call for volunteerism because overachievers must stay busy. *How long will that last,* wonder the directors of such organizations, overwhelmed by this surge of volunteers their staff can barely cope with. But perhaps when the economy rebounds, they hope, donations will pour in from these enlightened "consumers."

If consumer debt helped to sink our world, perhaps it's time to rewrite the meaning of consumption. Is there too much "aspiration" and not enough dream? To paraphrase American writer Delmore Schwartz, *in dreams we learn responsibility*. In aspiration, all we do is value the object or goal, without ever questioning why we aspire, because advertising tells us that we *should* aspire to all that is beautiful, hip, shiny, new.

Living in Middle America, I catch up on television, the cheapest form of entertainment besides the library. *Trust Me* is a new series about two ad men here in this country that gave birth to advertising, the creative craft of consumption. The art director is an overachieving workaholic family man who places trust in brands and the family he never sees. The copywriter is the single guy, an irresponsible Peter Pan who will not grow up because being creative is about placing trust in a childlike sense of wonder, regardless of consequence. In 2009 advertising is as much in our DNA as is Confucius. Google "Confucius" and he appears over 4 million times because we consume his thoughts and what he represents the way we consume everything else on the web. That advertising is an industry dating back only one, mostly American, century is irrelevant; search "advertising" and you pull up over *500 million* sites. In Google world, we place greater trust in the new. The etymology of "advertise" dates back to Middle English; its obsolete meaning is "to warn or admonish."

Artists dream, aspiring to remembrance and responsibility, not wealth for its own sake. *Protect!* warns Holzer in March, Women's Month. Is this an admonishment as well? February celebrated black history. Will this black president raise global consciousness about American culture other than consumption and advertising? Martin Luther King dreamed his country would judge people not on skin color but on "the content of our character." The world too needs this message. Instead of blaming America for the mess or expecting a lifeline, we should examine the content of our character and ask where responsibility lies for this mess we're in. This quicksand world where we all now find ourselves.

# WINTER MOON

*Where is love's magic?*
*Where has it gone?*

"WINTER MOON," MUSIC AND LYRICS BY HOAGY
CARMICHAEL AND HAROLD ADAMSON

You play his music, listen to multiple renditions of the songs he wrote. You think you know something because you've played "The Nearness of You" so many times that it flows from your fingertips, improvises, transforms, flies.

It's winter on the South Island, which means it's summer in New York and New Jersey, where the man in your life spends his nights and days. You do this distance thing because you've bought a "crib" in New Zealand—even though you're not Kiwi—and the first piece of furniture you install is this very heavy used upright. Its left front wheel has since fallen off, and the piano has been in a "lockup"—more quaint Kiwi English for the room sealed off from the rest of this getaway house-crib—to rent out in your absence for over two years now. But that's another story in the *yet to come*, the 沒來, as the future articulates in Chinese.

So it's winter on the South Island, and you're playing the piano in the green room. You had it painted pale green to match the garden. The painter should have been an artist, as should the gentleman contractor who restored your little villa (more quaint Kwinglish) to its former glory. You say "bungalow," I say "villa." *Let's call the whole thing off.*

It had been some years since you owned a piano. Having moved your life from Hong Kong to New York to be with the man, you join his family in New Jersey every Christmas as well, and graduations, christenings, birthdays, Thanksgivings. Once, you even went to Mass, lapsed Catholics though you both were, with his parents and your visiting mother who were not, who never lapsed. It was a good life, a wonderful life. The movies of your childhood and his soundtracked your America. Because you are American, became American long before this man in your life, except that he *is* the America you ought to have married because it was the one you imagined as a child in Hong Kong. Well, perhaps not quite. Your invisible America was greener, cleaner, larger than a railroad flat in Manhattan. You would have a piano because there always was one in your life. The American you did marry was a music man so there was a piano, and a drum set, and guitars, and an electronic keyboard, and amplifiers, sound makers aplenty. Until it all went silent. Marriages do that, go silent I mean, while *the music box plays on.* But that's another story of the 後景, *backward view*, as the past articulates in Chinese.

Was Hoagy Carmichael your America? By now you can't be sure because his music is mashed up with the soundtracks of memory. Didn't you *always* know "Stardust" or "Lazy River" or "Two Sleepy People" or, yes! "Heart and Soul," which every ivory tickler knows from even her tiny person time? *Hadn't* you seen him in the old black-and-whites late at night, gabbing in those Yankee accents you didn't entirely understand from a world glimpsed in the pages of *Life*? Or is this all just imagination because it's winter on the South Island and you're cohabiting with this man who can recite lines from *Rear Window, Casablanca, Cat on a Hot*

*Tin Roof*, and more, who identifies Tinseltown and Americana for you, filling in the knowledge gaps?

That's not quite right. You are not exactly living with this man right now. You're at the top of time, and he at almost the other end of the zone stretch across the globe that is Time. This was pre-Skype, which is less long ago than it sounds. You cannot see each other and New Zealand Telecom is outrageously expensive. He lives over there, and you live here in this villa with a garden and a green room with a piano that you play for hours.

That winter, "The Nearness of You" became your song. So did many others from the American Songbook. You tried to have the piano tuned but rural enclaves are seldom visited by tuners. Besides, it sounded good enough for an amateur like you. The music was more than America or him or you. The piano caressed your hands, danced melodies round your head, sang love songs to you.

And then you no longer lived together, because you bought a home, a real home in America, not the playpen of New Zealand. Greener, cleaner and larger than a New York City railroad flat, although still in New York, though not one you knew existed when you imagined the country from Hong Kong in the little-person era. You bought a piano, a bad buy you later discover, because this console will not hold its tuning. Regret passed soon enough. Nights and days of handholding and dancing. Consolation in your large and green space up north, where the piano was your constant companion.

You envied your ex-husband's guitar portability and considered learning a woodwind, even stopped to examine a clarinet once in a secondhand store. But the piano! You can lean into its body, stroke its keys, rise and fall to the rhythms of the pedal. Are you being faithful to the man in your life given this promiscuous flirtation with not one, but two pianos? Oh, his stuff is up north (including a bicycle), and your stuff is in the city.

You live together; your stuff is in each other's homes. You both embrace George Carlin's monologue on "Stuff," laugh, even though you've never watched it together. You even get mail in New York City, as you do up north, as you do in New Zealand.

So what is this silence into which you write, into which you stare at a photograph of silent keys? That piano sits in an abandoned space, and, like all abandoned spaces, holds a strange allure. They worry the memory, imprint themselves on your very self once you've left them behind.

Is it spaces or pianos you leave behind?

The South Island piano is a light-colored wood, like oak, and its action recalls a piano you used to play in another time, another space, on a dead-end street in New England. You sold that one and got a better one that thrummed through you, resonant. And then you sold that one to live for a spell in Cincinnati. where a swimming pool was the most desirable feature. It would be a long time before another upright entered your life, and when it did, the musician was abandoned, along with his guitars and amplifiers and drum set and the electric keyboard in Singapore on which you practiced "La Vie en Rose," a song he never heard you play.

These are years, mind you, we're discussing here. Decades. These are not the passing flirtations of youth.

You time-trip into today and find you cannot abandon Mother. She is old. She cannot remember. Instead, you abandon the hopeless piano that will not hold its tuning in northern New York. You rent out the South Island crib to strangers whom you never meet. You do all this in order to come "home" to stay till Mother is silenced forever. The pianos sit silent.

And now you really do *not* live with the man in your life in the upside-down time zone, and you sleep when he wakes and wake when he sleeps.

For a brief while, when abandonment was less certain, you spent half a year in the middle of America in a rented space. The house was on the historic register, large, and in the garage was an abandoned piano, wedged amid the detritus of a household. You opened its lid, tickled it awake, but it was a little far gone. Besides, it was heavy and immovable and this was the dead of winter. But desire smoldered.

At the music store you tested the weighted keys of an electric keyboard and brought that to your space.

This was when you still lived in almost the same time zone with the man in your life. He meant to visit the cornfields of Iowa, where you were settled for a brief spell, but Manhattan held him in bondage. That year, he never saw Middle America after all, this American lover of yours. You write about being American to articulate what it is you have become.

At the University of Iowa, the library had a section of music scores. You found the Hoagy songbook and in it the anthem for the next years of your life (although you did not know it then). When your brother the composer visited, you played it for him. *Listen*, you said, *I think this was Hoagy's heart.* Your brother, the church music composer, does not always share your taste in music, but this time, he asked for a copy of the score for "Winter Moon," and you made it for him, gladly.

"The American dream," Carlin said, "you have to be asleep to believe it."

In the little-person time, you dreamed yourself into an America of desire, to escape the Hong Kong prison into which you were born, where your voice felt continually silenced. Now, back in this birth city you abandoned to be with the man in your life, you install not one but two electronic keyboards. The multiple sound tracks—*vox humana*, every instrument of the big band and orchestra, sound effects—sit beside your bed. The weighted keys sit in your writing space. The simulation that feels almost like a real piano switches on, comes alive, holds your hand, caresses your heart.

The man in your life is on Skype when schedules mesh.

And you? You listen to Hoagy sing "Winter Moon." You play his songs. You sing the lines to his chord changes.

The other night at a dinner, someone actually sang "The Sound of Silence" and the audience sang along. Time journeys, nostalgia, lost youth.

And you. You wait, like a winter moon, for summer's return.

# THE SUMMERS OF
# MY DISCONTENT

August 2009

Arrival, mid-July, is too hot, but "time off" in America (longer than usual this year) means I must go home again to my city. On Mum's rooftop—my Alzheimer's mother who has forgotten our roof room exists—I swelter. I appear before my mother after an eight-month absence, and what she says is, *oh there you are*, as if I'd never left.

Summer is not the time to be in Hong Kong, but this year seems particularly inauspicious. To begin with, July's "solar eclipse of the century" only favors us a partial viewing while on the mainland some three thousand tourists flock to see the real thing. My consolation is that Shanghai's view is marred by rain, while our city gets six glorious minutes. We get plenty of rain though. Six typhoons hit us this summer, and signal 8 or higher is hoisted thrice. The first, Molave in July, rises to signal 9, and the mean temperature that month is 0.4 degrees above normal. Goni's visitation disrupts the annual secondary student scramble for form 6 places. What really hits home, however, is when my internet dies in August. Morakot, the typhoon and earthquake that shakes up Taiwan's government, forcing President Ma to apologize for emergency mismanagement, also damages PCCW's undersea telecom cable. I batten down discontent, my internet intermittent, unable to access life. Chastened by nature I bury myself in books. Even right into mid-September, Koppu rages the night before my departure until morning, and the plane sits on a traffic-congested tarmac more than an hour as the rains and winds subside.

What people do to nature is yet more galling. My old school, Maryknoll, is a heritage site graced by a seventy-year-old Norfolk pine, which is threatened by destruction. Supposedly in danger of crashing, and hence a safety risk, the tree withstands all typhoons this summer. The legal frenzy surrounding its destruction is absurdist drama, but it's safe for now, having won a reprieve thanks to conservationist common sense. Meanwhile, at Big Wave Bay, where my sister lives, at one of our more pristine and less polluted beaches, the government proposes to erect a six-meter-long wall, two meters high, supposedly to prevent further sand erosion that resulted from damage by last year's Typhoon Hagupit. This makes me think of numerous silly walls erected in China over the centuries—often more offensive than defensive—erroneously considered part of the so-called Great Wall, but which simply means "long" wall in Chinese, as Julia Lovell points out in her excellent 2007 book about the history of the wall. Residents and surfers are up in arms. With luck bureaucrats will rethink this eyesore plan because Big Wave Bay is where my sister lives and surfs.

In the meantime, two vacant lots, the controversial West Kowloon arts hub and the former airport site, are still in the Hong Kong Government's Property Purgatory. Development Goliath continually battles human well-being in our capitalist enclave.

Then, in mid-August, a new rail link opens, causing chaos, complaints, and confusion. The fast ride to my gym in Tsimshatsui, which averaged eight to ten minutes, is now a longer transfer trip that can take up to twenty-five. The integration is not yet seamless, which is what happens when a rural railway merges with an urban subway system. The former has outdoor platforms; the latter began underground. A railway builds public toilets; a subway does not but should now that the MTR Corporation serves all of Hong Kong and more, having swallowed up the Kowloon-Canton Railway (KCR). We will, however, adapt and adjust to our city's never-ending growth spurts—this hormonally challenged adolescent thing—as population body heat rises closer toward 8 million.

Confounded by the heat, my air conditioner hums more often than not, hastening environmental meltdown. On television *Mother's Dead Upset* is a Korean soap opera about discontented mums. Real news is grim. During high winds two workers fall off bamboo scaffolding and die. One morning a water pipe bursts, closing down the main artery linking business districts, further disrupting life. At the construction site of what will be the city's tallest building (stay tuned for this commercial phallic enterprise), six workers plunge twenty floors down a lift shaft, the worst industrial accident in years. None survive.

But these discontents are just another summer in the city except for this last. On Sunday, September 13, hundreds took to the streets to protest the beating of three Hong Kong journalists in Ürümqi and to condemn the Xinjiang government's response. In the Chinese University poll commissioned by the News Executives' Association, a sizable majority (78 percent) did not believe the Xinjiang investigation reports, and nearly 60 percent said the incident shook their confidence in Beijing. The situation simmers; a local delegate to the National People's Congress now counsels "patience," saying Premier Wen Jiabao is not the one raising the nightstick, as if a leader bears no responsibility for the actions of its government officials, as if a citizenry should accept violence and denial as norms. Is this what life must be now that *tianxia*—under heaven—we're all "one China"? Is the best recourse to stick your nose in a book, ignoring these murmurs of discontent?

And will Beijing one day, like my mother, simply gaze blankly at us and say, *oh there you are*, forgetting we ever left?

August 2015

The prediction for typhoons in 2016 is iffy because of El Niño's uncertain effect. At Maryknoll, the Norfolk pine is gone, despite prolonged protest, though the government's proposed wall construction at Big Wave Bay was defeated by a residents' group, much to my sister's relief. West Kowloon is now a large hole in the ground—reminiscent of Boston's never-ending "big dig"—this construction for the rail link to China controversially delayed, while the arts and cultural district is still more virtual than real. But the former airport is now a cruise terminal, a government project meant to revitalize the area with a new park, shopping, and the like but which most consider a resounding failure. The KCR is now fully subsumed into the MTR, which suffers notable service delays, and the public toilet situation at its stations has not appreciably progressed. However, the new line that extends to the western side of Hong Kong Island has opened, and the University of Hong Kong no longer exists in its former splendid isolation, at least not in terms of speedy public transport. Korean telenovellas have been shunted aside in favor of *Under the Dome*, a TV serial sci-fi horror based on Stephen King's novel on what is now more or less Hong Kong's *only* free station, the other now reduced to a shadow of its former self. High-rise construction sites still bring us regular horrors of industrial dangers, alongside the usual quota of suicide jumpers, enhanced these days by accidental falls from on high of the selfie-obsessed, stepping too far back. And China is one country, one large and super-powerful nation, flexing muscles under a president who knows what's best, like Father.

**5.** 哭 = cry. 父母為我哭了 我為將來哭了. Our parents are crying for us. I am crying for the future. *My parents . . . my future . . .* the cri de coeur of the young "Yellow Umbrella" Occupy Hong Kong protestors in 2014. Photo courtesy of the author.

# THE CRYING CITY

We cried over Occupy. We cry over Occupy. I will continue to cry over Occupy in the years to come. Our sadness, it appears, is measurable. The World Happiness Report ranks our city at 72, far behind Taiwan (38), Singapore (24), the United States (15), or Switzerland (1). At least we're ahead of China (84), Greece (102) or the seriously sad nation of Togo, ranked last at 158. But I am being unfair. Hong Kong's unhappiness is not only due to Occupy, seventy-eight days in 2014 during which my fellow citizens transformed our streets into a tented city to protest for a "democracy" that remains slippery, contentious, unresolved.

By 3 p.m. on Monday, December 15, deadline for the removal of Occupy, our streets were almost entirely cleared. We Hong-Kong-ers obey our deadlines. We turn in homework on time and pay taxes to our Special Administrative Region with minimal protest. In the days and months that followed, a slew of songs, photos, videos, and declarations shuddered through cyberspace, aided and abetted by the ravenous international media, starved as they always are for heroes and villains as icons for what they don't have time to digest and fully comprehend. Besides, young faces are the harbingers of universal hope, just as they were for Tiananmen twenty-five years earlier. *Time* always needs persons for the years.

Within our borders, nostalgia was quick to follow. Merely months later, we have ensured the preservation of street art installations and other remembrances. An attempt to rewrite that history via a Cantonese musical drama plays to a full house at City Hall Theatre. It was a muddled attempt, framed in a futuristic narrative of a dying child in need of a bone marrow transfer; a cross-cultural marriage between a blind, white *gweilo* and a Hong Kong Chinese woman with a dark secret; a Rosencrantz and Guildenstern–styled musical interlude; memories of Occupy muddied by rape. At intermission, I exited, stage left.

So why am I still crying for this city I currently call home? This city that we may perhaps no longer call home in our own future narratives?

Years earlier, the rain-soaked return of our city to China was a memorably muddied moment. We sorely needed yellow umbrellas then. Shortly after midnight, the new morn of July 1, 1997, I wandered through neon-lit protests by the same politicos who shout today for true democracy. They were and weren't about Occupy, because it was the students who led the world to our streets with tents and supplies, turning the city into a giant campground. At Admiralty, the main Occupy site, it was school vacation with study hall. In Causeway Bay, a giant map exhorted the passersby to *please, please* buy from the surrounding stores. Customers had vanished, inconvenienced by the barricades, fed up of the constant photo clicking by citizen journalists for Facebook, Instagram, Twitter, Tumblr, and *who knows* where *your face might end up, somewhere in the files of the PLA or CCCP?* A prolonged siege is fodder for speculation. On Hong Kong Island, tourists holidayed in the streets of these two districts during the days and nights of Occupy. Some international celebrity made a dumb remark that was quickly retracted, his China market too lucrative to offend. My city is prone to memorable muddles.

But we had to give the students ten thumbs up for their newly awakened political consciousness, even if some sweet young things muddied history, raising the Union Jack as symbol of some sweetly democratic past. They had not suffered the slings and arrows of unequal treaties, historically the most humiliating deal for a defeated China, the same deal that transformed this once-barren rock into the cosmopolitan, prosperous, thoroughly modern city of their births. Our sovereign master (or is it a mistress-dominatrix worthy of ten thousand shades of yellow?) still nurses the wound inflicted by that terrible time. Opiate for silver dollars. Gunboat diplomacy. An emasculation to surpass even our sad history of a eunuch serving class for entitled royalty. A national humiliation so unforgettable it will steer China's foreign policy into the next century and beyond. Displacement, denigration, discrimination by the marauding colonial conqueror. Trauma narrative, that universally popular genre.

Even so, you had to love those invigorated, passionate young hearts as they slept, night after night, on asphalt, forsaking their dorm rooms or Hello Kittyed bedrooms at home. As they packed up their tents, stacked their supplies, organized their departures with the same logistical efficiency that colored their occupation, those determined visages, too young to truly know sorrow, made us cry.

Why are we such an unhappy place? Our rankings in earlier World Happiness Reports did not fare any better. Meanwhile, our universities are desperately rising in the rankings while driving out as many of those leftover running dogs of the British as they can. Tenure track these days is north toward Beijing, and racing hounds countenance a brand new shade of whiteface. That's why academia weeps. Our government-funded universities are all English medium, and faculty command among the highest salaries in the academic world. These days, though, critical thought is being redefined as far away from that troublesome, Western-centric, democracy worship as possible, that polluting influence on our young minds. The English language is a slithy-tove lingua franca, either uttered with a masculine, mainland accent or assisted by a large research grant in anything measurable that raises a university's ranking.

Still, we can be consoled by the fact that Hong Kong is the only non-nation recognized in the ranks of a global report on the happiness of nation-states.

Is that the root of our unhappiness, that we are not a nation-state? Our unique international dialing code, +852, almost makes us one, but that is a hyperbolic claim. The city of Macau, that other SAR of China, has its own code too. Macau, however, is not ranked on this happiness scale. Which only leaves Taiwan (unless you count those rocks in choppy waters lapping the coasts of China). The thing about Taiwan, happily ranked under Malta and above Kuwait, is that it has less dystopia and other residuals on the x-axis of happiness when compared to Hong Kong. What we talk about when we talk about this other China, that only Chinese democratic world, is our trepidation. How long, we wonder, can Taiwan last before it too loses its nation-state toehold? Taiwan's greater happiness, at least from our perch, just might be delusional. Depending on whom you ask, it never was one in the first place, being a rebel territory of China. Of course, China lays claim to all kinds of disputed territories, reclaims at will for maritime rezoning, and then says, *so there*, drowning out further protest.

Perhaps Hong Kong's real problem is that for too long we playacted at nation-statehood. We design and print more and more new stamps, in all denominations, and Hong Kong Post collects revenue from philatelic sales from the Stamps-R-Us crowd. There is the SAR passport, with visa-free entry at last count to 162 countries, a step up from the colonial one that required a visa for Britain. Our currency is multicolored and issued by multiple banks; the hybrid bauhinia, our national *fleur*, is a favored design; our immovable peg to the U.S. dollar fulfills the Hong Kong Monetary Authority's first main function, to maintain currency stability.

Cantonese, a Chinese language with global currency for a large diaspora, is still an official language here alongside Putonghua and English. We even have our own legal system, so stick that in your pipe to those who bemoan *ceci n'est pas une pipe*. Our universities and the elite public schools teach in English. When university faculty resort to Cantonese, as they do, it's only because too many students have trouble fully comprehending this alien, *slithy* tongue.

There are some minor issues. Not having a military, for instance, but the PLA has proven a superior replacement for bagpipes and kilts that on windy days expose bare butts to the world. Or the lack of sovereign ability to negotiate foreign relations: one former bowtie-toting Chief Executive of this SAR racked up frequent flyer miles behaving *as if*, he's now pilloried for wasteful government spending, the breach of public trust, and just sheer bad taste. Or the lack of right to vote, except for student government, but our youth get to play at democracy in university, so what more do they expect? Just as the older generation in nation-states cluck and tsk at the younger, so do we. Freedom of movement, freedom of thought, a progressive, forward-looking culture poised to succeed in the twenty-first-century global economy, *that's us*, we say, bursting with national pride. *So tsk tsk*, we scold our spoiled and pampered youth. What entitled you to be freer than free? *Thus spake Zarathustra*, and we.

Back in the 1970s, I imagined a Free China Movement for my first attempt at a novel. The book was titled *Proximity* and foresaw my birth city in its post-1997 turmoil, where a nationalistic party wanted Hong Kong to secede from China. The territory's fictional futuristic fate was as that of an Atlantis in the South China Seas, a tourist attraction and historical reminder of the city that would be free. At the time in reality, Hong Kong was rising, and China was just beginning to peek out from behind its Bamboo Curtain. No one would publish the novel, which, from my perch as an author now, was probably a good thing since literary juvenilia can be embarrassing in retrospect. Today, the manuscript resides in the archives of a government university library for whatever posterity brings. That's the trouble with fiction and being a writer: you are too, too much a Cassandra foreshadowing dystopia. Which means you also cry too, too much, rather too soon, while the rest of your world still roars with laughter.

Today, a postapocalyptic video of an abandoned city is already doing the cyber rounds, a homage to the heroic failure that was Occupy.

In this post-Occupy here and now, the essay seems a more appropriate genre than fiction for the articulation of our tears. See, I even dare say "we" and not merely "I" or the indecisive *tutoyer* or *vous* second person because for the first time in the history of my native-born, foreigner-local Hong Kong existence, I know I am not crying alone.

The history of modern Hong Kong is fraught with crises and protests subdued. In 1857 poisoned bread from a Chinese bakery sickened many Europeans and was one sign, the British knew, that local nationalism needed to be squashed. In 1967 the leftist riots meant schools closed early and the British again squashed dissent. In 1984 the Joint Declaration was China's vengeance for unequal treaties, a checkmate move the British failed to fully anticipate. Now Britain's protests about the promised democracy in that declaration might as well have been signed in invisible ink, which, as any youthful would-be detective knows, can readily be made from lemon, squashed.

But these political moments are mere blips in our city's history and can too readily fall prey to the revisionist. There is no dominant narrative now. Besides, the real narrative, the one that anyone, especially China, actually cares about, is all about the economy.

Our survival instincts, once the British departed, were good. The Asian economic crisis proved a momentary burp for our Hang Seng Index.

Bird flu? A minor avian inconvenience. Birds will be birds, and we simply stopped chickens from crossing our roads by summary execution. When the global financial crisis shattered economies in 2008, Hong Kong's then-commissioner for economic and trade affairs ended his remarks at Johns Hopkins University the following year on an optimistic note: *We have confidence in Hong Kong's ability to rebound due to its sound fundamentals, can-do spirit, quality workforce, the great support from the Mainland, and the new opportunities arising from the Pearl River Delta development.*

We even survived SARS (the virus, not the plural of our political reality), which caused a serious economic setback in the autumn of 2003. It was spooky wandering through an emptied SARS city, as was flying to Hainan out of the new but silent airport where only a few, brave, masked souls ventured forth. I was reminded of that time as I walked through Mongkok, the main Occupy district on Kowloon Peninsula, where buses and cars were diverted away from Nathan Road, the main north-south artery, because the long vehicular access was closed for protestors in gas masks. The city wept differently in Kowloon, this Occupy by the working classes. They were older, madder, politically stubborn, and ready to fight. This Occupy generally got less attention than the heavily media-occupied districts of Admiralty and Central on the island. Until violence erupted, that is. The fundamentals never change, not when content providers must stay *on top of the News and ahead of the Times*, a New York newspaper's ad slogan from the days before newsprint disappeared.

It's the disappearance of what we have been, are, and could be that makes us cry. Never mind the economy. Milt Friedman was both wrong and right about our laissez-faire property bubbles because markets simply will rise and fall, there's no perfect time to buy or sell except to buy low and sell high, and past performance is never, ever an entirely reliable indicator of future returns, a caveat that never stops the saddest investors from plunging into debt or off tall buildings at a single bound. Our government hoards

our cash and ends up with (WTF!) a gigantic surplus each year, yet refuses
to spend on making nice for the poor and disenfranchised. After all, as
our financial secretary has been known to quip, he too enjoys his French
coffee and red wine, his nod to middle-class life. Did he conveniently
forget that our top government man (and for years it was always a man,
until a woman finally assumed the mantle in 2017) earns more than the
president of the United States? As the number one finance man himself,
he does not lag far behind. Only the willfully obtuse would name such
an existence "middle class" in this sad city where the GINI coefficient
measures an ever-widening gap of income disparity.

Meanwhile, conspiracy theorists abound. It's easy to be suspicious of
Big Daddy up north who might take our T-Bird away because their right
to raid our coffers is unquestionable. But in the end, we sigh, the economy
always does seem to take care of itself. The city heals, democracy remains
a complicated linguistic puzzle for all, so why gripe about politically
impossible dreams? Shouldn't we dream instead of *Dolce Vita* (as the
local TV program regularly reminds us), to eat, shop, travel and luxuriate?
What more should a SAR citizen desire? Besides, there is all that great
support from the Mainland, and its coffers are way larger than ours. Our
fearless leaders will make nice for our poor and disenfranchised, within
reason, naturally. Up north, the central desire is only that Hong Kong
be peaceful, prosperous, and patriotic. Reasonable expectations, don't
you think? Which is why we might as well adopt our usual pragmatic,
practical, prosperity-making selves.

Darling, the road more taken is apolitical. Destiny is survival.

I like to think, because I haven't given up trying to write, that my sorrow is
universal. That our little archipelago in the South China Sea is mourning
a disappearance that has global echoes. Perhaps those echoes resound in
fits and starts, in moments recognizable elsewhere. Yet this lament feels

decidedly local. Even within our borders, our tears are for variable sorrows. Parents of young protestors cried for their safety. The youthful campers wept for their future. In the homes of members of the police force, private battles raged. The police attempted to do their job with minimal force in subduing the protests. The protestors pushed back. People got hurt. Behind closed doors, other eruptions followed. No narrative can assuage the schism that ensued. We are and have been a civil, law-abiding, and peaceful society, and this unnatural violence terrified us. Yet Occupy returns months later, replete with yellow umbrellas, and the morning news is full of Mongkok's nighttime violence and clashes with the law. A few days later, the evening news is full of the protests for some kind of *democracy, democracy, democracy.*

The international world of my Hong Kong howls for the loss of our moment in time. We once dared to believe that *this* city, *this* global home, could and would embrace a transnational, transcultural, multilingual reality that welcomed myriad voices, ethnicities, desires, and dreams in a civil society under rule of law. Our world wanted freedom of speech and movement, tolerance for diversity, and a future as a global, unique city in China. We watched our children intermarry and become TCKs, third-culture kids with Chinese characteristics and Hong Kong roots. Admittedly, the successful TCK is still an elite minority, a product of international schools, economic well-being, privileged Western education, bilingual fluency in the lingua franca that is English alongside Putonghua to prosper in that shiny new nation, China. They cry for all that is being disappeared by a one-party, one-perspective, our-way-or-no-way shift in the governance of this city. They mourn while preparing their exit plans because if you have a foreign passport, you have other worlds and homes to embrace you. Actors depart, stage left. Heaven is *Murgatroyd, e-vun.*

But each time I consider Occupy, I know I weep for the majority local population, especially the young, who do not have an exit plan.

Besides, why should they even need one? This is their home and should be their future.

Besides, they must love Hong Kong because they have no other lover.

*Life is unfair*, howls the theme song of *Malcolm in the Middle*, an American TV series about that sad and luckless middle child. Our youth are caught in that middle between warring politicos, definitions of democracy, one country two futures, the conflicted ways of being Chinese. In Hong Kong, a small minority believes we could become a city-state, but worldwide odds on that run around a billion to zero. Even fewer must believe we should return to Britain, although the recent surge in renewals of British National Overseas passports is *curiouser and curiouser*, nostalgia for a Red Queen instead of the East that is Red. The truly desperate might seek passports to happier countries, those that hawk nationalities. Unfortunately, of the top five nations with easy entry in the BBC's report ("Where is the cheapest place to buy citizenship?"), only two, Malta (37) and Cyprus (67), rank higher than Hong Kong on the happiness spectrum; the other three tiny nations did not make the list.

Meanwhile, we all have our private sorrows. As I write this, an international explosion of writers is happening to protest against the closure of a creative writing program. Five years earlier, I helped a local public university set up the first Asian low-residency master of fine arts (MFA) in creative writing at their English department. Against my better judgment, I took my first ever full-time job in academia as their writer-in-residence to direct the program. Although I'd taught creative writing and lectured at universities around the world, and also at almost all the local universities as a visitor or adjunct, I'd never really wanted to work at one as a full-time faculty member. The low-residency MFA world I favor is flexible and independent and is in my mind more closely aligned to the writing life. That's the trouble with being a writer: you're wary of scaling slippery ivory heights. Besides,

I've always hated homework, and university, even for faculty, is still all about homework, whether it's grading papers, staying awake at committee meetings, or submitting repetitive reports that no one bothers to read. Agnes Lam, the writer I call Hong Kong's unofficial English-language poet laureate (and a happily retired linguistic scholar) has this perfect sense of humor. In response to my complaints about academic life, she gave me a green canvas tote bag with "homework" emblazoned as its designer brand.

But to start an Asia-focused, low-residency MFA program was irresistible for a transnational like myself. Since it wouldn't happen unless I agreed to work full time, I said yes. The day I reported to work, I already almost regretted my decision.

Here's the short history: the program flourished, and, somewhat to my surprise, the students began to successfully publish books of poetry, fiction, and creative nonfiction within a very short time. They also published more than a hundred individual pieces in literary journals worldwide, won literary awards, and went on to inspire others, especially around Asia. Perhaps the most important thing this outlier MFA gave birth to was an international community of writers from here in Asia who looked at the world through a wider lens than simply that of one country, one language, one culture, one religion, one race, one gender, because one anything was not our prevailing wisdom. Diversity ruled, with Asian characteristics and many Englishes. The resultant conversation signifies this increasingly global world we inhabit, where there can be no one way of being human. That's what we do as writers. We're observers of humanity and bridge gaps across ways of being. The conversation is one that will endure long after the rankings of the university have soared toward Babel and splintered into ten thousand fragments of silence.

And for a brief time, this global literary conversation happened in Hong Kong, until some actor without a cause disappeared it as directed. Turnitin homework. Easy A. Next problem?

So we have reason to be sad. The choices for a more compatible or enduring love appear to be Hobson's, at least in our Hong Kong. We perhaps deserve this below par ranking on the happiness scale if all we can manage for the love of our life is nothing better than a broken heart. You break it, you buy it. The Consumer Council will not entertain an appeal. Cry all you want. The patient parent will wait out your wailing to the tipping point of exhaustion, until silence once again prevails.

# MUM AND ME

# TYPHOON MUM

If you write, your world, however you define that, is your primary content. There are moments when those worlds suffer seismic shocks, volcanic eruptions, tsunamis, cyclones, and ice storms or typhoons of enormous proportions. There are also moments when those worlds are beset by milder cataclysms that are difficult to ignore. Whether natural or manmade, these moments alter or appear to alter our worlds as we know it, and somehow we recognize that things will never again be as they once were.

The typhoon that was my mother's Alzheimer's changed my world, shifting all its known compass points, altering the map so completely that I'm unsure I'll ever find my way back to the world I once knew and loved, the world where I once thought I knew who I was.

In Hong Kong typhoons are part of the natural rhythm of life. Some pass our shores with barely a breeze; others inconvenience us with more rain than our reservoirs require; still others shut down our city, and children shriek with joy at a day off from school, in much the way the nor'easter kid yelps *snow day, yay!* Typhoon Wanda, a ferocious one of my childhood merited signal 10, the highest storm indicator. Signage flew, rock slides halted traffic, lives were lost. From my harbor-front verandah on the seventeenth floor, I watched the South China Sea churn a frenzy of whitecaps.

If there was a single moment that altered my life in the series of typhoons that is my mother's ongoing Alzheimer's, I cannot name it. Yet her condition altered my world more radically than anything I've ever experienced.

In 2010 my mother was ninety and in excellent health. She climbed stairs with the aid of a cane, had a healthy appetite, was still able to manage her daily toilet. Her doctor had recently diagnosed her to be in the moderate to severe stage of the disease. She had begun to exhibit a change in behavior after a period of relative calm—an unwillingness to wash plus a refusal to allow my sister to help her shower, where previously she had submitted quite willingly; a sudden demand to "go home" until I calmed her and showed her she *was* home; flashes of unusual agitation and unease. Her doctor switched her to a stronger medication to improve cognition. For a while, this did ease the daily routine, and she was at least willing to shower again.

My mother's eldest sister, in a much advanced stage of Alzheimer's, had passed away a few weeks earlier in Indonesia at the age of ninety-nine. My sister and I told Mum together. She exclaimed in shock, asked about sending flowers, and then, as she always eventually does, forgot the entire conversation. She will likely ask us again at some future point about this sister whom she last saw some fifteen or more years ago, and we will remind her that she has died. My mother can usually recall that my father and her closest sister, her only sibling who also lived in Hong Kong, are dead. These deaths occurred, respectively, twelve and seventeen years earlier, but in the slow creep of Alzheimer's that evolved over time, my mother would sometimes say, out of the blue, *is Daddy dead*, or *where is Auntie*, meaning her sister. Such queries are relatively benign, unlike the outburst—*what are you all doing to me!*—shouted violently, as she banged her cane once, twice, on the dining room table, shouted at my sister and myself with little or no warning, frightened as she must have been at a sudden cognitive recognition of her altered state.

Her doctor cut back the dosage. An inconsistent cognition can be a dangerous thing.

My world had changed some eleven years earlier, although at the time, none of the family knew that my mother's Alzheimer's might have been a root cause. We were distracted by my father's sudden death, at home, from an abdominal aneurysm in July of '98. My mother went into a state of shock, one that lasted the next couple of years. She would often say, quite unexpectedly, "Daddy died so suddenly." For about a year and a half after his death, one of we four children would always be with her.

In January of that same year, I had just left an eighteen-year corporate marketing career to move back to New York City from Hong Kong to live with my partner, Bill, and write full time. Although I planned to return to Hong Kong for regular visits, I no longer intended to live there and had shipped my household effects into storage for what I hoped was the second-to-last major move until I could buy a place back in the states. I had long wanted to immerse myself entirely in the writing life—by then I had published three books—and apply to writing residencies and colonies, perhaps even take a workshop, hook up with writers groups in New York. In other words, I wanted to do all the things I couldn't with a full-time corporate job while writing on the side. My father's death changed things somewhat because it meant I *would* have to spend more time in Hong Kong than originally planned to be with Mum. However, that was still doable, and my mother even let me take over the spare bedroom at our home as an office since she would now have the master bedroom entirely to herself. Previously, she had used the spare room as a dressing room. Her flat was on the top floor with a guest bedroom on the roof, where I slept. So the seismic shift that was my father's death may have been emotionally painful, but grief is natural, and time does indeed heal all our broken hearts.

What my siblings and I did not count on was the fact of my mother's Alzheimer's.

I have often wondered what life would be like today if Dad had not died. Where would home be, what would I have written, and how in fact Mum's Alzheimer's would have affected my work. When my father died at age seventy-five, he still had his full mental capacity. His death directly informed my fiction. My fourth novel, *Habit of a Foreign Sky*, opens on a sudden death, and everything I learned about Hong Kong funeral homes—especially its macabre comedy—made it into my book. A couple of years after Dad's demise, I had a dream that he and I were walking past some building in Central, the business district—it resembled the old Bank of China, with a large door opening onto Queens Road Central—and piles of my books were displayed on the front steps. My father stopped, looked at these piles, and said, *it's good to have your books out there like this.* I woke suddenly and felt a tremendous relief. Dad had given his final blessings to my new life as a writer without a "job." A year or so later I published *The Unwalled City*, a novel of Hong Kong that is dedicated to him.

But Mum's Alzheimer's would not articulate itself in fiction.

By 2010 I had only published one book of nonfiction, a collection of essays, in contrast to my seven other titles, which were all fiction, except for one mixed-genre collection of stories and essays. My tendency as a writer, when confounded by the exigencies of life, is to disperse my confusion into fiction. I've been doing this for so long it's second nature, whereas in nonfiction I feel like a three-year-old, stumbling when I try to walk, the loss of baby teeth still a future shock. Also, much of what might be termed "traumatic" in my life was mostly psychological and almost entirely self-inflicted, just as much of what I wanted to reflect on or research or make social or political commentary about—in other words, everything that was my world—could be fictionalized. However, in my relatively newish head as an essayist, I discovered that parts of my world did not prove to be material for fiction.

Mum's Alzheimer's, it soon became clear to us, was going to be a very prolonged moment. The earliest stages were often frighteningly violent as my mother slipped in and out of memory control. Mum is strong, having been an athlete in her youth, and even at ninety, she could grip my hand with a tremendous force that belies her age. It took time, but I eventually came to understand that all her anger and recriminations and hitting out at us were an attempt to regain control, probably prompted by fear. Similarly, her often inexplicable behavior, which we at first took to be merely unreasonable, could not be understood through the rational and emotional intelligence we possessed.

Yet when I tried to disperse these emotions into fiction, every story I started was quickly abandoned. My mother's condition was beyond fiction. Meanwhile, the freedom I had discovered as a full-time writer was slowly being eroded. It soon became apparent that managing my mother's care was not doable from New York, and my one sister who lived in Hong Kong was feeling the pressures mount. The logical person to spend more time back home was me: I wrote about Hong Kong, had helped build its literary culture and therefore had a network, could readily get part-time teaching and other work, and, being a writer, could write anywhere, right? Well, more or less right. My home, I knew, was in America because by then I *had* bought a home and unloaded storage, and my partner and I *did* have a real life together after our first year or so as a couple in a long-distance relationship. Hong Kong–New York long. Yet I resisted making the move and continued flitting back and forth, simply staying longer and longer each time. It was temporary, I told myself; we would work out a solution for her care. My sister and I thought an end point would arrive, the way you convalesced a broken leg or managed depression or grieved the loss of a loved one.

The trouble with writing fiction is that it absorbs life as it passes but not my real life. Mum's Alzheimer's was real. It would also *never* go away. Rationally, we knew she would die one day, but death is natural, is the passing of life, unlike a life you are forced to live. We choose some lives; other lives choose us. Writing chose me.

Mum's Alzheimer's also chose me, accompanied by a whisper—*do this in memory of me*. Because my father's voice echoed every time I tried to tell myself that this was *not* my responsibility. Mum and I have almost never gotten along. Of all her children I am the one she understood the least. Dad, on the other hand, got me from the day of my birth, and even in death, he asks of me certain things as his eldest child—his eldest "boy" because my only brother and he did not see eye to eye—he will ask of me a Confucian filial piety that he did not impose in life. My mother never really gave me "permission" to write, despite a lip-service brand of support. She doesn't read and never quite understood that writing is in fact work. Also, despite her disdain of Confucius, Mum actually demands filial duties of her children. My father always gave me permission. All he ever asked was that I do the right thing.

And the right thing, whether or not I wanted to do so, was to help manage Mum's care. Being the eldest and the one who had to learn to curb her own violent temper, I am not afraid of Mum in the madness that is her Alzheimer's. My brother and I are the two who are least afraid—he because he was her favorite and I because I was her nemesis. I say "was" because the truth of Alzheimer's is that you must come to recognize that the person you once knew is no longer there, and that she will never, ever again exist as you once knew her. Certain traits are unchangeable—character *is* fate after all, as we say in fiction—but Alzheimer's is something about which we, at this point in human existence, are only just beginning to understand.

Which is why Mum's Alzheimer's eventually found voice in an essay because nonfiction contributes to knowledge without the indirection and artifice of fiction. You can state facts in nonfiction, articulate what actually occurred, and need not dramatize everything in favor of the story.

Typhoons no longer carry only Western female names. Nomenclature cuts across gender and ethnicities now, typhoons often adopt Asian names, and we get much earlier warnings than before. One thing, however, hasn't changed, which is the precarious feeling a signal 8 always engenders. Typhoon signals in Hong Kong are numbered one to ten, and in my childhood, the numbers meant a change in wind directions, which was confusing because a six might not actually be a worse storm than a four. Now, signal usage has simplified to its essence, signals 1, 3, 5, 8, and 10, to identify progressive levels of severity. Signal 8 is that moment before complete shutdown. While most schools, universities, and businesses will close when signal 8 is up, there is lead time before public transport stops. Signal 10 is when the city comes to a virtual standstill.

But signal 8. The city's longtime residents know enough not to tempt fate by straying too far afield. Signal 8 can look benign or fierce depending on the permutations of climatic synapses. There might be rain, there might not, there might be wind and flying debris or not, but an 8 lacks the certainty of a 10, which the Hong Kong Observatory raises at the risk of incurring public wrath if it turns out to be a false alarm. An 8, however, we can forgive even if the typhoon veers off in another direction or peters out.

In March 2010 I moved back to Hong Kong and accepted a full-time position at City University of Hong Kong as writer-in-residence. On the face of things, this was a good career move because I also helped establish and directed the first low-residency MFA for writing in English in Asia. I converted our guest room into a minimalist bedsit studio and use the separate gated entrance by going up the building's stairwell. My mother thinks I live somewhere in Hong Kong as I used to.

But did I really want a full-time position after twelve years of doing just fine with part-time work and full-time writing? Of course not. Would I have taken on the job when I had books to write, people to see, and places to go? Of course not. But will I obey my father's voice that whispers: *be responsible, Su-Su,* the name he called me as a child? Of course I will, although there are more than merely moments when I wonder if I must. A full-time job means a return to a long-distance relationship with my life partner in New York. It ties me to Hong Kong, and Mum, for as long as signal 8 is up, before that inevitable 10.

Meanwhile my new novel is out there, the book I wrote for Mum and which is dedicated to her, even though she doesn't know this. Vivien, one of our Filipino helpers, read it and said it was "very exciting," so at least Mum's copy didn't go to waste.

How long will I have to "forgive" Mum this signal 8?

It is 2013. My mother is ninety-three. The "moderate" of her moderate to severe state has tipped a little closer to severe. There are moments she no longer recognizes me or my sister. She speaks less these days, although she still startles us with sudden declarations during flashes of lucidity. Her health is excellent, as is her appetite. She uses a wheelchair but can still walk with a cane and assistance and manages her own toilet with only infrequent accidents. She climbs two flights of stairs most mornings to attend Mass at the neighborhood Dominican chapel, except when it's pouring with rain or she doesn't feel like going. She does not remember whether or not she's gone to church on any given day, not even on special occasions such as Palm Sunday or Christmas or the first Sunday of Lent. At Mass, however, she can recite all the prayers. *I confess . . . Lamb of God . . . thy will be done*, and she never forgets what to do when the communion wafer is presented by the priests who come to her, saving her the walk to the altar.

On June 21, 2013, Anthony Marshall, the eighty-nine-year-old son of the late Brooke Astor, was sentenced to jail, having been convicted of stealing tens of millions from his mother. He was accused of tricking her into altering her will, when she was one hundred, to unduly enrich himself. The accusation originated in a lawsuit filed by Marshall's son Philip, who also alleged neglect by his father in caring for his grandmother, although the charges of neglect were never proved. Anthony Marshall was his mother's legal guardian for the latter part of her life. Brooke Astor suffered from Alzheimer's and died in 2007 at the age of 105.

On May 27, 2013, James Sisnett, the second-oldest known man in the world, died at the age of 113 on the island of Barbados.

Next year I turn sixty. Meanwhile, my real life remains on hold.

Am I a prisoner of a self-imposed filial piety, doing the "right" thing, in order to be praised by this culture I came from? This Confucian command has always been a false value in my books, a poor reason to procreate in order to enslave the next generation to care for you in old age. Or am I merely a waiting woman, like Hong Kong's famous Amah Rock on a peak in Kowloon, the woman who waits with a baby on her back for the husband who went out to sea and has yet to return? The gods took pity on her and turned her to stone so that she need not suffer the agony of the futile wait for a dead man. My wait, however, is not futile, because Mum will die. But is that really what I'm doing, waiting for my mother's death like a heartless wretch? Or am I a truly ungrateful, hopelessly childish daughter, moaning *why did you give birth to me*, like some self-centered teenaged grown-up wannabe, whining petulantly, so that the world may revolve constantly only around *me, me, me*?

Or is this really about the soul, the one Dickinson says *selects its own society*, watching life's passage in an existence that chose me, regardless of my mother's Alzheimer's?

*Writing chose me*, I say.

So write.

# MATERNITY LEAVE

Mothers frighten me. The weight of their worlds—so often borne alone as their demeanors imply—is a presumption of responsibility that eludes me. For Gen X and younger women, the task seems less onerous, more shared perhaps, less vile. But that might just be wishful thinking by one in midlife who evaded this condition of her gender—willfully, deliberately with a tubular ligation at twenty-five—until blessed menopause eliminated the fear for good.

My mother in early Alzheimer's terrified me and my three younger siblings as we caucused secretly back home in Hong Kong. Mum's widowhood and world felt crushingly weighty. Number two sister, the MBA, took over finances, transforming a complex tangle into manageable accounting after Dad's demise. Number three sister, the criminologist, took charge of keeping our extended Indonesian family at bay; only she had lived in our parents' country of birth, so foreign to our own, and was conversant in the language and culture. As for Mum's Catholicism, the keeper of hope was our brother, a liturgist and church music director, the last of the flock. But it was the power vacuum that frightened me most, and not because of any power struggle among the sibs (there was none). Instead, it was my mother's clinging to a long-absent power that threatened to overwhelm me. And as I was 大家姊, or "big sister of the family," the job of wresting away that power fell to me.

There was a moment, when I was just shy of forty, that Mum no longer frightened me. Unlike Dad, she had at the time only just retired from paid employment as a pharmacist. My father never saw the point of working for a living and was only too happy to dispense with it as soon as he could so that his days could follow a clockwork of self-actualization. Breakfast and the morning paper: thirty minutes. Daily toilet: one hour. Public transport of choice (the neighborhood free shuttle to the stop for Kowloon Motor Bus number 7) and the walk to his post office box to retrieve materials of self-actualization (*Kompas*, the *Far Eastern Economic Review*, *Time*, *Newsweek*, letters from the world where relatives, friends, former business acquaintances and the occasional stranger via an introduction regularly wrote him their geographies of time, distance, longings, and desires): one hour, forty-five minutes. Purchase and consumption of one lunch box (chicken drumstick or roast pork or some other *soong* with rice) at 大家樂, Hong Kong's answer to Macdonald's, where "everyone is a big happy family": one to one and a half hours. And then the return journey, an overlong, rambling trip of under four miles that would have taken much less time by MTR (the subway, a higher fare), to return home to read and clip articles that were neatly filed under various categories ("China Today," "American Presidents," "Sex," "Chinese History," "Indonesia," "Viagra," plus some clips set aside to be sent to his correspondents) or to write letters on aerogrammes or sheets of thin, airy light blue paper in his tiny, cramped hand to the rest of a world where you would travel but had no desire to move to and live in.

By then Mum would be back at the flat, or almost back, having spent her day asserting power at church, at the market, at shops. Her power was most apparent in the kitchen, and their long-suffering domestic helper would hope that her boss was happy, unsuspicious of theft and other sins (although no helper in more than two decades ever stole or was unduly sinful), and satisfied with dinner preparations. By dinner my mother would have made a few attempts at conversation with Dad, to which he might respond, depending on his unpredictable moods.

But dinner! I tried to stop coming home for dinners, even though my parents had desired I attend since my return from New York to a job in Hong Kong in '92. My second sister, returned the same year from London, came over even less. Mum's obsessive nagging would begin sometime earlier in the day—calls to our offices to remind us, usually in the middle of meetings—and our secretaries and staff soon learned that "your mother" was not the call we ever needed to take. You could not be late, even though both our management jobs careened into overtime against our wills, well past the sacrosanct dinner hour of seven, even though Dad said, *it's okay, never mind, you have your work to do*, stunned as he was by how much we were able to earn in our inflationary city. Neither of us really wanted much to eat, especially when summer rolled round and the temperature rose to an ungodly degree, and soup, rice, meat, vegetables were beyond the limits of our appetites.

But dinners. My sister and I won some reprieve when the two younger siblings came home to visit, from Jakarta and Ohio respectively. Our sister-in-law, a vegan, gave up telling Mum that vegetable soup cooked with pork is not vegetarian. Dinners meant the evening news on TV blared for Dad, while Mum continued a conversation stream he ignored. When the news ended, both parents would vie for conversation space, talking at cross-purposes, neither one listening to the other. Even the visiting sibs and sister-in-law would exit, stage left well before dinner had ended with some excuse, *must see so-and-so before I leave, sorry!* Dinners were easier outside the home at a new restaurant or old favorite that would please both parents. That became my strategy because by then I was no longer afraid of what Mum thought of me or what she would try to tell me to do (because she did try), of how she wanted to interfere in my second marriage (because she would), because by then she was just my mother, whom I could ignore on anything that mattered, since she had little idea of what my life was really like, because all she wanted of me was to listen to her complaints about Dad, which I had been doing since my early teenage years.

So dinners at home disappeared from my life, and then I was transferred to Singapore, which distanced the daily despair but still left me closer for visits home than New York.

Then Alzheimer's appeared. We dismissed it at first as the usual melodrama, the known exaggerations of suffering and sacrifice, the post-traumatic shock of our father's sudden and unexpected death at seventy-five, he the younger by four years. It's like that, this strange disease that only now, in the early twenty-first century, we think of as an "illness." You do not notice the onset because an intimate like my mother had long been a familiar stranger. A physical malady would at least generate a known response. Confabs with medical professionals. Fear. Anxiety. Grief at a prospective demise. The desire to make up for lost time sooner rather than later. But Alzheimer's, like dinners, can be ignored for quite a time, and then one day even the idea of dinner disappears and then you wonder, *where did it go?* Didn't I once eat dinner around a table with a family and chopsticks or silverware and cloth napkins like civilized persons do, instead of nibbling cholesterol-laden hors d'oeuvres at fancy receptions, downing free liquor paid for by business clients, ordering room service at some five-star at 10:55 at night, just before the dinner menu ends, because your flight was delayed but who eats airline food if they don't have to? You ingest what passes as dinner, and then run or swim to keep off the weight because, even in your forties, you are still young in the late twentieth century, unlike in an earlier, more benign era when forty-something signaled the path to the grave, ending corporal torment.

Our brother, who, unlike me, is not allergic to doctors, was the first to declare: *something's not right*. There had been a traumatic trip to Europe with him and his wife, the problem being, according to Mum, our sister-in-law. Understand, mind you, that we three girls call her our "fifth sib," that we like her sensible, down-to-earth disposition, admire her intelligence in her chosen field of psychology and, most of all, love her for loving our brother. Understand, mind you, that even our mother did reluctantly acknowledge our brother had married well. Yet what Mum now saw was only the woman who took away her son. Even though she no longer asserted the kind of control she used to over my brother when he was younger, that power remained alive in her head. So this trip, arranged to occupy Mum in widowhood, this trip had turned into a disastrous meltdown, one that in retrospect might have been partly due to Alzheimer's. You are not quick to name it that, though, given your own arriviste American identity. After all, you have been called foreigner, minority, alien, and suffered those arrows, stings, and slings before letting go of that barrage of names. Yet still at times, in moments of stress, you do revert to the outsider who doesn't belong here, one who will denounce the American way of naming everything a disease. My brother, being less of an arriviste, and for whom America represents self-actualization as well as segregation from Mum, appreciates the value of good medical care with benefits. In a reversal of power, he asserted control and took Mum for a complete checkup that returned the diagnosis: *Alzheimer's.*

In time, even my two non-American sisters agreed. It was not just old age. The odd behavior our mother exhibited was real, was beyond her control, was not simply more of her extended fictions. She did lie, outrageously now; she did hide things down rabbit holes of drawers and closets; she did confuse personal history and incidents and insist she was right; she did behave irrationally for real and not from the habitual passive aggression we all knew too well. Once, when she and my youngest sister accidentally locked themselves out of the flat, she declared she would climb from the roof down to the veranda and get back in that way. We are at the top of a twelve-story building. My mother was once a budding tennis star and swimmer, an athlete who might actually once have made such a climb. But by then it had been more than thirty years since she played tennis or swam or was in any way physically active. Her declaration was not just ridiculous, it was delusional.

There is, as Naipaul says, an enigma of arrival. The thing is finally here and known, as was my mother's diagnosis. However, the one arriving is not the subject but the state; Alzheimer's arrived and now my mother would never entirely be herself again. I arrived and re-arrived and re-arrived again in America; along the way I acquired citizenship and became a subject of the state. But I did not disappear. If at times I sounded patriotic while at others mildly traitorous, my behavior was controlled despite any anti-American sentiments expressed. What I vent does not lead to irrationally exuberant acts. More significantly, my actions are not potentially harmful to others or myself, and I do not dwell in the perpetually frustrated misery of almost-memory, in an exile of near-control, delusion and slippery power. Unlike my mother, in Alzheimer's, whose feelings cannot be easily artic-ulated and remain only what I can guess at—*How contentment is always denied me, despite my age and the years I've given to children and family, putting my own dreams and desires aside because this was the life my God handed me! How I wish I could say, in those moments of my real self, that I am grateful for that life, and happy, more or less.* Or perhaps that is only my wishful desire, to imagine my mother's tiny moments of happiness, despite this miserable state to which she has been condemned.

At church, the priests who had known her for years noticed. Other parishioners, the women with whom she once would lunch or organize the flower arrangements, called, concerned. Would you like to join us for afternoon rosary? May I drive you across the harbor to the Catholic Women's League meeting? Will you come with us to lunch, someone can bring you? *No*, she insisted, *no, no, no*, because she had lived in this city for forty-odd years, knew it well, and should not need anyone's help.

Meanwhile, Mum's domestic helper Maryam, a young woman who had worked for our aunt in Java and whom my mother employed to be her companion after Dad died, was going through a slow crack-up. Her original employer—the woman who bought her conversation tapes and books to teach her English and Cantonese so that she now spoke both passably well enough to get by in this bilingual city, the one who taught her to cook and shop in the local markets, the one who consoled her when the boyfriend left her pregnant, the one who paid for the abortion, the one who taught her to save money for the house and business she would eventually buy back in Java—that woman had turned into an uncontrolled shrew who screamed at her daily, disparaged her cooking and work, accused her of stealing, and told anyone who visited, loudly, how stupid she was. This woman was no longer the auntie with whom she watched television or reminisced about Indonesia. Maryam sat on the kitchen floor for hours, muttering to herself, counting the days, hours, and minutes to Sunday, her one day off, when my sister would come over and take Mum out to lunch, relieving her from further obligation for at least a day.

We children who lived abroad caught on slowly. I visited regularly from New York but only stayed for three weeks or less each trip. On one visit, Maryam told me she was being underpaid. I asked to see the accounts. My mother had misconstrued a new government ruling on domestic help pay and cut Maryam's salary for well over a year. That was rectified quietly, behind my mother's back, as there was no longer any point reasoning with her. On one of her visits, my Indonesian-fluent sister had a long conversation with Maryam, and all the pent-up frustrations, repressed anger, and genuine concern—because she was and had been a trustworthy, faithful employee who cared deeply for my mother's welfare—tumbled out. One morning, my mother went to town to meet my uncle for lunch and got lost in the neighborhood she had previously lived in and knew extremely well. She dared not move from the street corner until Uncle came to get her. After that, she never would take public transport alone again. One day, we realized she had shunned all friends and acquaintances from church, muttering angrily about these women of whom she had become insanely suspicious, as opposed to being benignly suspicious while still on friendly terms.

We each of us tried to talk to Mum about her condition. We did not talk. We screamed at each other. At times I felt I was losing it, reverting to a long-forgotten state of clinical depression when I would scream at myself, lost in the America and marriage to which I had arrived, only to find a state so alien I wanted to tear it out of me. Except now I was screaming at Mum, trying to get through to her because I still did not fully believe in that "arrival," because I would rather have had the mother I knew, despite the gulf between us, because that woman would either ignore me as I ignored her or sigh melodramatically about her sacrifice and suffering, which at least made a good story to share with the sibs.

And so the screaming continued until the crisis of the spiral staircase.

Sometime in the eighties, my father built the rooftop structure and connected it by a spiral staircase to our home below. It was a guest room for relatives (we have so many!) or "the children" when we were home from whatever foreign place or lover currently claimed us. He designed it like a Japanese hotel room—stacked, tiny, only for sleep—but equipped it with a spacious bathroom and its own compact refrigerator for fruit, cold drinks, and coffee and tea supply because civilized people would take breakfast before descending the spiral staircase that connected it to the flat below. *Rubbish!* said Mum. What guest would stay upstairs when breakfast was served downstairs by "servants" (as she called the one helper) who "waited on them hand and foot"? Which is why my mother considered it her job, however exhausting, to scale that staircase, knock on the door at breakfast, lunch, and dinner to get that guest down to meals, even if the guest were sleeping off jet lag or if a couple was perhaps making love. No guest would be hungry in her home, not as long as she ruled and could serve.

My father had been the host who loved visitors; my mother tolerated their presence because that was the way things were and who was she to argue? Once, when my now-ex-in-laws were visiting, I found Mum scrubbing out their underwear by hand, complaining about the work. *Why?* I asked, shocked. They certainly didn't expect it, had only given her their laundry because she insisted, saying the servant would do it. Their very Americanness was alien to her (my mother-in-law was with her fourth husband, the keeper, finally) and nothing my husband or I could say or do would lighten the unbearable responsibility of their presence.

After Dad's death, the guests disappeared. And when Alzheimer's arrived, stayed, lingered, outstayed its arrival like some of our less-welcome guests of the past, we children no longer invited relatives or friends to stay. Yet it was now that Mum suddenly wanted guests, her own family, the last blood relatives who peopled her childhood. None of them had visited much when my father was alive because either his family or we four siblings dominated the upstairs room. Mum had three elderly sisters left in Indonesia, one in an even more advanced state of Alzheimer's or dementia; the other two were frail and only traveled if a younger relative accompanied them. So when the latter two sisters were traveling in China with a niece from Australia and called to say *we're coming to Hong Kong and wish to see you*, Mum welcomed them all because of course she had a guest room now, one under her control and not Dad's, so *yes, please come, please visit, please stay.*

But what she forgot about was her existing guest, the hovering arch-angel, relentless and merciless like Gabriel announcing to Mary, *you will bear the son of God whether you like it or not because this visit I'm paying you, it's an honor, see?* But she forgot that the guest room could only house two people at most and forgot, naturally, to tell our Hong Kong sister, or anyone, the date of their arrival. One day in the middle of life, my sister received a frantic call and rushed over to Mum's to find ten people waiting to stay with her, having just arrived from Guangzhou. Mum was as surprised as my sister. The niece was with her children and other relatives, and fortunately, this stranger-cousin whom we had never met was with it enough to make alternative arrangements once she took stock of the situation. Mum's two sisters stayed upstairs and things settled down, and Maryam coped as best she could with these two unexpected guests. Meanwhile, that other invisible guest hovered, saying, *hey, don't I get rights of first refusal here?* and we knew, we understood, that this must be the end of guests, regardless of my mother's desires.

Which meant redirecting phone contact by our network of relatives, many still strangers to us, whose language we barely knew. The Indonesian sister took on primary responsibility, although the culture being what it is, they still called or even just showed up without warning. When you live in huge homes, waited on hand and foot by an army of servants (in my mother's childhood, I think the family had at least ten or more), guests are a minor inconvenience. But Mum, the one who left her country because life was too slow there, too corrupt, too lazy and unproductive for her, too lacking in personal independence, too uneducated, especially for girls, Mum was afraid to say *no* to the horde who wanted to descend. Like the middle-aged nephew whose name she barely recalled, whom she had perhaps last seen when he was five, arriving from the Netherlands with wife and children in tow, looking for a free hotel room in expensive Hong Kong. *No.* That became my operative word. *No, no, no.* If you want

to visit, call me or my sister, I insisted, and then of course I'd accentuate
the negative. Suddenly, all the bad cop training from my former corporate life (laid to rest, I thought, the "skill" of firing people) was back, an
equally unwelcome guest. My Indonesian sister did the diplomatic thing,
pouring oil in mellifluous tones, talking around the subject as the culture demands; my Hong Kong sister monitored information flow, with
Maryam as number one spy. But I, I became bad cop with the really hard
cases, and who wants to be that when the older you get, the kinder you
would prefer to be, but how else to protect Mum, how else to prevent the
agitation of guests? Because she was agitated, frightened by the weight of
responsibility, which she confessed to in moments of lucidity, because she
no longer managed much, not even her kitchen, having relinquished the
marketing, menu, and food preparation entirely to Maryam (unthinkable
in her younger years). *My mother*, I said to stranger-relatives in emails,
over the phone, in person, *has Alzheimer's and is too elderly to have guests
anymore*, and they, as naturally suspicious as her, poked, pried, wanted to
be sure their (suddenly!) "dear" Auntie Klin was okay, was being cared for,
was not sitting on some vast fortune they stood to inherit since everyone
who makes it to Hong Kong gets rich, or so my mother's world believed.

Who was this obnoxious horde?

Some years earlier when my aunt died, her older companion Christine
(lesbian, halfway out the closet) fell into the hands of blood relatives.
These two maiden aunts were rich, or at least had wealth enough for a
comfortable retirement in Indonesia and looked forward to living in the
Bandung home they built. Both had worked in Hong Kong and were
among our closest relatives, much like immediate family. Yet Christine,
after almost a lifetime in Hong Kong, was cast adrift. Where do such
elderly people with no spouse or children go to die? She went to a nephew
in Indonesia. My Indonesian sister and I assumed her power of attorney,
but her nephew kept a joint account with her in Jakarta. Yet this "dear"

blood relative, this son of her favorite brother (long deceased) bilked the joint account until we finally caught on and turned off the flow of funds from Hong Kong. She was eventually cared for by a distant cousin who did inherit the fortune, deservedly, but it was my lesson in how to look beyond blood in matters of money.

My mother is not rich, but she did inherit half her schoolteacher sister's fortune. It keeps her well cared for. What assets my father had when he died were long in Mum's name—the home, some joint accounts, and modest savings—and he did not die a rich man, as he once had been in his younger days. But her relatives! They hovered and nosed around like a pack of bloodhounds on the wrong trail. *Desist*, I cried. *Cease this relentless trail in the pursuit of phantom wealth*. Finally, they did.

But Mum continued to climb the stairs, the slippery, narrow, spiral affair that Maryam would beg her not to climb, afraid she would slip and break her neck. Who did she hear above her head? Which guest, which unwelcome visitor from which sector of memory past? When I came home to stay, as I increasingly did, I learned to lock the door to the roof room so that Mum wouldn't burst in on me. Once, I left some jewelry up there while on a side trip to Shanghai. The jewelry disappeared and did not resurface by the time I needed to return to New York. I dared not breathe a word to Mum, knowing for sure she would blame Maryam. Over the next few months, my sister snooped through Mum's cupboards. She eventually found it hidden in a drawer. Mum had climbed the stairs, found the jewelry, and probably thought to safeguard it in my absence. In one of the lower-pitched arguments over her condition, I mentioned her doing this. She denied it, did not recall, the memory lost to heaven or hell, who can say which?

Yet still she climbed. *Oh, there's no one here*, we sometimes heard her say. *What*, we wondered, *was it she really heard?* because my mother continues to hear footsteps often, as someone in the building invariably is renovating, this favorite Hong Kong pastime, and nearby, workers always lurk. *Workers, men(!)*, this was her great fear, harking back to 1960s Hong Kong when crime was rampant and break-ins common. Or is it my father's two half-sisters she recalls, who lived with us when they were teenagers, in our previous home where the guest room was a separate flat on the same floor? For years Mum could not release the burden of that responsibility. The older sister lied, told stories about being mistreated by my mother, was a royal pain in the neck. Do their spirits fly back from Canada, where they live, to dance on my mother's ceiling, taunting her with their presence? Or is it some other young woman, the Japanese perhaps, of whom Dad was so enamored? Mum hisses at moments: *your father wanted to move upstairs, away from me!* We have no evidence of this, just Mum's repeated accusation. An unhappy marriage is like that, although, unlike an Alzheimer's spouse, even an indifferent but real husband will keep you focused on life as it is because you must make sure he gets his breakfast and dinner even if he does take lunch out, must deliver any phone messages from friends or acquaintances, must oversee the laundry and ironing because Dad needed his shirts and clothes and things just so, and, above all, must keep the home clean, every speck removed, all the silverware shined, the crystal sparkling, the parquet polished, the hair swept off the bathroom floor because my father saw hair everywhere— *your hair!* he cried through our childhood—because in a household of too many girls, hair always lurks.

It's hard work being a mother when you also have to be a wife.

One day, the crystal came tumbling down. The wine and liquor glasses were stored in a wood cabinet on the wall above the sideboard in the dining room. The cabinet had two glass sliding doors. I heard the crash and descended the spiral. The weight of crystal and a host of other junk had finally collapsed it. Between Maryam and me, we salvaged what we could and trashed the wreckage. Mum might have climbed the stairs for all I know because I finally had to move her aside from where she hovered, monitoring the cleanup but only getting in the way. What shocked me, though, was the layer of black dirt on the glass shelves, on all the crystal, a layer that clearly hadn't been cleaned for years. It was after this that I began to look for dirt, channeling Dad's detective eyes, and saw the piles of papers and unopened mail thrown higgledy-piggledy into drawers; the caked, ancient makeup on top of and in my mother's dresser; the clothes, the rows of unworn clothes, some brand new, two closets filled with my late aunt's clothes, my aunt who predeceased Dad; the sets of unused dishes, appliances unopened since the 1960s, chipped vases, Pyrex plates, birthday cake candles, a dormant rolling pin . . . the exhausted mess crammed into kitchen cupboards, the ones Mum no longer dared open. My mother was never especially neat, but this, I knew, was beyond even her limits. She hadn't discarded any of our ancient schoolbooks, old report cards, or unwanted gifts, filling up rooms with stuff. Maryam slept on a narrow single bed in a tiny room, the one formerly with bunk beds my brother and I shared in this home I had lived in for only a year before disappearing to college in the States, and so was relegated to the top bunk for my transience. The room was so chock full I wondered how she slept.

Meanwhile Mum climbed and climbed and climbed the stairs until I thought I would go mad.

In this home of accumulation and slippery stairs, there were moments I wept. I came home more and more frequently, staying longer each time. Although there was a literary career that occasionally demanded my presence in the city, I knew, as the spiral staircase nagged at me, that work was the least reason of all. I could write just as easily in New York, and more happily too, at home with Bill. I teach at the Vermont College of Fine Arts MFA in writing, a low-residency program, and even though I could be away most of the time, my presence was required twice a year in Montpelier. What teaching I did in Hong Kong—and slowly I found myself accumulating gigs—was to fund my time at home, babysitting Mum.

Because I found myself being, for the first time in my life, a mother. And the thing about motherhood and maternity is the fundamental desire to protect a helpless being whether in the womb or out. Mothering frightens me; how is it possible to watch another being twenty-four-seven, to make sure she will not climb and climb and climb that spiral and finally break a leg, or worse, her neck?

My mother frightens me because she is still quite healthy, with a straight back and good appetite, but her balance is shaky and only getting worse. Alzheimer's arrived, stole her mind, but fooled her into believing herself physically as strong as ever. It's like that, this unwelcome guest, downing the bottle of your best liquor but leaving just enough so that you think you've still got some left. It tramples your roses while helping you garden, pulls out the new shoots instead of weeds, leaving your garden in a state of despair. I once knew a man who confessed that hostesses would not let him help with dishes: he always managed to break their best crystal, not deliberately, mind you. Alzheimer's is like that, crashing clumsily into your life, "accidentally" scratching a key across your memory chips so that you loop around endlessly, round and round, up and down the spiral, while the hard drive refuses to reboot.

*Once an elderly person breaks a leg, a hip, and ends up in a wheelchair, deterioration is rapid.* This received wisdom, from the medical community and those who know, nagged me more than Mum ever did. It is the dependency, to be strapped to a wheelchair, unable to negotiate your way around, that is crippling, more than the physical state. Watching her climb and climb and climb those stairs, I became the mother trying to prevent this accident in the making, trying to preserve the last measure of independence for Mum's survival.

And so it came to pass that we built a metal cage around the spiral, with a gate, and locked it. Mum screamed and shouted, demanded the key, took a screwdriver to the lock to force it open. *Will you lock me out of my own home?* she demanded. This was worse than Dad and his threat of removal upstairs, worse than me implanting myself in her home, taking over command of the kitchen and helper, managing her day to day, establishing foreign routines she simply knew were wrong, wrong, wrong. Divide and conquer, her longtime strategy with us, failed. We passed the buck to each other whenever we spoke to her; A said talk to B, B said talk to C, C said talk to D, and the loop began again. Meanwhile we powwowed on email so that each knew the latest developments in our corners of the globe.

It was the criminologist who said, *we need to blow up this apartment.*

When I told my friend Jenny about the spiral, her first response was *remove it! Just take it away*, she said. After all, we could access the roof from the building's stairway. In fact I had begun to do that, so as not to go home through the front door below. Mum locked me out more than once with the dead bolt, and I had to wake Maryam to let me in. The alternative was to have Mum sit up and wait, which she did, and I would return at one or two in the morning after a night at the jazz clubs or drinking with Jenny, and there was Mum, asleep in her armchair, her eyelids fluttering awake as soon as I entered, saying, *I wasn't asleep, of course I wasn't*, followed by *how come you're so late*, a question to be answered through clenched teeth if I didn't want to scream.

You simply cannot be both daughter and mother. It is too schizophrenic, even worse than simultaneously being corporate bad cop and writer. You can justify bad cop as the exigencies of paid employment, since a literary life can leave you leaner and meaner than you want to be. And you can blow up the apartment. Which was what we did.

Her new home, or rather her new-old home, cleaned and refurbished, does not have a roof room. It does, of course, where I, the part-time babysitter, now reside. But the spiral staircase is gone, and sometimes, my mother stares at the empty space and asks, *didn't we have another room*, and one of us replies, *no, you're thinking of G flat*, our old homestead with the separate flat, or *no, I don't think so*, and minutes later, she will be focused on something else, dinner most likely.

The excess clothes I gave away to the Salvation Army, filling ten boxes. The crystal cabinet is gone, as is the sideboard, as are all the plastic filing cabinets filled with dead letters. The kitchen I emptied at breakneck speed in between transpacific travel and work, blessing the advent of laptops and high-speed internet that connected me to my world. Her old closets, which she locked constantly and then forgot where she put the key, are gone, replaced by wardrobes without locks, just as the doors to her room and bathroom no longer have locks, just as she now no longer holds a key to the flat because she is never alone anywhere. Two Filipino helpers watch her twenty-four-seven and alternate their time off.

Now I am the employer, the one who has to show the helpers how to acclimatize to Hong Kong, who handles visa applications and medical insurance, who must prove she is locally employed and solvent enough to afford these foreign workers. Who must, by law, reside in the home where these helpers are employed. When my Hong Kong sister and I conceived their job description, our top priorities would likely not pass muster for most want ads today: the candidate must be pretty and clever—otherwise my mother will loudly criticize her appearance and lack of intelligence— and Catholic, because she must take Mum to church every morning and on Sundays and holy days of obligation. It helps not having to go with Mum to Mass as often, but I still occasionally do, lapsed though I am, and the priests approve, as do the parishioners, glad to see her cared for and happy, looking more alert and better groomed than she has been in a while, and proud to have a daughter so filial as to take her mother to church. It is hypocritical, I know, but at least it quells the screams.

My Hong Kong sister still takes Mum out most Sundays for lunch, and on a weekday as well if I've run away home to New York for a spell. Now I shop for my mother's clothes and shoes, bringing home packages that she unwraps like a happy child, and before she can ask I say, *it was on sale, 70 percent off,* and then name some impossible price of fifty years ago (U.S. dollars stated as Hong Kong ones work, given the exchange rate, and this way I do not tell a total lie), and this she will understand, nod happily, pleased that she has taught her daughter the value of a dollar. I bring her flowers when I'm there or surf FTD. com when I'm not. The flowers brighten the home, for both her and her permanent houseguest. If things get too much, I call Jenny and we meet for drinks and bitch about life and old age. You can do that if you're not a full-time mother.

Mum no longer screams. But the agitation never completely disappears because Alzheimer's is like that. She's good one day, crazy the next, and benign immediately afterward. My Hong Kong sister likens it to Kafka's *Metamorphosis*, in which both the protagonist and his family must learn to live with their new reality. It is its own beat, atonal and arrhythmic, improvisatory at best of times, but always complex and never easily assimilated.

I am less afraid of my mother now because I don't know how much longer she will remain my mother, so fear seems pointless. One day I'll come home and she'll say, as her eldest sister does to my cousins, *who are you? Do I know you?* It isn't the tragedy I once believed it was because at least now she is in control again, bossing her two "servants" who take their real direction from my sister and me. Now she is Queen Mother again, whose children are "home." My youngest sister arrives, my brother departs, I come and go, our Hong Kong sister shows up, and each time, it is as if she saw us only yesterday, or the day before, or *it doesn't matter because my children will all come home again eventually*. Alzheimer's time is like that. As in a novel, time skips, you arrive at the next dramatic moment of the story and ignore the missing time. My mother no longer needs the facts. The illusion, the fiction is, for her, the more significant and comforting truth.

**6.** My mother, Kathleen Klin Phoa (潘吉林), circa 1948. Fact. A student at Saint Mary's Canossian secondary school in Kowloon, Hong Kong. Fact. My mother's Hong Kong school ID photo, 1948. Photo courtesy of the author.

# MY MOTHER'S STORY

## The Fiction and Fact

Despite the hiatus that was the war, she was still a girl. Oh, she knew she was almost a woman, but inside, she felt like the schoolgirl she still was who had to matriculate, to further her studies, to become a medical doctor. That was the plan in the run up to 1947.

By then the Japanese had left Singapore, and she must have wondered what the Convent of the Holy Infant Jesus, her former boarding school, looked like now. She had gone home to Indonesia when the war began, but her father had sent the family to the hills of Wonosobo in Central Java, away from the occupation. In Tjilatjap their family home was gone, leveled by the bombs, as she would tell us all through our childhood, when she was still "Mum," long before that got lost to Alzheimer's. Her version of the war in Indonesia may be fiction, but we have the documents to prove she did indeed attend the Singaporean convent school and that she later did attend Saint Mary's Canossian in Hong Kong, from which she did indeed matriculate, and that the University of Hong Kong did indeed offer her a place to study. Medicine is another story—she never attended university. She qualified as a pharmacist instead and either apprenticed or worked for a brief while at Queen Mary Hospital. Then she met Dad, got pregnant and became "Mum," and could no longer be a girl.

But in 1947, well before she met Dad in Hong Kong, she was, perhaps, really already too old to be a girl.

It already feels like summer even though it's only May. It is 2011, and my mother and I are in a taxi on the way to her regular medical checkup. Dr. Pei is a geriatric specialist. About half a year ago, her Malaysian GP recommended specialized elder care. Her GP, Raymond, I've known for years as the author of a memoir because we once shared a publisher. He became our choice when Mum first needed medical supervision after a lifetime without a regular doctor, and he speaks to her in Bahasa Malay. He's my doctor now as well since I moved back to Hong Kong. This return "home," after a dozen or so years of a freelance life, inhabiting the flight path connecting New York, Hong Kong, and the South Island of New Zealand, though New York was home base. It's a life I miss.

*That's Kowloon Tong Club*, she says. *And Maryknoll School. And Saint Teresa's Church.* Yes, yes, yes, I say as I do each time she exclaims at these passing landmarks, as if these were sightings after a long time away. Perhaps for her they are. She and Dad held their wedding reception at the club, just as I did for my first marriage. *Champagne flowed*, but that's Dad's story, not hers, for both weddings, theirs and mine. She sewed her own clothes, including the white dress—more cream than white— which doubled as her evening gown, to fit an eighteen-inch waistline. Except that's fiction, because by the time they married, her waist could no longer have been eighteen inches, assuming it ever was, but that is my mother's story and has been ever since she heard Vivien Leigh utter that svelte ideal in *Gone with the Wind*, one of the very few movies she ever mentions or recalls.

We "the children"—as we forever were to our parents and even to ourselves—shredded Mum's wardrobe in play over the years and now, few of the dresses she sewed remain, except the wedding gown, which is wrapped and preserved, and one Thai silk cocktail dress. It's black with a pattern of large golden blooms, less garish than you might imagine, with a shawl of the same material. When I unearthed it while clearing the horrifying accumulation her home had become in the nine years after Dad's death, no one was sure whether Mum or Aunt Caroline sewed it, or if it even belonged to her. But there it was, never worn, and I kept it thinking it could be taken in to fit me. Five years later, I'm still thinking. Recently, I tried on a dress that was almost a dead ringer for one my mother taught me to sew when I was a teenager. Brown and blue batik shaped from a Simplicity sheath pattern, to flatter my cheongsam-perfect figure—just slender enough for that high-necked, tight, Sino dress-glove—the most Chinese thing about me.

*Pure Chinese*, my mother declared of her wah kiu Indonesian ancestors in Tjilatjap. The wah kiu or "overseas Chinese" of Southeast Asia were more Chinese than the ones left behind on the mainland, even after five generations, their purity preserved by racist distaste for dark-skinned Indonesian natives. Mum was not inclined to reflect on the wrongs and rights of racism. It was simply pride, pride in the family she left behind to pursue a girl's ambitions in Hong Kong. And yet. *Cuckoo! They were all cuckoo*, she would exclaim, when telling family tales of her inbred cousins, nieces, nephews, in-laws, the irony of this racial "purity" completely lost on her. Like her memory now. *Cuckoo.*

*Don't get so dark—you'll be ugly*, she yelled at me and my second sister, for as long as she could be Mum, in charge of herself and us, for as long as she could deny us our Indonesian bloodline and pigmentation. *Pure Chinese*, unlike my father's mixed-race heritage. Our dark skin was Dad's fault, not hers, of that she made sure we knew.

She got pregnant in 1953 and gave birth to me exactly nine months and sixteen days after her wedding, just in virginal enough time. *I'll bring you the moon and the stars if you'll marry me* is what the girl fell in love with, but the woman muttered over a lifetime of bitterness about *men(!), sex(!), prostitutes(!), geishas(!), concubines(!)* loud enough for all her girls to hear, for all her girls to doubt most future declarations of love, despite our inbred susceptibility to same.

The problem, I believe, was the elongation of her girlhood.

In 1947, at the age of twenty-seven, my mother was too old for school. This is probably fact. What is also more than likely a fact is that she (and later, Aunt Caroline) adjusted her legal age upon arrival in Hong Kong by shaving off four years. When you've heard a story all your life it becomes fact even if it's fiction, especially when you cannot verify anything from Indonesian birth certificates that, in any case, appear not to exist or have vanished from my mother's papers. What does exist is my mother's Hong Kong identity card with the birth year 1924.

Power of attorney for an aging and confused Mum is a curious thing. We the children are "responsible" for the feeding and care of a woman who was nothing if not responsible for everything about our family, even when that responsibility was no longer required and had become an annoyance to us, the children. Squatting in my mother's former guest room, converted into that British horror, the bedsit, I am now the "responsible" adult-girl in this home, as my mother once was for me.

Because girls are not responsible for anyone other than themselves, which, I suspect, we pretend to believe, my mother and sisters and I. *Heavy, so heavy*, my sister whispers, stooping her shoulders for our imaginary burden, as together we watch Mum age.

> *I flip when a fellow sends me flowers*
> *I drool over dresses made of lace . . .*
>
> *I'm strictly a female female*
> *And my future I hope will be*

*In the home of a brave and free male*
*Who'll enjoy being a guy having a girl like me.*
"I ENJOY BEING A GIRL," LYRICS BY OSCAR
HAMMERSTEIN, MUSIC BY RICHARD RODGERS

It *was* fun being a girl. At nineteen, when she came home after finishing Senior Cambridge in Singapore, she was still her daddy's girl, the "flower of Tjila," a talented tennis player and the one the other girls envied, the one all the boys chased. Meanwhile, her brothers were here and there, she claimed, helping to run Daddy's stevedore operation at home in the village, preening in their sharkskin suits while flunking out of school and generally frittering away the family money. That could be fiction, but it has the ring of truth. The sisters, however, were becoming nuns or marrying and popping out babies, and the one who got married off to the homosexual and couldn't consummate her marriage had at least married money and could afford to adopt.

She and Caroline did not have to marry, not yet. They were still girls running wild and free, and Mum the smarter and younger and prettier by far. A girl can dream about becoming a doctor before the grind of medical school is reality. A girl can make plans to shore up her science and math for when summer days are over and the academic year begins anew up north in Hong Kong. It was always summer in Indonesia, though, where the food was rich and fatty, yummy and fatty, around-the-clock plentiful and fatty, since everything is fried in palm oil. Breakfast served at dawn, snacks at eleven, lunch at one, tea later in the afternoon, dinner at seven or eight, snacks at night before bed. Daily. Her mother had eleven children and ran a household of servants who cooked and cooked and cooked. And then she died of diabetes, or so we think, since we can't be sure if it was that or cancer (which several of our aunts and uncles had) or both, the result of a diet of wealth instead of health and common sense.

But unlike her mother, Mum was not illiterate, this ambitious girl who dreamed of higher learning.

Meanwhile, she enjoyed being a girl.

Eight years later, two years after Japanese hostilities in Southeast Asia finally subsided, she was still, unfortunately, a girl. And she was probably twenty-seven. And not a doctor. And not yet even a wife.

Even in the twenty-first century, mutton does not pass for lamb, Hollywood nip-tucks regardless, just as décolletage fails on skinny women as leggings do on the fat. A smart girl can memorize formulas and skeletal parts and cram for exams. A determined girl can force aside fears to head out alone, on board a ship bound for Hong Kong, where she must make her own way without family or friends. An outgoing girl can rely on personality to win friends and influence people. A tough girl can endure winters in a subtropical climate when all she has ever known were the tropics. A pretty girl can smile at men who continue to fall at her feet.

But a woman is a woman growing older even if she thinks she's still a girl.

Here it is, 2011, and I am, unfortunately, no longer a girl, although I am not yet a woman growing quite as old as my mother. My life is on hold the way Mum's was when war raged and her education was postponed. I think she had more fun, though she may have paid more harshly for it later. *I had a life once,* I sometimes say, one that trod a path less trodden, a path that was mine. But then it forked away, like memory.

So there it was, 1947, and my mother was either twenty-three or twenty-seven, getting the best marks she could. *An A in math! My male teacher said I was the smartest student!* Did she prettify and flirt, seducing with her womanly form? Or was it nose in books, the grindstone wearing away time, time, time?

In the report cards we found, there was indeed always an A in math; she neglected to mention the C's in other subjects like music or history. *You can do math if you try!* she shouted at my baby sister, then aged around seven or eight, as I tried to help her with arithmetic, not ever her strong suit. But that sister did eventually pass all her public exams in math and got an Ivy League PhD in criminology. One day, to her own horror, she even taught college-level statistics for social science research.

But a favorite child is lost without her daddy to confer that favoritism.

A handsome suitor who adores you confers the favoring even if somewhere, deep inside, suspicion rankles. A potential mate from the right background, even if it's not quite as good as your own, likely engenders *he'll do, he'll do, he promised me the moon and the stars,* even if this is something you don't say aloud.

I have tried to write fiction of their meeting. It fails every time. The romance of my parents' love—because I must believe that they were once in love—has lost its girlish innocence. In the womb of Mum's bridal gown and fancy shoes, amid the rhinestones and perfume we rummaged through as children, my parents could *only* be in love. Dad was handsome; Mum was beautiful. The faded photos and our memories do not lie. Many years later, long after the engagement diamond and marriage and children, long after my father's near bankruptcy and philandering, long after Mum's tumble down the boulevard of shattered dreams, Dad bought her a diamond to replace the one she sold, along with all her other jewelry, to feed us when we were broke. It was large, not especially beautiful, and she wore it for a while but then removed it. Despite her bourgeois upbringing, despite all her carping about money till we the children drowned her out, despite, despite, despite, despite it all, what she wanted most was love, not things. She taught us that well, even as she gave us diamonds and gold as insurance against disaster. *You can run with gold,* she repeated through our childhood, as if we too would one day have to hide our valuables when the fill-in-the-blank military might descend upon her adopted city Hong Kong, and we too would have to sail away, run for the hills, or find a seat on the last flight out of Shanghai for Hong Kong, as Dad did in 1949, the wrong year for a young Chinese Indonesian guy to be a student at Saint John's University, playing the violin and saxophone in his spare time, extolling the pleasures of the capitalist's dream life when the Communists came to roost.

I sold my diamond necklace back to Mum when I was in my early thirties. My then-second, now-ex-husband, a jazz musician, and I needed food, shelter, drugs, and drink more than bling. I threatened to sell it, and she finally relented and gave me the cash I needed in exchange for her gift. *Never look a gift horse . . .* but I did.

It is 2011, and life is lonely in Hong Kong. The man who has loved me for the past fourteen years and has been my friend even longer is back "home" in New York. We email; we Skype. We christen the bedsit "the squat." I fly back whenever I can, en route to conferences, in between work. My mother met him a long time ago, back when she still was Mum. Sometimes, I mention his name, and this, strangely, she seems to recognize, even though she's rarely seen him. He continues to love me, despite, despite, despite.

And for those brief times we're together, this fellow brings me flowers.

My girlhood was filled with cheap romance. Champagne flowed while the guests danced downstairs in our penthouse flat, the home with a view of the Hong Kong harbor. Another fact. I used to imagine other harbors from up high—Rio de Janeiro, San Francisco, Monaco because Grace Kelly was a princess. A beautiful life. But Mum could have done with something else—the moon and the stars perhaps—because a life is only beautiful if you are.

When did he turn away from her beauty?

I remember the Japanese woman in her kimono. She was young (they always are, aren't they, the eye candy of men who stray). More important, she was gentle and sweet, probably bright, but this could be my fiction of remembrance. The niece of my father's business associate. When Dad died, we the children sorted through dozens of loose photos of strangers. There were several in Japan, very few included Mum, and what remains is the memory of her plaintive, broken recording, *your dad wanted to take a second wife, a Japanese geisha! I said, then I'll divorce you*, over and over and over again until we stopped listening, stopped caring, stopped arguing the illogic of her declaration, since part of the point of being a geisha is *not* to marry. Mostly. Besides, I'm not so sure Dad ever visited a geisha because a hostess who serves drinks—the stuff of those photos—is not necessarily a geisha. He did go to Japan, sometimes for weeks at a time, until the business collapsed, and those trips of pleasurable business ended. I was ten.

Dad never took a second wife—which was legal in Hong Kong till the midsixties. He simply tuned out his first one over time. Mum never did get a divorce, not even after that bout of the clap when she was older, much too old, really, to suffer such slings and arrows, although medical evidence is lacking. By then I had long been defending her against Dad, since this oldest child was always the one, the *only* one who could argue with him, being Daddy's favored daughter, at least when I was still a girl. Despite being my mother's least favored child and lifelong nemesis, even I knew when my talent ought to be used—that verbal ability she so despised— despite my unconditional love for Dad and the conditional one for her.

Somewhere along the way, Mum the girl stopped flipping and drooling over the lace of romance. Somewhere along the way, she became Mum the woman.

Was it when I got tonsillitis and had to be hospitalized for the operation, or when my sister tumbled off the slide at school and sported a
gigantic bruise on her forehead? Or when she had to fire my youngest
sister's baby amah, the nanny, because *she was dirty, so dirty, she didn't
wash your sister properly and she got a rash all over her bottom!* When Mum
flipped, it was to shout at servants, sometimes at us, and most of all to
complain about Dad. Until my brother was born.

Things changed with the boy, the one and only boy. My father was
not unusually boy-crazy at the expense of his daughters, the way so many
Asian fathers still are, but the boy-at-last *is* cause for excitement, even
among us girls. For my mother, it was her female-female moment. My
brother had asthma and needed the special care that her pharmaceutical
training could provide. Now, at last, a raison d'être as woman.

Chinese motherhood is a social-climbing affair. Having delivered the
boy, at last she could relax. Oh, she was *such* a girl! Behind closed doors
she would say of all those aunties married to uncles who were part of our
parents' circle, *only a secretary, that's all she is, none of Mum's daughters
will be secretaries . . .* or flight attendants or nurses. No, we girls would
be the CEO, the pilot, or doctor—so Mum decreed. And yet. There she
was, playing house with Daddy, having given up her own profession as a
pharmacist because a well-kept wife is the ultimate sign of success. Better
than the woman who has to work.

A harsh downslide when she returned to work because my father was
broke. She did it though and could still brag of being a professional, not
*only a secretary,* because only *she* could sign for the "dangerous drugs" at
the pharmacies and pharmaceutical manufacturers that employed her.
She was happier then, an almost-woman then.

In 2011 "second wives village" in Shenzhen is already old news in
Hong Kong. Since concubinage has long been criminalized, Chinese
men cross the border to the mainland, where a factory girl or karaoke

hostess or hardworking rural miss will "marry" the one who can set her up to play house. *Pretty Woman* is fiction. The fact is that the pretty girls trade their faces for their fates. All she need do is give birth to a boy to assure her husband of his virility. That the Communist Party once placed women alongside men as equals—in the factories, on the farms, to fight in the military—feels like ancient history.

> *With a pound and a half of cream upon my face.*
> "I ENJOY BEING A GIRL"

But Mum was educated. Mum was modern. She was proud of what she achieved, this girl who would be queen, *independent*, the way she urged us all to be. *Girls need to be educated*, she told us all through our noisy childhood, *in case their husbands can't support them*. Girls, not women. Girls who won't grow up.

*Your daddy wouldn't let me work when we got married. He insisted I give up my job.* Over and over and over again through our noisy, noisy childhood of messages and media that did not jive until we stopped listening. The girl who would be queen could not shed the princess brat who wanted it all.

Yet it was as Woman and Mother that she finally found her face.

It is 2011, and I am much too conscious of my conditional love for Mum. This is the rebel girl who must tear down every social construct her mother holds dear, the girl who is still the daughter trying to prove herself better than her mother. Meanwhile, Mum is old and has slid into the moderate to severe stage of Alzheimer's. That much is fact.

It is 2011, and the harsh heat of Hong Kong is finally moderating with November. At our last doctor's visit, I tell him my mother's latest story. That she asks to go home to Tsimshatsui because she is time-wandering back to our penthouse home by the harbor in the sixties and doesn't realize she *is* home; that she thinks it's time to go to work; that her memory for faces is slipping because she did not really recognize our visiting Seattle cousin, whom she knew only a year earlier. That she took a fall recently, bruising her shoulder. It happened on the verandah when she went out and must have been bending down, I say, probably to check the potted plants, and lost her balance. *Were there witnesses to the fall?* he asks, and I say *no* because our domestic helper was in the kitchen at the time, and I wasn't there. So her green encounter may be fiction because I like to remember the flowers my mother planted, the orchids that graced the verandah of our childhood, the mini orange trees she brought into our home at Chinese New Year. Her green thumb that kept her rooted to the soil in this harsh city of her womanhood, where the *best years of her life* were stolen by the cheap romance of being a girl.

It is 2011, and Mum is dying.

It is 2011, and I am trying to be a woman, not a girl, for the mother who would be queen.

# MUM AND ME

*How do I love thee? Let me count* . . . but wait I may possibly lose count because the mind loops back and around, down and up, around the world and back until Chaos! whenever you appear.

Revolve. *How do* you *love me? Let me count* . . . but no, you would never count, would you, because you've always loved me as only a mother would, unconditionally, which you'd undoubtedly say if you still could. Undoubtedly. Wouldn't you?

Restart. Revise. *How have I* not *loved you? Let* you *count* . . . Dad made the great mistake of giving me a sizable sum as a down payment for a home, the second home I purchased. This was long after the great crash, Dad's virtual bankruptcy, the cause of my straitened circumstances in college, and the years of never asking for money, of always earning my own way. My unforgivable mistake was to marry and make that home my second husband's and mine. Which was when you disowned me, when you said I was no longer your daughter, when you accused me of "running away with the family's fortune." Melodramatic, yes, because it was hardly a fortune or the family's only money. But it hurt.

Replay. Recall. Dad loaned me the down payment for the first home that we—Mum and I—purchased and jointly owned. It was a good flat, a post-first-marriage home, a place for me to hide in Hong Kong after that Greatest Folly of My Youth. A flat that increased in value several hundred percent by the time Mum sold it. We jointly paid the mortgage, and then when I left home to be a writer, you rented it out and gave me the rental income to live on for my one belated gap year in Greece, until I could support myself again on a graduate assistantship for the MFA.

By then Dad's new business was making some profit, and you were earning well as a pharmacist and assumed equal stature to Dad in your own Marriage of Too Many Flaws. Those were the years of Mum and Me, when I stood up to Dad for you, verbally countered his mean remarks, said that you could divorce him if you wished, as I had divorced my husband. You complained about him, knew that without your income he could never have survived his shame and depression and years of genteel penury. You discovered the power of having your own money in marriage and other sins.

Do you remember, Mum, that time of liberation and freedom? My brother, the youngest sib, had departed for college, and the nest was completely vacated. *Leave him*, I told you, when dinner table arguments grew heated and hateful. When I accused him of bullying you, of belittling you, of humiliating you, of making himself the Big Man and you the little woman, of making you cry and feel unloved. The way he never made me feel, the way he never dared treat me. Was that because my tongue could be as devilish as his, my outlook on life enough like his to chafe against the boredom of the bourgeoisie, my longings and desires as expansive as his? While you, Mum, simply wanted a good husband and father to your children, the way you were the good wife and our mother, sacrificing all for family.

Do you remember, Mum, how often you came to me for support, how willingly I gave it, jeopardizing Dad's love for me?

I never laid claim to that first home, the significantly more valuable property, because the considerable profits from its eventual sale rightfully belonged to you. A small starter home, even in upmarket Amherst, Massachusetts, cost less than fifty thousand dollars and eventually sold for less than ninety, a mere fraction of the value of a flat in an upscale neighborhood in Hong Kong's insane property market. What profit I made selling the house was peanuts compared to the value of that flat. It never was about money, Mum, not for me, except when you made it so.

Which you did.

Replay. Recall. The first financial fiasco for Mum and Me. Even earlier, the first husband wanted land to build his kennels. That was before Dad had regained enough financial footing in the marriage and Mum completely ruled. *Yes*, my then-husband told Mum, there was this village land he wanted to buy that could—or so he was assured by an expat Brit "village land expert" who made promises with other people's money—be converted from agricultural to residential and commercial. We could build a home there, establish proper kennels for his business. I was reluctant. We had moved twice into village homes for this business that was going nowhere since he drank away what little he made and was uninclined to work more than a few hours a day. Meanwhile, I held down a full-time job, paid the rent, ran the household, and after hours worked for his business as well. By then I had been carrying his weight long enough to know the mistake of that marriage. Even Mum knew. But here was her chance to be the savior, to rescue my marriage. *No*, I said, do not lend him the money, do not do this, it's a pointless proposition. So naturally she gave him the money but asked that the land be in my name, to which he happily acceded. The land remains in the family's fortune, unused for years, worthless except for agriculture. After my husband gave up trying to build on that land, I finally left him. The whole process took less than three months.

Dad used to say, at least when it came to family, *we keep no accounts*. This Chinese turn of phrase renders the ledger invisible as debts are disappeared and what fortune a family has is simply shared in times of need. He was that way with his cousins, brothers, and the two half-sisters who lived with our family back in the sixties, never mind the tsunami of his and Mum's relatives who squatted with us. With my sibs and me. It was always *that way* with Dad and money. What he had he spent as lavishly as possible on himself and others, even after the money was gone.

Mum was everyone's mother. She took care of housekeeping, stretched the budget, ensured we all were fed and warmly clothed in winter, especially those relatives from tropical Indonesia who shivered on arrival in Hong Kong's subtropical climate. Most were grateful, called her *older-sister-cousin*, the almost-Chinese honorific for the wife of an older male cousin or brother.

Mum was a rich man's daughter, unlike Dad, who came from lesser circumstances. Until Dad's bankruptcy, she had not really known anything remotely resembling real poverty. Oh, she understood hardship, she liked to say. In stories of her postwar years in Hong Kong, this pharmacist-in-training only owned two wool skirts to wear one on top of the other, alternating each day, in order to stay warm. But isn't that every petty bourgeoisie youth? To have "suffered" hardship while staying up all night studying for exams, eating little, working hard, sharing rooms with other equally hard-up students? Buying secondhand books or clothes? Counting pennies in every currency? All to be praiseworthy by proving your mettle in higher education, the professions, that white- and pink-collar gentility? And then, when you finally marry a rich man, don't you *deserve* the money? Isn't that what you are owed for treading the right path in life? Isn't that simply your destiny? It never seems to occur to the privileged just how much of a difference that privilege makes to succeeding in life. Mum, unfortunately, was no exception.

Mum could be generous. I don't remember her as stingy or mean when it came to money, not when I was a child. She taught us pity for those less fortunate and insisted we give alms to the poor. She also taught us the value of money, doling out allowances we were expected to budget. We were privileged by her good sense as a mother. Unlike Dad, who showered luxuries on us, who would slip the children extra cash behind Mum's back for treats, especially to the two younger sibs as his business revived after the leanest years. Overcompensating with money, until Mum put a stop to it.

But something happened to Mum after Dad's bankruptcy. The shock to Dad's system was readily manifest—the disgrace, the inability to accept his failure, the need to hide from the world, resulting in a prolonged depression (clinical, probably, but that's another story). With Mum, though, Dad's betrayal—because it was a betrayal, this reckless disregard of family responsibility—resulted in a prolonged PTSD, a form of post-traumatic something or other that lasted the rest of her life, long after money wasn't the problem. For years afterward she would repeat, *gone, all gone, all his money was gone*, and then she'd gaze into space, the shock visceral. That face looms in my memory, harboring all the pain and torment of her broken life. Even after Mum's memory played tricks on recall, she still occasionally muttered about money. It was like Dad's death, abrupt and unexpected, the vanishing of a known life that lingered far beyond the moment, something even Alzheimer's could not completely eradicate. *Daddy died so suddenly. All his money, gone, not even one cent left.* The two incidents, some thirty-five years apart, signaled what was forever wrong about this marriage of hers to Dad.

And there I was, the prodigal oldest girl, the difficult one, the dark-skinned one too ugly to land the right husband, running off with the "family fortune" that Dad was foolish enough to give me, unleashing a second coming of penury and horror on the family. There I was, the oldest child who was supposed to be the responsible one, who should not be so greedy as to need money or even a man. Besides, I already had my BA, hard-earned by Mum's humiliation at having to borrow from her sister so that we could afford an air ticket and expenses that my scholarship did not cover. Later, Mum even swallowed resentment when I left my well-paid job and dumped the banker fiancé of whom she approved, disappearing to Greece to write (surely a wasteful luxury since *anyone* can write) because at least I would go to grad school. She approved as long as I would get a higher degree, even if it was in English, because at least I could teach. But a second marriage! To a man she hadn't met, *and a musician to boot,* well, wasn't that simply *beyond the limit*? When Mum refused to talk to me number three sister intervened to explain—she was the responsible one at the time who required little money for her PhD, who hadn't yet married and divorced, who had done well in school (even if her math was not quite up to Mum's standards). The sibs all have their tale of "Mum and ——," including a money story. Only I had the temerity to ask Dad, not her, for money and to receive such a sizable sum without her blessing. With all the others, Mum doled out the family's fortune as loans and gifts and remained supreme leader.

The family survived. Mum gave money to the two younger sibs, willingly supported their lives. Partly because by then she could, and partly because sister number two and I were already managing and needed little. As for myself, I keep no accounts, will never do so with family money among us, the sibs and our families. I owe Dad at least that much.

But, Mum, let us go further back to the origin of our species. *Did I not love you enough because my love for Dad was greater?* Was that really why you disowned me? Why you said you no longer had this daughter? Because Dad wanted to make things up to me with the monetary gift, an apology for not taking care of me as he would have wished when I was younger? To Dad I was never too dark-skinned or ugly. When I danced with my father, I was always his beautiful girl.

Many years later, after the quarrel over money was forgiven if not forgotten by Mum, she still could not call me beautiful. By then I had left the second husband, the one who presented Dad the gift he liked, a Bose boombox that broadcast opera and classical music from Europe. The husband Mum was always a little afraid of during our twelve-year marriage. She had reason for alarm because she exerted no control over him. He never tried to please her, only Dad, and the two men are a lot alike. If not for him, I might not be a writer today, but that too is another story.

With Mum though, it happened like this. I had come home to live and work (and eventually divorce) and also published my first book. More books followed. In Hong Kong I became a little bit famous. Mum's church friends saw my picture in the papers, as she announced one day over lunch with some of the family. This was shortly after my third book was released, a year before Dad died. *My friends asked about my daughter the writer*, she began. *They said she looked beautiful in the newspaper photo. So, I told them, that can't be my daughter, because my daughter isn't pretty.* Dad's shock was palpable, and he immediately changed the subject, speaking loudly over my mother's words. I don't know if anyone else heard or fully absorbed what she said. But I heard, and so had Dad. Our eyes met and I knew right then that nothing had changed, that the mother he had asked me to be patient with when I was a teenager, that woman would never truly love me no matter how hard she tried.

That moment might have been one of the early signs of Mum's Alzheimer's. She did get angry at me often, but she was never really mean, not as mean as Dad could be to her and others. When I picture her in that moment, making that unkind remark, I am not sure if it was her or her muddled mind. Even as a young teen, when I knew local boys didn't consider me pretty because of my dark skin and less than perfectly Chinese features, Mum would assure me that one day, some boy would like me. Some boy of a lesser god, it was clear, because unlike her I simply wasn't attractive enough. But she meant well, despite her warped idea of beauty and love. Mum simply isn't good with language and often couldn't really hear the meaning of what she said. Her mangled verbal utterances were the cause of much hilarity, and pain, among us sibs. I came to understand more than she ever would about the meaning of beauty and love. It was my good fortune to be born when I was, to be educated and offered myriad opportunities and alternatives to marrying a rich man. To not have suffered the gap years of war, to have had a mother who looked after me as responsibly as a mother should, even if I did not rise to her satisfaction, even if I could not vindicate her with Dad, even if I would not become the woman or the doctor she herself wanted to be.

And one thing I do know about Mum and Me is that I'll never completely know which Mum was real and which Mum was victim to the twisted creep of Alzheimer's. The two intertwined as time stuttered away from both of us until all that was left was a Mum and Me, genesis uncertain, and not the one we both had hoped would be.

Replay. Recall. Dad forgave that loan and gave you the gift of a second, valuable property in that flat (the family flat was the first, which he put entirely in your name). Dad never had to ask me to hand over ownership of that flat to you because he knew I would. A long time ago he taught me not to be greedy, and by helping me buy the home in Amherst, he reckoned that would be enough for me. And it was. Dad best knew how to show love with money. His fatal flaw.

And Mum, what was yours? Your fatal flaw, I mean.

Restart. Revise. *How have* you *not loved me? Let me count* . . . did I really ever believe you did not love me, that you seriously could abandon me forever? That you hated me because Daddy loved me more than you wanted him to? Was I vain enough to think he would choose me over you? Or was that just the ego of youth? This daughter you found too ugly to be princess, her birth became an insult to you, the queen, queen, beauty queen? *Mirror, mirror* . . . cannot, does not lie. You were always more beautiful than me, more athletic than me, so much cleverer than me (than all the sibs) in math and science, and maybe even the better student who always tried her best in every subject, even in music, which was not your talent, and you memorized "The Blue Danube," a feat to demonstrate diligence. And most of all, you were the good wife to your man, even when he didn't deserve it. So why couldn't you recognize my talents, in literature, music, the arts, why couldn't you understand my willingness to forgo marriage to the "right" (read: rich and predictable) man for my life?

Let us start from the real beginning before once upon a time. *How do I love thee?* Till the end of time I'll be counting the ways. Yes, Mum, you bested me in math, which as *everyone* knows is a far, far superior subject to English, in which I excelled. Yes, Mum, you memorized "The Blue Danube" on piano (did you really? I never once heard you play it), proving that my musical talent was nothing much and was perhaps why you never bothered to hear me perform on piano. Yes, Mum, you lost everything because of me, this first child who imprisoned you in motherhood but couldn't even be a boy and who perhaps also was your shameful secret, the reason for marrying in haste.

So now we're finally at once upon a time, when Mum and I was all about me. *How do I recall thee, let me count . . .* but *I was too young! I cannot possibly recall!* Mum and Me lasted exactly sixty-eight days before my first sibling was conceived, and the rambunctious womb activity that followed confirmed it must be a boy. That birth, unlike mine (I slid out, obediently, as soon as I could), was longer, more arduous, as the fetus kicked and turned, insisted (disobediently) on emerging feet first, almost, but alas not a boy, my tomboy sister number two. It did not take long for her to shoot up taller than me, fairer than me, more athletic than me, the gorgeous one of whom Mum could be proud and with whom she enacted yet another version of "Mum and ——."

But mine are mundane longings blown up out of all proportion, transfixed in memory. *Remember, remember, the fifth of November . . .* there were fewer bombings and explosions as age took over, Alzheimer's appeared, and the persistence of all memory became unreliable. Now I no longer shout at you, argue with you, defend those longings. You've simply forgotten, not just me (or my sibs), but all of you. As far as you know, there never was a Mum and Me, a you and I. All I am is the woman who shows up before you, sometimes kind, sometimes grumpy, this person who seems familiar somehow but who is otherwise irrelevant. Even Daddy is gone, and there no longer is any need for me to defend you against his mean tongue, his mean spirit, his mean heart. His mockery. *You're mocking me!* my baby brother used to cry when, frustrated by all his "big sisters," he would run to you to claim his version of Mum and ——.

There will come a time when none of this will signify because no matter how mean-spirited Mum might have been over money, she showed me a longer time ago that her spirit was not essentially ungenerous. She couldn't help being the spoiled little rich girl or the beautiful young woman with too many desirable Chinese suitors or the woman who fell in love (perhaps eventually out of desperation) and married the man who was both so wrong and right for her. I wasn't so unlucky as to live in her time and place, to harbor prefeminist longings coupled with postfeminist ambitions. She couldn't help the state of her world, where a woman like her didn't know how to be king but craved it. And for all her harping on about playing Strauss's waltz, she could not hear the irrelevance of such a boast for a tone-deaf, unmusical person. She was superwoman, or thought she had to be, the one who was a princess but never quite the queen. #MeToo has nothing to say to her: Mum's womanhood was all about doing, doing, doing, with little time for saying her heart. Doing is seldom about absolute rights and wrongs; in the end, she did not disown me. Saying, on the other hand, demands words that parse the difference between wrongs and rights, even when she didn't know what she was saying, because she never did say she could not really love me, even if that truth was close to her heart.

But I need not be mean about money, the way she was with me, because it's meant less to me than to her. If I can earn myself a reasonable life and fulfill enough ambitions, then I need not lust after money the way I lust after Mum's love or empathy. Mum felt sorry for me—sympathy, not empathy—because she did not understand me. But she did her best to mother me, the way she strove to be best in all she undertook. I was not, I was never a motherless child.

Begin again. Once upon that time there was just Mum and Me, the first and only girl child to love and adore. Now it's me and Mum, where I am—or whoever next appears before her is—always the first and only girl who loves and cares for her, the one she will love for a moment until she forgets her existence. Isn't that enough, isn't that the best I can hope for? To live in this present tense of love and appreciation? To surrender all resentment and anger and desire, even without a bodhi tree? To simply be the daughter who will care for her mother until the end of time, the way her mother once cared for her? Unconditionally?

Maybe, just maybe, that's all there really is to say about Mum and Me.

# PRECARIOUS PRECISION

*Daddy was precise. Precarious! So precarious,* Mum complained, as long as he was alive, about the way he was, the way he couldn't help being. When he died, we the children found in his wardrobe several clear plastic bags of coins, sorted by value: the tiny, golden ten-cent coin, so light it barely feels real; the curvy dodecagon that is the twenty-cent piece; a bauhinia graces heads on the elegant fifty cents, the way it does all the other new coins; "1" declares the value on tails of the one-dollar coin, the way roman numerals do them all; the two-dollar piece apes the twelve-sided polygon that is twenty cents, except that this is larger and silver like all the coins that cross the dollar bridge; five is weighty, the largest coin, thickened by layers; at ten, coinage reshapes, smaller, more manageable than five, although similarly stacked, and the only one to mingle silver and gold in its minting (fig. 7).

But mingled among each denomination were numerous foreign coins and the old, colonial coins, many with Queen Elizabeth II on heads. My favorite are the really old ones with King George V because these are solid, larger, weightier, real value in my childhood (fig. 8). Fifty cents (the largest denomination) bought two soft drinks with change to spare; at today's exchange rate this is less than an American quarter, while a soft drink is at least ten dollars in vending machines.

The king: KG5 we called him, echoing the name of the English school that Chinese children could not attend in my childhood. A precarious notion, this once-separatist colonial attitude, because now these same English schools survive only because upper-middle-class and wealthy Chinese pay as much in tuition for their children to attend these so-called international schools as you might for an Ivy League education. To perfect their offspring's English. To keep them away from rote learning at local schools (*memorize multiplication tables, trigonometry formulas, historically significant dates, Chinese dynasties, the elements table, and the odes of Keats!*). To prepare them for an ever more globalized economy where

**7.** Tails of all Hong Kong coins in use in 2018. Photo courtesy of the author.

**8.** King George V and Queen Elizabeth II heads and the bauhinia flower image on tails of some Hong Kong coins from the colonial era. Photo courtesy of the author.

pennies from heaven rain most melodiously in English and Putonghua (or Mandarin), not Cantonese, the language of the city's teeming masses.

Isn't it precarious, this thing we call history? Almost as precarious as money.

Daddy wasn't a collector. Mum collected, or at least she did once upon a time before motherhood got in the way, the way it did for some women of her age and times. Stamps, mostly, although she liked currency as well—bank notes—the greater value of paper compared to silver or gold simulations. But Daddy was precise, and the mini bus from our hilltop flat we call home cost exactly $3.30. Fourteen years after his death it costs $3.90 and is likely to go up soon. This mini bus is yellow and green and seats fourteen, its route from our hilltop locale to Kowloon Tong rail station and back.

Kowloon Tong. The station where you connect to life: trains that whisk you across the border to the Chinese mainland or take you to the island of Hong Kong (where the Fong, that international nightlife slope, is located) or to Lantau Island (site of the city's airport that is rapidly running out of runway space). At Kowloon Tong, taxis line up patiently at the rank each day, buses head for hither and yon but mostly to the New Territories where verdant nature is sacrificed to house the teeming masses. At Kowloon Tong, Festival Walk gleams, a high-end shopping mall and commercial complex that is a little less high end now since its "breathtaking" completion (marketing language is *so* imprecise) the year my father died. Daddy might have liked this mall with its myriad restaurants and fancy groceries and designer goods, but I doubt it. It doesn't feel either exclusive or marketplace-messy enough, the way the city used to be when he was alive. It's just another shopping mall in just another globalized city, sanitized, where Bally reigns and imported Japanese tchotchkes cost twice those from China. But he would have liked the regularly cleaned toilets, a sign of progress, especially after SARS. Pestilence and war are the most efficient cleansers of humankind. Public toilets used to be as absent here as they still are in New York, and about as clean as the ones in Paris aren't. Measuring civilization in toilet stalls.

I live on this same hilltop today, not entirely willingly, to help care for an aging mum with Alzheimer's. The other day, I watched myself stack the last of my father's coin hoard in neat piles: two, one, fifty, twenty, and two tens, exact change for the fare on the mini bus. The mini bus today, like all public transport, has a card reader for the ubiquitous Octopus, a transport cash card you refill (electronically through your bank or with cash at ticket machines) to travel to the world and back (it works on the airport express train line), to buy soda and snacks and medicine and tchotchkes from 7-Eleven or other messily unchained shops. Few still drop coins into the fare box or bother with cash. The other day, my young colleague at the university where I now work laughingly told me of an older woman friend who does not use Octopus, preferring to buy a ticket with coins from the machine instead to ride the trains. I laughed too because I also depend on my Octopus the way I once depended on Daddy to be his usual, precarious self, even after retirement, balancing coins in neat piles on his wardrobe shelf, piles *so precarious that anyone could knock these over*, although who this *anyone* is is a mystery known only to Mum, since their maid would never have dared open his or my mother's wardrobe, especially not Mum's, because she locked wardrobes and safes and front doors and gates, fearful of thieves—*mainland refugees!*—who would break in and rob us in this dangerous and precarious city. The city my parents emigrated to after the war and called home and raised us, the children. Not entirely willingly.

Can we precisely name these emotions we harbor about life and change? We, the children, are no longer children, any more than we are "we," an emotionally charged foursome who hid life from parents and dreamed of lives away from our city. Three of us returned for a time as adults to live and work, and all of us come and go, come and go, following flight paths from wherever we happen to have last landed. Time, tides, and deregulated air transport. It has been precarious, keeping a foothold in this rootless city that survives on precision. Buses and trains run on time, and transport fares are calculated to the tenth cent (it used to be the fifth), even though only the elderly and eccentric use change these days. No flat fare for trains in this city-village of bean counters who once clicked their abacuses, long replaced by adding machines, calculators, computers and spreadsheets, eyeing that bottom line. Just like property developers who rule this city, our economy built on a paper tiger that roars the price per square foot, a number that rises and falls as unpredictably as the tides of the Yangtze and now even of the Mississippi.

My father had an adding machine in his office. The metal hammers imprinted long rows of figures onto its paper roll. Meanwhile Daddy inscribed numbers with a fountain pen onto large sheets of accounting paper, notebooks, invoices, bills of lading, bank deposit or withdrawal slips, back when human tellers were ATMs. His handwriting is almost as indecipherable as a medic's scrawl, although we can read it. Genetics, perhaps, like my penchant for precision, despite my hopelessly messy life. Daddy was a neatnik as well, forcing crap into order the way I do my life.

Despite all attempts at order, when imprecision rears its ugly head, the result can be catastrophic, as it was for Daddy when his business collapsed. The problem with precision is that you will watch the collapse in disbelief and move numbers around so that things look neat enough again. And move them and move them until there are no numbers left to move, and you must face the empty bank account, the worthless share certificates you held onto too long and finally confess to your wife, *it's gone, all gone.*

My mother echoed *all gone* for years. Bemoaned it. I heard it from the time I was ten or so for much of my life until her memory collapsed (*almost all gone*) and she could be spared the pain of remembrance.

I think about money these days, because I have a full-time job again (not entirely willingly) for the first time in over a decade.

For more than two decades, I embraced a parallel business existence to my writing life, working mostly as a marketing and management professional for multinationals in Asia and the United States, tripping around profit-makers that included printing companies, ad agencies, airlines, architects, corporate and private security, logistics and media, even a Wall Street law firm. I also briefly picked up contracts as a freelance research consultant for corporate trainers and venture capitalists or ran nightly production lines for design firms during periods of unemployment. Most of those years, I was employed full-time, except for a five-year hiatus spent traipsing around Europe trying to be a writer, after which I hung out at grad school in Massachusetts for as long as possible while completing an MFA in fiction.

When I quit my last corporate position in 1998 (the *Asian Wall Street Journal*, sometime before Murdoch besmirched the news of the world), I had no desire to work full-time again. Instead, I traded stocks and futures. Taught a little. Bought inexpensive property that accumulated value. Consulted occasionally, edited here and there. Wrote the odd commercial article or book review. Traveled. Instead, I reveled in the literary life, secluded at writers' colonies or in far-flung lands, and wrote and published several more books. It was messy, precarious, and thoroughly imprecise.

But then Mum's memory became precarious, and Precision blinked, looked me in the eye, declared: *darling, it's time to make order again.*

Funny thing, the changes of life. Menopause wasn't a big deal, but Mum's memory loss was. Alzheimer's is a way bigger deal than menopause. The latter is only physical and can be managed, the way money can. You cannot manage that which has no shape or physical certainty, and to date we still know too little about this change of life that mucks up memory to make any precise declarations that mean a hill of beans.

So instead I bean-count, making small hills of change atop an old chest of drawers, one that has come upstairs to my space through my parents' lives. This small, oblong four-drawer piece was acquired many years ago, when exactly I do not know, but it is solid, crafted of wood and not modern pasteboard that collapses and warps. All it needed was a coat of paint and *voilà*, I can avoid buying cheap furniture that will end up on the garbage heap when Mum passes away. You cannot gaze too long at trash in this city, or any city, because the sight will repulse you, scramble your emotional circuits, paralyze your brain cells, even as you continue to consume. A material madness defines civilized life, and we measure progress by exporting garbage that we soon must lose in space.

Money appears in my bank account each month, a regular amount that is more income than I've earned in years. Cash accumulates because there's little I really need to buy anymore. I pay off the last of my mort-gages, buy new clothes for work, eat out and take taxis more often than I used to because time is again of the essence, with no more space to loaf. I measure my life in iPhone calendar segments: a breakfast meeting to counsel an anxious student at 8 a.m. because he must go to work after-ward; a conference with my department head at 10 a.m.; remember to show up at the committee reviewing evaluative measures at noon and the subcommittee where gender matters at 2 p.m.; meet an overseas student in town at 3:30 p.m.; my publisher at 7 p.m. And so it goes. To where did time vanish, I wonder, now that order and precision reign again?

Daddy's precision was leisurely, like loafing, because he eschewed working for others. As a child, my great treat was to visit his tiny office on Ice House Street, where giant ice blocks once were made and stored, but which was, by the sixties, Hong Kong's version of Wall Street, more or less. My father is a Bartleby who laughs. I wonder if my willingness now to reinstate a full-time work life is partly due to his own unwillingness to do likewise. When his business collapsed, he refused to take any job. Mum begged, borrowed, and perhaps even stole, not money but dignity, all through Dad's refusal to accept his situation, so that he could wear the public face that pretended his business was well. Even when I earned a pittance (as a grad student for instance), I was never really broke. Pennies hoarded, purchases postponed till money returned because in this messy, imprecise life I lead, I always manage to find a way to have money. Money did return to my father eventually, but at home we witnessed his face of depression and shame.

This face haunts me still.

I talk to Daddy here in his room, this creation of which he was once so proud, this solidly constructed mini house that has survived typhoons, subtropical humidity, and the Hong Kong Government's bureaucratic angst for more than forty years. This UBW or unauthorized building works has outlived him and several decades of the Building Authority's orders that demand it be removed, the way the owners of every "illegal" structure in Hong Kong have been so ordered but who regularly ignore such orders until that ultimatum. To date we have received several ultimatums but not the fatal one.

*Daddy*, I demand, *how did you know when that time would pass, so you would one day wear a happier face again?* He is silent, unwilling to reveal the secret of his existence. *Did you ever doubt your choices in life, the responsibilities you shouldered for marriage, family, di wei?*

*Di wei*. 地 位. I can speak to Daddy now in Mandarin—Putonghua, the People's Party calls it—because that was his Chinese, the Chinese I did not learn to speak in Hong Kong, the Chinese I studied in Massachusetts at grad school. 地 位, your place in life, in society, the space that

**9.** The "squat." Exterior view of my rooftop bedsit home for some fifteen years, approximately one hundred square feet of an unauthorized building works above Mum's flat in 2018. Peak of the Lion Rock visible above the roof. Photo courtesy of the author.

**10.** A view from the "squat" looking north toward Hong Kong Island in 2018. Photo courtesy of the author.

gives you face. An awfully precarious face, one that dominates socially conscious Hong Kong. Much more than mere status, it cuts so deep you might throw yourself off a building someday, as Leslie Cheung, the AIDS-infected actor, did, because it cuts into your hetero-loverboy face, your homoerotic beauty, your precariously real existence on screen that was the heart and soul of you. Or so we surmise.

If Daddy contemplated the jump—as an insurance salesman friend of mine did, fatally—he never said and still does not say, although I sometimes think he did. Once, when I was in my thirties, I called home from New York at Christmas as I did each year and told Daddy my life was a disaster. I did not mean to say that. What I wanted to say was that my then-marriage was fine, that work was going well, that I was earning a decent living after my penniless years as a writer in grad school, that he would not have to worry about me anymore. But I couldn't utter the words I knew I should because they simply weren't true. It did not matter that every Chinese gene in my body screamed *stop it, stop crying, stop with the depression and shame that you've failed in your marriage, lost your job, maxed out your credit cards.* My move to New York had been precisely planned. A corporate job offer, more money than I had ever earned in my life up to that point, my first paid-for-by-a-corporation move. A move my ex-husband agreed to, not entirely willingly, since he was doing fine as a jazz musician impresario in Cincinnati, his hometown, the city where I was simply too globally weird. A year and a half after our move to New York, the company was sold, and I was among the first downsized casualties. It was the irrationally crashing eighties, the bubble deflating, the air sucked right out of me. I was not to find another full-time job again for over a year.

*It's okay, it's okay,* he told me through my crying jag. What was okay? Was shame and depression just the nature of this precarious moment, the way it once was for him? I never spoke to Mum that year. Dad knew better than to pass her the phone.

I am luckier than my father. I have no family to feed, no face to lose among an extended family of global relatives who expected him, the eldest son of his generation, to be a pinnacle of success. We the children make few demands of each other. My sister picks me up from the airport when I flip between New York and here. I bring her jelly beans and sweet-smelling handmade soaps from America. Years earlier, this same sister lugged a heavy electric typewriter for me from London to Paris by train during my itinerant literary youth. Genetics perhaps, doing what matters to the other even if it makes no sense to you, the way Mum once did for my father.

*You want me to do this, right?* I ask thin air, hoping his voice will reassure me that this too will pass, this looking after Mother, the once-furious woman who made my life hell but toward whom I must be filial.

*You want me to do this, right?* I say to the air, as I make order out of Daddy's coin hoard, living my days on our rooftop, working for a living again. The job forces me to live in Hong Kong. The job is at a university down the hill, walking distance in winter, a five-minute mini bus ride in summer, the easiest commute ever. It is certainly easier than the F train in the eighties that often broke down between Brooklyn to lower Manhattan, or the hour-long bus trek to the new office tower that leaked in Singapore, or the forty-minute drive around the ring road to the architects in Cincinnati, or the two-and-a-half-hour public transport relay (one way) to the ad agency in Hong Kong. *Thank god for small favors*, as my sister would say.

*You want me to do this, right?* I ask Daddy, when life with Mum gets too much, when I'm homesick for Bill and the life I left behind, freed of an employer. *Do not bite the hand that*—and I do not, never have in fact, because once you oblige yourself, your face depends on meeting that obligation, even if it is a contract entered into not entirely willingly.

Because he cannot answer me right away, as he did that Christmas years ago, I parse time by sorting through his coins. First, a separation into foreign and local because there were numerous coins from elsewhere, evidence of his travels, the global life he bequeathed us that made us who we are. We the children have lived here, there, and everywhere as if such precarious peregrinations are normal. It has made for a memorable life so far, so what right have I to complain?

But I do complain, and to shut me up there were Daddy's coins.

Now the foreign coins are in their own hoard, awaiting future separation. The pre-handover colonials and post-handover Hong Kong ones are almost separate, and I think about how to cash in defunct money.

And each day, I make hills of the usable change on that flat white surface. Two dollars, one dollar, fifty cents, twenty cents, two ten cents. The hoard dwindles. When I remember to do so, I snatch a tiny hill on my way out to catch the mini bus; other times, I default to Octopus. It is life for now, and *it's okay, it's okay*, this precarious precision until the mini bus fare goes up and the hills must be rebuilt, or my mother's condition worsens and new medical care is needed, or life intervenes and sends me another curveball of shame or depression, although these seem less frequent now, more manageable, like money.

I never did get Daddy's answer.

Summer is at its peak, but eventually the air will cool into bearable again. The rains will be less drenching, the sun a lot less blistering. The coins sit silent in their precarious mounds. Life changes. Life's changes. One less complaint.

# JOURNEYS THROUGH PAST TIMES

## A Norwich Narrative

June 2011. Resistance. Not to Norwich but to The Journey that begins badly, with a robbery. My unlocked garage has fallen victim to intruders. A lawn mower and generator are missing; my car is untouched. The state police boy-man will later tell me that techno-ready autos no longer fall prey to the *Too-Dumb* to keep up with the times (*proper-nounhood*, mine or Pooh's). We, my neighbors and I, noticed the loss too late (I because I am never home anymore, given my current residence in Hong Kong), and another neighbor further north up the road recalls footprints in the snowdrift by the garage door in late February. (Who in god's name hovers around this rural route during a northern New York State winter?) Footprints aren't necessarily suspicious though: my next-door-but-one neighbor revs up my car and checks on the home. This home through which I transit on my journey to Norwich, a Journey to the East. Violated.

Leaving for the airport in Burlington, Vermont, I forget to set the security alarm. An unforgivable memory lapse given That Incident of a Foot-Imprinted Snowdrift. Passport, ticket, sterling pounds. Hong Kong dollars are left behind for the final leg of the journey back to that other home. Complicated and tedious, this traveling between homes, despite excitement about the journey eastward to the West, to Norwich, where, for a whole week, I shall not have to eat Asia-Asian or see my mother. Later, the neighbors who set the alarm through my lapse will tell me the house between our homes was burglarized. Only ten dollars stolen, nothing else missing. I sometimes hear these people (even though tall trees block sight of their dwelling and the multiple vehicles on their lawn) when they play music too loudly or shoot rifles out of season, shattering the peace. Discomfiting, both their presence and the burglary.

At JFK, I board a KLM flight to NWI (the airport at Norwich supposedly is international) that is really Delta's. I rarely travel this U.S. carrier. As one whose youthful livelihood began at an airline in the East, customer service is in my blood, the way it is not quite the same in the United States. So I expect the worst. Overall, an uneventful leg, except for the arrival into JFK's *Catch Me If You Can* terminal that Delta occupies. The trouble with the preservation of the old (and who in their right minds would destroy this temple to early global aviation, the era of PanAm circling the globe?) is that it takes too damned long to retrofit for modernity. We, the pax, haul carry-ons through makeshift walkways, up tentative metal stairways, into a crowded terminal. I beat a path to Terminal 2, international, and pretend I'm *Up in the Air* with Clooney.

NWI. Summertime (almost) and the taxis are missing. The taxis, I suspect, are always missing at Norwich's sweet little airfield, hardly international. But I am back, this is familiar, and suddenly I am deliriously happy to be journeying again to Worlds, the annual writer's symposium at the University of East Anglia (UEA), by invitation only. *Love is lovelier / the second time around* (Jimmy Van Heusen and Sammy Cahn, 1960). Whose voice do I hear? Sinatra's? Is this too a home of sorts for one who traverses the globe too frequently, racking up mileage, hearing melodies, constantly homesick?

The streets of Norwich conjure visions of Christchurch. Like New Zealand at the zoo. My writer's paradise, between Christchurch and Dunedin, is a small villa-bungalow (Kiwi-Yankee Englishes compete). Furnished from the op shop. Hidden by a macrocarpa hedge, fruit trees, hydrangeas, the garden sheltering forget-me-nots in corners beneath the porch. Sacrificed at the Altar of Confucian Filial Piety (Mother is ninety-one, Alzheimer's is impossible, Eldest Daughter is *haau seuhn* 孝 順). When I moved my writer's life back home to Mother's Hong Kong, I relinquished that getaway home; my crib-bach (South-North island dialects compete in a nation of fewer inhabitants than most major cities) was rented out over two years earlier. Driving through Norwich to the UEA campus, I briefly regain paradise. *It's lovely going through / the zoo!* ("Manhattan" by Richard Rodgers and Lorenz Hart, 1925). Audio memory-home.

It takes a few days to sight them, but eventually, the rabbits are rampant again. I run around the lake-pond (Anglo-American tongues compete) contemplating our worlds. Narrative instincts declare: *it's all about the journey*. Monkey journeyed west to India in a bid to gain Paradise. Compass points and literatures compete. *Paradise Lost* outbid *Regained* in the West's collective consciousness. I journey east to go to the West, where my languages coalesce around Worlds at Norwich. Back home in New Zealand, my English falls off the cliff. Back home in New York, my English slangs, bangs, and elides into jazz. Back home in Hong Kong I create a world for Asian students writing in English who redefine, rewrite, reimagine Asia. In Norwich my worlds collapse into narrative, having finally arrived at the Destination.

Exiting the Land of Rampant Rabbits, my flight is delayed. Flybe charges me £30 to check one bag. Where the hell is Robin Hood when you need him? Transformed into a Kiwi Crowe, out of reach. At Manchester

International (all airports seem globally soulful these days; is life imitating Pico Iyer's *Global Soul*?), I race between terminals, barely making my flight, grateful to UEA's lake-pond running track that prepped me for this leg of the journey.

I fly home. I no longer know where the journey began. Was it New York (city or state?), Hong Kong, Burlington International, or the last time I saw Norwich, two years prior? Or did the real departure begin years earlier, in colonial times from Kai Tak International, long before this peripatetic journey took root?

Sometimes, it's not about the journey. Sometimes, the Still Point is arrival.

# HOME BASE

My mother did not want to leave home. She never quite said that before her memory collapsed into its present state, but we knew. My brother and I tried, after Dad's death, to move her to the states. We were the two American citizens among the siblings, and he worked for the Catholic Church in a small town in Ohio. My brother was tapped into the medical community, his wife is a psychologist, and we felt he could organize good care for Mum in a home for the aged near his church. Our Hong Kong family flat would sell for a sufficient sum, which, coupled with my mother's liquid assets, would be enough to cover her care. I could easily visit from Manhattan, and the other two sisters could travel. Back in Hong Kong, only our surfer sister still lived there, and she could not exactly abandon her dog or then-husband or beachfront home to live with Mum. The other sister was in Australia with her husband and their dog. Yes, decided the sibs, what did we have to lose? It was worth a try.

So we collected all the documents from U.S. Immigration, contacted lawyers, and inquired at rest homes. Mum even seemed willing. When we presented her the papers and plans, she received them, saying she would look through these before signing.

Months passed. Nothing happened.

Each subsequent conversation ended with delays and inaction.

Meanwhile, the prions did their worst and she recalled less and less of what had been said. I was staying longer and longer in Hong Kong with her each trip, wishing I could be back in New York or at my writing retreat home in New Zealand. We had to do something before Mum or I turned into pumpkins. Eventually, we resigned ourselves to the fact that Mum was not going to sign and never would immigrate.

*I'm finally going home, going back to Hong Kong*, declares the unnamed female protagonist in "Blackjack," a story I dashed off the night before the *South China Morning Post* short story contest deadline. The story that won first prize in 1992.

In 1992 New York City was home for my then-husband and me, but Hong Kong beckoned economically. As one city sank beneath the weight of irrational exuberance, another rose on a cloud of hope in its last years of British Empire before submission to eternal Chinese sovereignty. In 1992 the theme of the story contest was "Five Years On," a nod to the handover back to China in 1997. In 1992 my father was still alive and my mother's Alzheimer's not yet apparent, although the prions may have already begun their misshapen prowl. Prions, a still-evolving science, proteins in the brain that fold incorrectly and gum up memory. Origami gone wild.

So in 1992 my father, who understood that his daughter "writes," handed me the newspaper with the contest notice and said I still had a whole day to enter and win two tickets to London. *What did I have to lose*, I decided.

We move from home to home in our globally nomadic world and consider it our good fortune to be able to do so. At least I did, back in '92, when Hong Kong welcomed returnees like me to their birth city. *What did we have to lose*, I persuaded my jazz-guitarist-turned-commercial-real-estate-broker, now-ex-husband. *I'll work, you go back to playing, we'll live there for a few years and come home*, by which I meant the Brooklyn house we owned in Greenpoint-Williamsburg. Federal Express had offered me a huge pay increase to "go home," plus relocation expenses. We had some savings, and our two-family house rented out easily to cover the mortgage. It would be an improvement over our joint malaise—me worrying over the likely layoff at my Wall Street law firm marketing job, he over his abandoned musical career in favor of making a lot of money. What *did* we have to lose? I was not like my "Blackjack" protagonist who no longer felt at home in New York after her divorce, who had no real choice *but* to "go home." Besides, we ended up with a trip to London and had our first taste of cream teas in Devon. And I even got a fancy new pen as part of the prize.

In 2014 my HKID permanent right of abode card is the envied identity of young economic migrants from the United States because it carries the right to live and work in Hong Kong without first having to find an employer-sponsor for a visa. In 2014 my primary home base is in a city that no longer feels like home, to help care for a woman who no longer knows who I am.

For a while, my sibs and I had contemplated the China Coast, the only English-speaking home for the aged in Hong Kong. Mum's Cantonese has never been fluent, and as the prions continued their maniacal Play-Doh twists and turns, her tongue lost more Cantonese—her fourth, mostly illiterate language—than her literate third one, English. The China Coast held bingo Fridays, at which my Hong Kong sister and I became regulars for a time, calling the bingo that is, as recompense for regularly bringing our mother. Sometimes I even played the piano for their sing-alongs. But each time we went, Mum would gaze at the other residents, including a colleague from her youth, a doctor at the hospital where she had been a pharmacist in training, and, after winning at bingo, ask to go home. It was a pleasant enough residence, with a garden, goldfish pond, and flowers, but the rooms were small with no bathrooms attached. We would hate to live like that, we agreed, and eventually surrendered to keeping Mum at home, after cleanup and renovation, forever after. For a while, happily.

Meanwhile, I was still living the pumpkin life, transient along the flight path connecting three "home bases," or, as Bill says, headed to where my stuff resides.

When we renovated we made sure we kept enough of Mum's stuff. The small green safe in her wardrobe, for instance. For one thing, it weighs a ton and isn't easily moved. For another, she would open it regularly, just to make sure she could, to see that the jewelry was in there. We left a few trinkets of minimal value and locked up the valuables in the safety deposit at the bank. It kept her happy.

For years, Mum would lose her handbag. This always happened just before we had to go out, to church or lunch or dinner, and we would scramble around in search of the missing appendage. My sibs and I learned to commandeer the search before accusations flew, that Maryam, her helper, had stolen it or that *someone* had moved it. Sometimes, it was under the bed. At others, stashed away in the bathroom, the kitchen, behind her armchair. For a time, we were confounded by the locked wardrobe, and the missing key Mum couldn't find, and we searched through the containers of spare keys—none were ever discarded, even keys to locks that no longer existed—until we found the one that opened her closet. Her handbag was hidden inside, along with all the other things she had to hide from *the servants, workmen, thieves!* Somehow, Mum had locked the wardrobe with her own key, but where that key disappeared to only God or the devil of her memory knows.

So when we moved Mum back into her flat after the massive cleanup and facelift, she looked around the more or less familiar space, and settled into her home of some forty years. What she didn't know and would never remember was that there were no longer any locks on any inside doors or wardrobes.

The thing about fairy godmothers is that they're only interested in the forever happily ever after.

*This is not my home*, shouted Mum, a few years after she had been living in her renovated home. Our two Filipino helpers were in a panic. This was when my mother was still reasonably mobile with a cane and would go out with us or one of the helpers for lunch, walks, and church. By the time I got the call and rushed back home from my university office, both our helpers were following Mum down the hill away from our building, one with the wheelchair, trying to coax her into it, the other nervously trying to hang onto her so that she wouldn't fall, while Mum kept shoving her hand away.

I caught up with the convoy. *Hi, Mum*, I said, *let's go home*. She glared fiercely at me. *Who are you?* It was still early in her not recognizing me, and I had not yet accepted this eventuality. *Your oldest daughter of course!* I told her. *No you're not, you're cheating me.* I let her walk away, trusting time and prions to do their work. A few minutes later, I approached her again, and this time she asked me to help her and shooed the helpers away. *They're trying to take me away*, she confided, pointing at them. *Don't worry*, I said, *I'll make sure they don't and take care of you. Where do you want to go?* I asked. *Home*, she replied. We were a few hundred feet away from our building, past the park, down near the mini bus stop. *Where do you live*, I asked. Now, she hesitated, unable to answer, and finally retorted, *don't* you *know?* I waited a few minutes for her to forget again. *You live at number 67, don't you?* I asked. *Yes! Yes!* she exclaimed happily, reassured by the familiar number. In order to confuse her, we walked a circle downhill and around the block to bring her home because she refused to go back up the hill. Soon, she succumbed, exhausted, to her wheelchair and said to the helper, *can you push me please?* By the time we brought her back home, the security guard did his best to make her recognize him, greeting her in Cantonese by name, pointing to the name of our building, which we repeated in English and Cantonese, hoping some memory would trigger. It did. She returned home without further incident.

This home-that-is-not-home continued for a time. There were other incidents, including the time she tried to hail a taxi to take her home. She managed to run away from us, albeit never far from our reach, almost all the way down the hill, which is at least a seven-minute walk. We got into the taxi together and brought her home. Her doctor modified her prescription of psychotropics, and things calmed down.

These days, Mum no longer carries a handbag, money, or keys.

She used to confound us, weighing down her handbag with things. Cutlery. An extra pair of glasses. Used-up tissues. Keys she unearthed from her minefield of a wardrobe. A weighty number of coins. When we cleaned out her home prior to renovation, my sister and I counted over HK$25,000 (approximately US$3,000) in various currencies of bills and coins and Chinese New Year *laisee* packets of new money squirreled away in her wardrobe. Before my sister took over her accounts, my mother would storm into the local Hang Seng bank branch, demand to see the manager, and insist that someone was stealing her money. Fortunately, the manager was patient and honest. He showed her the balance, gave her the desired withdrawal, and, in time, learned to call one of us. But what worried us most were the locked doors. We did not want her to accidentally or deliberately lock herself into her home or bedroom where we could not get to her. So off went the deadbolt to the front door, away went all the locks on the doors, except the one to the main bathroom our helpers used. Into her handbag we placed a minimal amount of money, tissues, prayer book, and rosary. Now even that phase is over. William Carlos Williams was only partially right: there is not meaning but in things, but meaning evaporates when things reside only in memory's fold.

The thing about pumpkin life is how easily you fall into that waiting game. The prince will come, you'll fit that shoe (were there really so few others sized 7.5?), and then life's just a bowl of bananas as you go off happily to the promised new home. I began to wear a lot of orange. At some point, I counted five distinct orange outfits in my wardrobe. My mother and I, we've both been waiting to "go home" for a long time now, so long I've lost count of the days, months, and years. Now, I no longer count.

*Where are you based*, the Asia corporates ask, accustomed as they are to the constant movement here, there, and these days mostly north to China. I was like that once. My first corporate move, back in '86, was when Pinkerton's relocated me from Cincinnati to New York, and we stayed in a downtown Manhattan hotel room for a week, where heaven was resident in the mini bar. We found a spacious, two-bedroom apartment in Brooklyn, at the southwest border of Park Slope, that could still be had for $900 a month and did not panic until a year and a half later when Pinkerton's then-parent, American Brands, sold it to a California company, and one by one the directors were laid off, me in that first batch of last in, first out. A few years later, gainfully reemployed, we purchased a home in Greenpoint-Williamsburg, where a two-family house, on a quiet street with its own driveway and garage, could be had for $250,000.

The trouble with divorce is that the home base, your most valuable asset, vanishes into a breakeven sale just so you can be done with all that. You can't look back on home because it's never there when the neighborhood shoots up in value, and besides, Thomas Wolfe and you know perfectly well, you can't, you really can't go home again.

Federal Express relocated me to Hong Kong, into a much nicer hotel room, until we found a place. A studio flat opposite the Royal (today, a commoner) Hong Kong Yacht Club, with its magnificent view of the hills of Kowloon, this shoebox cost over $2,000 a month; the car park space nearby was another $500. Then my aunt Caroline died, her companion Christine moved back to Indonesia, and their large flat in the building where my parents lived was empty. I reluctantly moved across the harbor to Kowloon for the same rent (family rate) to accommodate my ex-husband's car in the parking lot below. Three months later, I was promoted to a regional job in Singapore. Uprooted once again into even more luxurious hotel life for a couple of months, and then there was this house on the east side of the island state, tastefully furnished, open, modern, and spacious, with its beautifully manicured garden and a backyard to hang washing on a sunny day, of which Singapore has many, for only a little more than the shoebox in Hong Kong.

*Where are you putting up*, Singaporeans asked, a Singlish turn of phrase I particularly like. Changi, I replied, which was always met with exclamations of *oh, my goodness, so far!* Distance to home is relative if your driving commute in Cincinnati is forty minutes from work to home, or if you've suffered New York City's subway at its worst, to commute forty-five minutes (and usually longer) one way. A taxi to work in Singapore took me less than twenty-five minutes, which, on an island you can traverse in less than a day, is long. Paradise, however, has its drawbacks, not unlike pumpkin life. It's the brief respite before the fall, because fall you must, culminating in your politely agreeing to disagree with the boss with whom you cannot see eye to eye (corporate speak is nothing if not excruciatingly polite when you willingly accept the proffered financial handshake), and before you know it, you're off again, looking for home in all the wrong places. Paradise is also where Adam says to Eve, *but how could you do that*, even though he too succumbed to the bitter fruit, and before you know it, marriage, like home, vanishes.

More easy living followed that summer—Leo Burnett was generous with my month at the Park Lane Hotel—and before you know it, you're back in Hong Kong, where the parents are still alive across the harbor, as you move from that corporate home to your final one at the *Asian Wall Street Journal* and find solitude in homes along the escalator, uphill on the island.

And then, when you least expect it, you fall in love again and move back to New York, surrender completely to the writing life, and the rest becomes history still in the making.

All that confusion is past us now as Mum settles in "at home." Even I've settled down into pumpkin life on the roof, with its magnificent view of the island to the south and the university where I currently am "in residence" to the west. A bedsit smaller than the shoebox in Causeway Bay, with a makeshift kitchenette and an outdoor "kitchen sink," to be avoided when lightning strikes, which occurs with disturbing frequency these days. But it's free. On good days, Disney's granny fairy godmother sings *bibbidi bobbidi boo*, and my mother's smile is benign, not hostile, and she tells me she's feeling fine. On good days, Mum still talks a little, although the prions have robbed her of most of her speech. On good days, I forget that Mum is ninety-four, still recuperating—from a broken hip and hip replacement operation in March this year—better than even most seventy-year-olds can, and maybe, just maybe, since we've both stopped counting, could live forever.

There were bad nights after her fall. Her sleep was wracked by complicated dreams and shouting at invisible ghosts. We, the sibs, watched her for a couple of months in her hospital bed, taking turns to keep vigil. By standards, a fractured hip is nothing. Old people fall. Old people with Alzheimer's fall, and then forget they have until the pain prods their body into submission. Physical therapy was slow and difficult. Also, this was more than our two Filipino helpers had signed up for in their live-in, rotational, twenty-four-seven elder care, despite their six years with us and genuine affection for Mum. Her fall meant a new phase of "life at home with Mother."

Months passed.

In our home, the visiting nurses came and went, talking of bed sores and the care and feeding of the elderly. I hired a live-in Filipino nurse and reconstructed the living quarters for our grateful helpers. There were evenings and mornings I watched Mum dream or was told of her incoherent conversations with the dead who call her home. There were nights when the only thing I knew how to do was gaze at that pumpkin patch and, like Charlie Brown, wonder, *but why?*

And from time to time, when Mum's awake, she still asks to go home. *You are home*, we tell her, then wait. Eventually she will forget, and Mum can live more or less happily ever after again until the prions prowl a longer trek and further confuse her. I'm waiting and wondering about the next phase of Alzheimer's. Mum went from mild-to-moderate to moderate-to-severe a few years back. At that tipping point of "severe," the patient literally forgets how to chew or swallow or breathe. She forgets how to live. It will be excruciating. Right now, though, her doctor and we know she's doing extremely well.

A few weeks ago, the last of her ten siblings died. She's waiting, I think, for the right moment to "go home," back to where dinner must always be prepared for Dad, to where Aunties Caroline and Christine will stop in from their flat downstairs, to where all her children and even that first great-grandchild—currently in waiting in her/his mother's womb in France—will eventually fly home to visit her, to where all the relatives from Indonesia, Holland, Canada, Australia, and the United States, as well as friends from other far-flung homes, can come visit and stay awhile in the upstairs guest room as they used to.

As for me, I'm just waiting forever to go home to Bill. Patience, they say, is a virtue, and orange, I hear, might just be the new great white hope.

# AND THEN, FILIAL TIME

Three and a half years ago, I left home and my man in New York to "move home" to Hong Kong. Many of my generation have made similarly global-contortionist moves (or rack up thousands of frequent flyer miles) to care for elderly parents. *What else can we do*, we say to each other. We're Chinese, and being filial is our destiny.

My mother turned ninety-four last year, and her Alzheimer's is now in the moderate to severe stage. She is extraordinarily healthy—excellent appetite, in charge of bodily functions, able to daily scale two flights of stairs up to a neighborhood chapel for the 7:30 a.m. Mass. She has raised four citizens of the world who are not a menace to society. It is possible she may live to a hundred or more; her eldest sister with Alzheimer's made it to ninety-nine. *Waaa*, my Chinese world exclaims, *good for her*, confirming belief in longevity's virtue.

Also, I'm privileged. Our family can afford two live-in Filipino domestics to look after Mum. It's a very Hong Kong thing, one not readily replicated in the West unless you're extremely wealthy. The city's largest minority population is Filipino, and the majority of these nationals are women—employed as live-in domestic helpers by mostly middle-class families—women who leave their own elderly and children to care for those of others on two-year contracts, after which they're entitled to a one-way ticket home if their contracts are not renewed. They get one day off a week and are legally entitled to public holidays, but these are often granted at the whim of the employer. Many work unduly long hours under this legally sanctioned indentured servitude. *Two helpers!* My Chinese world exclaims. *Does she really need two helpers?* What's left unsaid is that helpers shouldn't really need all that much time off.

Coincidentally, I was handed an enviably well-paid position, walking distance to home. I live rent free, complete with a separate entrance. I did not have to abandon either children or pets, and there *is* Skype for virtual love. Others with aging parents aren't so fortunate.

*Accentuate the positive.*

Last year, the Chinese government legislated obligatory visitation and care for aging parents. That filial piety, this grand Confucian virtue, had to become law underlines the problem of our twenty-first-century fractured lives. Thomas Wolfe discovered that you *can't* go home again, but the question is, did you even *want* to go home in the first place?

The United States had been my home for eleven years when I returned to Asia in '92. Then, I still had a corporate career that paralleled my writing life, and I still had parents. After my divorce, I fell in love with an old friend in New York. We did the distance thing for about a year before I quit corporate life to move in with Bill and to lead a full-time writing life. Dolce vita.

*That* was home.

That was also the grown-up version of my prodigal past. At twenty I returned from college in the United States and almost immediately moved out of home. You don't do that in Hong Kong until you're married, not if you don't want to break your mother's heart, and especially not back in '74. But I was 大家姊, with no big brother or sister to guide me. So move out I did, to shack up with the man of the moment. Mum may have never forgiven me this trespass that all my younger siblings were afterward liberated to emulate. As much as the times are a-changing, most unmarried locals still live at home, and some continue to do so even after marriage in this city of unaffordable real estate.

*Accentuate the positive.*

My parents bought a large flat in a good neighborhood when property was affordable so that Mum could live comfortably at home. My home, "the squat," is at least the size of a decent hotel room.

As the now-filial daughter who used to be prodigal, I know that despite the grin-and-bear-it countenance that marks my daily existence, this filial time bites.

The parallel lives of our Filipino domestics give me pause. *What a warm culture,* Westerners who live here say, *they're so sweet to our children and really are suited to caring for others.* The local Chinese attitude is pragmatic, *they earn good money here, better than back home, and they get a place to live, so what more do they expect?* It's true that our helpers are loyal, kind to my mother, and very good at their work. One woman is a mother of a teenage boy, and her husband is home looking after the family. The other is single and the primary financial support for her family. She has an Indian boyfriend who works as a chauffeur. Both women have been with us six years, and we're hoping they'll stay as long as Mum is alive. All the other domestic helpers in our building consider them lucky because they get real time off (including all public holidays); we pay for a ticket home once a year, as opposed to once every two years; they get to stay out with visiting family or even weekly with the boyfriend; each has a proper room to sleep in, one that is a decent size, and not a closet or hallway; they're provided Wi-Fi and a laptop; in terms of cleaning and cooking, the work is much lighter than working for a family of six. They do my laundry because I don't have a washing machine up here, but they're not expected to clean my space or cook for me. We've hired them because our mother needs twenty-four-seven care, and they know she is their primary concern. Yes, they're "lucky" and are warm to Mum, just as we say we're "lucky" to have found them.

But their contract is still one of an indentured servitude.

Even though we're good employers, I have no illusions about the enormous sacrifice each has made in this luck of the draw. They are employees, not "servants," as domestics are still often called. Their nation's economy sucks; Hong Kong is a wealthy city. Filipino helpers are despised by the local Chinese community and condescended to by self-righteous Western and other foreign employers. Yet they smile and smile and smile, congregate with friends in the streets on Sundays when most get their day off, and exchange stories of their lives of servitude. Some are not even given keys to their home and are not allowed to stay in when the family is out. Others are called back on their so-called day off to come home and work. Abuse happens, sexual or otherwise.

Their *bad* luck is to be born Filipino.

As is mine to be born sort of Chinese into a culture that worships filial piety beyond a reasonable doubt.

Earlier this year, I turned sixty. My *real* life has already been suspended for almost four years. Even though Alzheimer's is classified as an illness, no one recovers, just as excessive longevity only has one terminal point. But for us caretakers of all this increasing, forgetful longevity, can we, in fact *do* we recover from suspended life?

To my fiction students I say, *write in real time*. Suspended time, e.g., *Mei Mei usually goes to the beach*, lacks drama. Readers don't care what your protagonist "sometimes," "often," or "usually" does, they want to know what your protagonist is doing *right now* in the story.

In Mum's muddled time, she believes she must go home to her long-deceased parents or meet her late sisters or husband or go to the office or market. A year and a half ago, she refused to go home because she thought we had imprisoned her. Now, she stares blankly at me and laughs or smiles at the funny faces I make. It's clear she has no idea who I am.

Mum and I, we're living in suspended time.

The problem with being at least part Chinese is Confucius's legacy. You can't ignore the man any more than even the Chinese Communist Party can, despite their brief respite of cultural revolutionary fervor. His famous analect that begins *At fifteen, I set my heart on learning* tracks the path of the civilized gentleman who at sixty listens to a "truth" that must be obeyed.

Like obeying my filial duty. All my siblings are married and have less movable homes, spouses, children, pets, or careers. Only one sister lives in Hong Kong. In the earlier stages of Alzheimer's, my mother feared the loss of her home. At Friday bingo in a home for the aged to which we brought her for therapy and company, she stared at the residents and said *so pitiful*, knowing she could go home.

For several years, I resisted the idea that I needed to move back because my sister was in Hong Kong and could look in on Mum weekly, and I could pop over for short stays of a few weeks. Mum also still had Maryam, the faithful helper and family friend from Indonesia.

But Alzheimer's fractured life.

There is nothing comparable to watching a rational, intelligent, independent human being go completely nuts. Which is what happened to Mum. The problem with Alzheimer's is that it is a disease of the mind, and it was horrifying to witness my mother so out of control. Her behavior became irrational, uncharacteristically cruel toward Maryam and others, and ultimately, dangerously irresponsible. Even before Maryam quit, it was apparent that radical change was needed, but we didn't have the heart to move her out of home. When the job offer came up unexpectedly, it was a convergence of the inevitable, an Aristotelean reversal of fortune worthy of the best fiction.

So for now, time is suspended. Like Mum, I go through the motions of life and hit the gym often. My man and I break weekly records for how long we can remain on Skype before getting kicked off. Meanwhile, I rack up frequent flyer miles on dazzling platinum.

In fiction, what follows are climax and denouement, which can still be surprising. In this nonfiction, however, what will follow is predictable, the one and only ending.

And then, when that happens, perhaps time will finally become real again.

# OFF-SEASON WITH SNAKE

There should not be typhoons in November, but this Chinese year, the snake one that began mid-February 2013 and straddles early 2014, everything is in turmoil. Typhoon season lingers too long into an Indian summer, that quaint romantic *idée* no longer *fixe*. Friends die too young, succumbing to the cancer they fought too long. Sanctuaries disappear, sold to the highest bidder, because they remained occupied too long by renters instead of occupied by you as they were once meant to be. Yet none of this is tragic nor anything to bemoan because the weather is merely the victim of climatic change (or cycles), death cuts short enduring life (the way curveballs shortstop ambition), and the property market is perennially profitable because you always, always, only buy low and sell high (the way Auntie Caroline taught you to do before she died) for all your locations, locations, locations.

Only Mum's life feels like tragedy.

Consider Ophelia, or *La Dame aux Camélias*. Was it so bad to die young? Is tragedy so much finer where Mum forgets every morning that there was a yesterday?

Consider your life. Would you really choose to die now and have Mum survive you, the healthy nonagenarian sans memory? Wouldn't you really prefer memory over longevity while your own ambitions still rankle? When there's still life at stake?

As this snake year comes to an end, Mum's mind cycles and loops home. Arduously. For the past few weeks, she has awakened halfway through her nights to exclaim, *my parents are waiting, my sisters and brothers expect me, I have to go home*, until calmed by our helper, who says, *it's still dark, there are no taxis, let's wait till morning*, and back to bed she goes. We all see dead people. We must. At some point in most lives the known dead precede us, and there they are, those pied pipers tooting siren tunes of invitation: *break on through to this* outré *side*.

Travel is pleasurable off-season, or at least, it used to be. Tourism has gotten fat, as obese as our global warming tragedy, and unseasonable waistlines follow. The crowds thin out less and less because too many are always traveling, on- and off-season. I first went to Greece in the fall of '79, just before the island bars and tavernas closed up for winter. Few tourists were around. Even Athens was civilized then, well before the Parthenon was roped off to visitors, and you could wander these pathways of the dead. The Olympics belonged to ancient memory and was not yet the fiasco of twentieth-century showtime, and the Euro had not precipitated the protests of the twenty-first. Greece was as far away from Mum and Hong Kong as I could flee to in my twenties. And so a year later, I fled my job and life, stayed, was gone for almost a year. The drachma was cheap, the airfares and winter rentals affordable.

No one spoke Cantonese.

I never did learn Greek. All I learned were the basics—παρακαλο, *kali mara*, "where's the toilet," numbers to bargain with, how to read and sound out the alphabet. It was a liberation from the familiar. All sounds were foreign, and language a deliberate tool for incomprehension. The louder they spoke, the less I understood. It was heavenly.

One night, Mum spoke Cantonese to her Filipino helper. *Speak English*, said the helper, *I don't understand you*. In another moment of nocturnal confusion Mum said, *jalan, jalan*, her mother tongue Javanese breaking through, sure of its command: *let's go*, or literally, *walk walk*. My mother looks through me sometimes, and I wait for which language she'll utter, which hippocampus synapse will trigger, which mysterious random access memory will figure in that moment. This snake year has been anyone's guess.

My mother might have preferred a life without Cantonese. It was not an easy language for her, this cacophony of nine tones. Being tone deaf, she could not hear the subtle differences between polytonal homonyms, such as *jung*: 種 lower register, "to plant"; 鐘 higher register, "clock"; 粽 middle register, "steamed rice and meat dumplings wrapped in bamboo leaves," tossed from dragon boats to feed the sharks to prevent them from devouring Wut Yuen's body—*dumpling overboard*—or so goes the legend of the Dragon Boat Festival. Mum first encountered Cantonese in Hong Kong when she was in her early twenties, having only studied rudimentary Mandarin as a child. Being visual rather than verbal, language acquisition did not come easily to her as an adult. She does however still recognize the odd characters, the large building signs we pass that say *bank*, *company*, *hotel*. And she says these in Cantonese, very occasionally even in Mandarin, and it always startles me, these linguistic snippets that emerge, persistent. A melting clock is still a clock as long as it continues to tell the time.

Off-season Greece was a sort of life. I had escaped Hong Kong, abandoning a good career in marketing with an airline, to become a writer. You can do this when you're young, when life is only about ambition and the individual. My first marriage at twenty was short-lived. Back from college in the United States, stifled by life back home in Hong Kong, I lit out, shacked up with the first boyfriend who asked, and, unfortunately, married him to mollify my mother's shame. Her first horror, when I moved out to live in a rural village with him, was that I would not have a telephone. The phone company simply didn't extend service that far. She could ring me at work in the city instead, which she did regularly, but work offered the best excuse for *sorry, no time to talk*. Today, the rural village is long gone, replaced by expensive high-rises that are electronically hooked up to the world. Life was slower paced then, even in Hong Kong, when escape from my mother's control was the faster pace that felt urgent and necessary.

One morning, just at the tail end of the snake year in late January 2014, my mother slipped and fractured her femur. Our helper called, and I quickly came downstairs. Mum was in bed, complaining her leg was sore. She rubbed her thigh as she spoke. There was no bruising. It was not the first time she had slipped and fallen, and it was difficult to tell, initially, how badly she was hurt. *Let her stay in bed for a bit*, I told our helper, *and see how she does*. I had a meeting that morning I had to get to, as my return "home" as the less rebellious adult daughter was facilitated by reluctantly accepting a full-time faculty position at a local university. A university job, like the wrong husband, wastes an inordinate amount of a life.

Only two years earlier, my mother had still been able to say where and how she hurt. Her training as a pharmacist made her medically quite accurate. This time she was way off. Fortunately, my sister was able to stop in later that morning, and by then it was apparent something was seriously wrong. At the hospital, however, her operation was considered routine, as the elderly constantly fracture bones. *No big deal*, says the medical community, unless of course, it's your mother, at age ninety-four, who can't remember that she's broken her hip and can't get out of bed. *Your* mother is *always* a big deal.

Still, she is of relatively sound body. She heals, more slowly perhaps than a younger person, but with a residual determination of her formerly sound mind. *Such a good girl!* exclaim the physiotherapists and nurses as they infantilize Mum. They watch her rise, clutch the walker, push her body forward to *jalan, jalan* around the block of the hospital wing before returning, fatigued, to bed. In the evenings, I stand by her bedside, rub her shoulders, kiss her forehead, watch her dream. Her lids flutter over the REM of sleep, and you try to imagine her watching you as a child, when she was the mother instead of you.

Motherhood at sixty is off-season. My entry into this unanticipated state began around a dozen years earlier, but it is only at sixty, at the tail end of this snake year, that I've finally accepted becoming a mother. Resistance, perhaps, to this reversal of circumstance, one that has no place for that long simmering rage at Mum. The thing about off-season, though, is that it is the time to unwind, to allow a mellowness to settle in.

I used to vacation only in the off-season. The dead of winter in Berlin, autumn in Greece or the coastline of New England, the searing summer heat of Florida or the desert in Arizona. This was when hotels were less expensive, flights not fully booked, and destinations emptied of families with children shrieking or hordes of tourists snapping photos. This was before I had turned forty, when global travel was less prevalent. My mother in hospital forced us to forget about work and our lives, to rearrange our schedules, to focus on the logistics of turning her home into a hospital room, and to reimagine her subsequent care when she returned home. Our two helpers were exhausted. They took turns sleeping nightly at the hospital with Mum, their working days elongated. We the sibs were exhausted. We sat, in rotation, through the mornings, afternoons, and evenings by her bedside, trying to understand her new physical needs, afraid of all the complications that emerged out of this prolonged monitoring by the medical community, and oversaw the initial physiotherapy.

Mum has virtually no medical history. Dad was the same. They self-medicated (especially as Mum had access to pharmaceuticals), were generally quite healthy, and seldom complained about physical ailments. I take after my parents but am a little better at getting the occasional checkup, once every five to seven years or so, but the result is always a clean bill of health. We all should be so lucky. Until diagnosed with Alzheimer's, Mum took hardly any medication, rarely saw a doctor, and never had checkups. Even after we began regular visits to a geriatric specialist, it was clear that she was healthy of body if not of mind.

But hospitalization meant a whole new circus. We were suddenly made frighteningly aware of Mum's fluctuations in blood pressure, the persistence of urinary tract infections (caused, we felt, by the undesirably cramped conditions in the public hospital where the staff are overworked and diaper changing a scheduled but low priority), a heart murmur that could (but might not) be her undoing, bed sores, the extent of physical therapy required. Clearly, this was going to be another daunting new phase in Mum care.

I no longer travel only off-season because it makes no difference now. The world is always buzzing with travelers, hotel "deals" are make-believe, and airline "security" a myth for the desperately gullible. The more you travel, the more the world merges into yesterday, today, and tomorrow that could blow up anytime. A lot like motherhood.

Mum is home now. After a prolonged period of extremely expensive visiting nurses, we've finally found a third live-in helper, an experienced and mature Filipino nurse, to oversee Mum's care. Our two other helpers are relieved. It was their suggestion to employ a third person, even though they knew she would be better paid, would get the single room, while they would have to share smaller spaces in a divided room, that she would, in effect, be their supervisor in the care and maintenance of Mum's health. The logistics are just logistics. After having swooped in as a unit of four siblings to takeover Mum's life, this part was a cake walk by comparison.

I imagine it's not unlike the end of postpartum.

The exhaustion of pregnancy has ended, the pain of childbirth is over, the waistline has shrunk back to almost its pre-pregnancy cinch through disciplined exercise, and the turmoil of *holy shit, what the hell have I done!* is no longer the shriek of your soul.

Some mornings, I pop into her bedroom and watch her eyes open. *Oh*, she says, *have you come to wake me?* I smile, nod, and kiss her forehead. She beams back at me as her eyes accustom themselves to the sunshine. *That's very good*, she says. I ask if she would like to get up yet. The attending helper of the day smiles, because lately Mum is lazier, wanting to have a lie in. For a woman who has gotten up every morning at 6 a.m. or earlier for most of her adult life, it seems right that she is finally able to relax.

Some nights, I help to tuck her in. I lean in close to her ear, to compensate for her increasing deafness, and say *good night, sleep well*. She sighs as a contented infant must. *See you tomorrow*, I add, as her eyelids close.

If she could answer I imagine she'd say, *and tomorrow, and tomorrow, and tomorrow.*

Or perhaps not.

Some days when she walks well, eats well, expels well, the tomorrows seem real, and my Hong Kong sister and I look at each other and say, *she'll make it to a hundred*. Then we panic briefly at what that means, financially, logistically, emotionally. Once, in the hospital, pumped up on oxygen, Mum became surprisingly lucid and spoke in full sentences. Her speech did not stutter in its usual halting pace, and she could call at least my Hong Kong sister correctly by name. It's been a long while since she was last able to call forth the names of her children or husband or the sister who moved to Hong Kong with her. A little more than a year earlier, she still occasionally could. Now, I wonder who she thinks I am when I hug her, massage her, walk her, feed her, get her up, or put her to bed. But she is happy, or something like happy, because she smiles and even sometimes answers me when I ask how are you feeling, *fine*, or *okay*, she says. One night, I kissed her forehead, and she suddenly opened her eyes and said, *thank you for the kiss*. She saw someone, or something, some angel perhaps.

Other days, she turns to jelly, unwilling to push herself up out of the wheelchair, waiting for one of us to lift her. This old lady is shockingly heavy, dead weight when her body goes on strike. As dead as her eyes that stare at me blankly, as dead as her voice that will not respond to any stimuli.

*Now, Voyager*. Mum's journey is, as we would say in Cantonese, 沒來, *the yet to come*. Cantonese, the language without tenses, where past and present are muddled and imprecise. Cantonese, the language that muddled my mother's tongue, and my tongue, perching precariously on its tip, ever ready for utterance in my birth city where it is the mother tongue of the majority population. Cantonese, not English or Putonghua Mandarin, our two other official languages now that we are back in China, returned to the Motherland, just as I have returned to my mother's side. Yet Hong Kong must know that, despite our seemingly global, cosmopolitan veneer, despite our historically English origins, we are indeed China whether we like it or not. The torrent of Putonghua in our city's streets, the hordes of Chinese tourists from the mainland that prop up our economy, is the future-past of who we should have been and probably will become. It is complicated, being native to a city without true "native" origins. Despite some attempts at revisionist history in this neo-Chinese era, Hong Kong was more or less a barren rock when the British redrew China's map, and its rise into a modern city is entirely due to British colonization. My mother's Javanese English smattering of Mandarin-cum-atonal-Cantonese muddled language is as much a part of Hong Kong's history as the Cantonese of the majority population.

Mum once tried to move our family to Hawaii. This was sometime in the sixties when pharmacists were in demand, and fast passage green cards were being offered by U.S. Immigration. Family lore has it that she applied and was granted visas for us, at which point my father put his foot down and declared, *and what will I do there, clean their toilets?* Thus ended my teenage fantasy of life among the surfer boys and Hawaii Five-O.

My mother, a little like a young Bette Davis in *Now Voyager*, sailed into the Hong Kong harbor in 1947 as a beautiful young woman, radiant with hope. The harbor, she says, was the one she had seen once before in a dream and she knew, right then, that this city would be her home. She used to tell us that, and I believed her, wanted to believe her, because it softened the rejection by locals of this city for being different and speaking the wrong language at home. In the end, despite her brief flirtation with an alternate American life, this city did become her home. What I've never questioned is my mother's declaration that she never wanted to go back to Indonesia. That is Mum, typhoon et al.

The snake year is over, and we're now riding a horse. The off-season has ended and the horse has brought prolonged spring rains and a too-early summer heat. My schedule has begun to settle into a new normal with our resident nurse and the minor reconstructions at home. There is a hospital bed with an air mattress for Mum to prevent bed sores and a companion bed in her room. Recently, I spent a day assigning the sleeping schedule and arranging the weekly days off on the new-normal calendar for the staff. Operations management was never my forte, but it is another skill to acquire in my unpredictable fate as a late-in-life mother. At least I got to skip childbirth.

But it is T. S. Eliot's "Burnt Norton" that echoes footfalls in my hippocampus. *Time past and time future / What might have been and what has been / Point to one end, which is always present.* I am back in Greece, during those endless days and nights when the 沒來 was a dream of the writer's life. I am back in Norway, in that spacious, empty, soundproof studio by the sea in Bergen, for three summer months of endless light, at the residency in a former sardine factory where I wrote and wrote and wrote. I am back in my New Zealand home, sold in the snake year, where *Other echoes / Inhabit the garden. Shall we follow?* If I can continue to inhabit relative time during off-season motherhood in my squat, perhaps tomorrow will be more than just another day.

It's not so bad, I tell myself, even if my mother does live forever.

# WAITING WOMEN

*I am waiting eternally for my life to begin*, I say to Bill, my husband-to-be. He has heard this lament for years now yet patiently continues to indulge my hyperbole. Once upon a time, he too waited eternally for his life to begin. It was a time when all his weekends were lost. The Saturday morning train ride from Penn Station in New York to Perth Amboy, New Jersey, to shop for groceries and cook and care for an elderly father, the father who had fallen and broken a hip, convalesced in a facility, and was now, happily, back home again with Bill's older brother, the sibling who had never left home. Weekends were when the weekday help had time off, a neighborhood lady who cleaned and prepared meals. Every Saturday, he would take care of chores in his childhood home, the home his widowed father prized. He would make sure his father and brother had their supper, that the dishes were washed and the kitchen cleaned, that his father would get to bed, that his brother had what he needed for the week. Sundays he made their breakfast and lunch, checked that the household was in shape for his father and brother to make it through the week ahead. Only then did he board the train back to Manhattan, to scramble through what was left of his weekend before work Monday morning. And then next Saturday, the cycle repeated, seemingly forever, until one day that eternity ended, and a new one began. Which is why he's still the man in my life, after twenty years of our too-often too-long-distance relationship. Which is why I've finally agreed to marry him next year, when "we" turn twenty-one, when both our lives will be more completely our own again, although at the time we were betrothed, we did not know quite how true that would be for me.

In my mother's home, I live half my life in her city and wait. It is 2017 and my full-time position at the university is finally over. I have ensured the last student of the defunct MFA program could complete his studies and graduate. I remind myself—I must tell the Department of English to remove from their website my name and those of all the writing faculty, those writers who generously lent the university their reputations so that once upon a time, a new program could be launched. For now, though, the program sits on their webpage, along with the literary programming that helped raise the department's ranking, along with the students' many achievements. The same students the university thoughtlessly, carelessly betrayed. It will take them too long to remove that site, but they will eventually do so, and those six long years of my time will vanish into nothingness.

Now, I am no longer held captive in this city by a job, only by Mum. I am in limbo, uncertain what my future will be.

It's been more than four years that my mother has been unable to walk on her own, and much longer since she's really been Mum. Recently, her condition has taken a slight turn for the worse, and she is even more silent than before. Earlier in the year, she would still utter the occasional phrase, a *good morning* or *I am fine* or *hello*. She had several bouts of urinary tract infections, a common malady for the aged, less to do with hygiene than we once thought, but that has cleared up for now. Our latest challenge is an upcoming hundred-day loss of the lift on our floor because the building is undergoing a massive renovation. The lift one floor below will still be running, but for Mum, this means she will be imprisoned in her home for more than three months. No walks in the park, no daily communion in the vestibule of the church, no outings for occasional dim sum lunches or drives to the Peak or the New Territories. We simply cannot risk carrying her down and up a flight of stairs in her wheelchair. *Poor Mum*, we say, *it'll be awful for her.*

As October ends, the weather is finally cooling. My mother turns ninety-eight later this year. Her Alzheimer's is still her Alzheimer's. This fall we three sisters managed to time our lives to be in Hong Kong together briefly. We mourn our brother, who died a year ago. Number two sister's divorce to the parasite she should never have married is finally, truly over, and despite his greedy attempts, he could not grab her home or steal her share of our mother's property that Mum signed over to us, the home she lived in. The judge, when presented with his absurd demand, shut down his lawyer with a terse *But the mother's still alive*. The law means well, but after this man moved in with my sister, he neither paid toward the upkeep of their home nor contributed any real assets or love to their marriage. The law is wrong in applying a fifty-fifty asset split in this instance, depriving my sister of her hard-earned savings. There are no children; he is younger than her and quite able to earn a living, and he does. But now this ex-leech no longer can verbally bully my too-generous sister into submission. His departure from her and our lives is timely, at a moment when women worldwide are finally speaking up about patterns of male entitled behavior to abuse, harass, dominate. To terrify women into bad life choices. My sister had to call the cops on him toward the end, as he hung around and shouted abuse, refusing to move out until the very last moment of the fifty-day grace period granted by the courts when the divorce came through, unwilling to give up his free room, board, and storage for his so-called business (an abject failure at everything, he blames everyone else, including my sister, for his own irresponsible blunders and sloth). We arranged to employ private security guards the week he moved out in case he tried to hurt my sister or further damage property, which he previously had done. He hurled filthy abuse at the stoic Gurkha guards we employed, these dignified men who remained a silent force, the ones who bore witness to his at-home Mr. Hyde face. My other siblings and I have waited years for our most beautiful sister number two to throw him out, wishing she'd done so much earlier when he cheated on her, or threw money in her face when she requested contributions toward utilities and household costs, or failed to show up on time, again, even for her sixtieth-birthday celebration dinner that he didn't pay a cent toward but ate and drank his share, or as he hoarded and stored more and more junk on the property, asserting his rights to the marital abode, doing his best to drive her out of her own home. Et cetera. Meanwhile, he swanned around his fancy private yacht club, did charity events with the Masons, ran a "business" that only bled money, kept large amounts of cash in our safety deposit box to hide income from Inland Revenue until I objected. To cry poverty, as he did, in the face of such excess is simply shameful. He's already snagged a new, much younger girlfriend and has been heard to brag about how rich she is. Through the divorce while he hunkered down and refused to leave, he and the girlfriend chattered phone sex into the night, loudly and lewdly in my sister's small, less-than-five-hundred-square-foot home, until my sister got a legal order that he cease and desist such wanker behavior. Of all the ex-husbands in our family, he is by far the most deplorable. At least he now can no longer brag to everyone about the house he owns, the same one he declined to purchase a share of when my sister offered, but up to the very end he screamed loudly at everyone within earshot about *my* house, this is *my* house! His tantrums echo those of many, far more powerful men who, if nothing else, at least paid for their properties.

All he did was take and take and take. Had our father lived to know him he would have pegged him from the start—*greedy, so greedy, and talking nothing but rubbish, a braggart.* He eventually junked many of the broken toys he hoarded on her property, most likely because a condition of the agreement was that until all was cleared away he could not touch his ill-gotten windfall held in escrow by the lawyers, to swell his bank accounts, all the monies he refused and refused and refused to fully declare into the marital assets until my sister, in desperation, simply gave in and surrendered almost 50 percent of all she had saved, just to get rid of him.

How long should women wait for relief from our mistakes, from our gender-imbalanced society, from the myriad responsibilities we undertake because women are taught that taking care of others, even the most selfish ingrates, is their lot in life? At least now my sister has her home again, and her son and his wife in France can come and stay with her second grandchild the way they couldn't when the first one was born because so much junk littered her home, even though the ex-husband had promised more than a year earlier to clear out space for their visit. It was the last straw, this stupid, thoughtless assault, to be denied the right to host her only son and his family, in the home that had been her son's home until this irritating and entitled man took over, ravaged, raged and wasted fifteen years of my sister's life.

I am 大家姊. My job, as Mum used to tell me, was to be an example for the younger siblings, to look out for them, to be the "big" and responsible sister. I am luckier than my sister, tougher perhaps, less willing to succumb to the male of the species that tries to bend my will. Yet all I can do for her now is just to be there, to lend a shoulder, to reassure her *it's only money, he's not worth your time and energy,* and when needed, to stare down that ex-brother-in-law, this coward who goes silent around me, who is afraid of me, fearful I'll turn my sister against him. In the end, he did that job himself. If I could, I would be her avenging angel, but all I have are words. *Where* are Medusa's eyes when you need them?

Amah Rock or 望夫石 stands approximately fifteen meters high on a hilltop in Shatin. This waiting woman, who carries her baby son on her back, was transformed into stone as a merciful act by the sea goddess. Her Chinese name means "rock watching out for husband," which is what she's been doing for who knows how long. Her husband went to sea and did not return, having drowned. Yet still she trudged each day to the peak to stand lookout, ignorant of his fate, hoping, waiting in this futile act of loyalty and love. All over China, numerous 望夫石 wait and watch, the stuff of poetry through the ages.

But it is her English Hong Kong name that speaks truth to power. Amahs are nannies, domestic helpers who cook and clean, traditionally indentured servants employed to cater to those who have more than their fair share. What amahs must learn is how to bow humbly and carry large burdens. Of course, they are only and always women. Even in love, women bow in submission, as Eileen Chang's protagonist does to her lover in the story *Love in a Fallen City*. He remarks on her tendency to bow her head, this "charming habit" of hers, but continues to withhold his offer of marriage, remaining silent, while she frets about her reputation as a fallen women who has foolishly spent too long in waiting. We women, we're all amahs to someone, even if it's not our man.

There are days I gaze at Mum and wonder if I'll turn to stone. She is in a semipetrified state by day, unable to speak except to cry out, howling when she doesn't like the shock of water on her skin in the shower. She no longer responds to my touch when I try to massage her shoulders or arms. She no longer hears when I ask her how she is. As the weather cools down, she less and less wants to walk and becomes dead weight when her helpers try to lift her. *Where are you, Mum*, my mind calls, trying to reconnect that ESP-ish line we've always had through joys and sorrows, no matter how far-flung I was. But she no longer hears me as she once did. She has vanished, like the children in English fairy tales who run *widdershins* the church, never to be seen again. Like the sailor husband who will never return.

Medusa was a fair-haired beauty once, a celibate priestess of the goddess Athena. Her mistake was to fall for Poseidon and fuck him on the temple floor. Sacrilege! The goddess was furious, and as punishment Medusa's gorgeous locks were transformed into snakes, her beauty destroyed and her eyes cursed with a petrifying force. Her gaze. Her terrible gaze. All because desire tripped her up into the arms of a watery lover.

Picture this: in despair over her lost beauty and repulsiveness, wandering around Africa with eyes that screamed *the horror, the horror* of her eternal darkness. Eyes into which no man would ever lovingly gaze again. Did she complain about the man who ruined her life? Or did she pine for him, railing against the woman who made her a monster? At least her fury had agency, and she could terrify men into leaving her alone after that. Meanwhile, Poseidon continued to rule the ocean, on the lookout for the next beauty to seduce.

I gaze into my mother's eyes, her cataract eyes, her dying vision. Does she see me at all? Does she remember the fury she once lashed out at me, disowning me, telling me I no longer was her daughter? Was I her fallen Medusa, succumbing to not one but many Poseidons? Was I the sweet, obedient girl who disappeared, transformed into a monster, defiant at every turn? Had she forgiven me my many, many trespasses? *Answer me, oh my love.* But she does not speak.

The days disappear with frightening alacrity. Blink and another day and another day and another day passes. Nothing changes. My mother sits silent, a being without agency, her history lost to the mythology of waiting, waiting, waiting, even when no one's there.

Up close, Amah Rock is just rock. There is no beating heart in her eternity.

Lately, my mother's helpers are scared at night. *Someone's always there*, they say. *She has lots of visitors.* Between my sister and I and the three women, we talk-story of dead people, the ones with whom Mum must be conversing in her sleep. It is only in sleep that her tongue loosens and speech returns. Sometimes, the conversations are long and involved. At other times, they sound like a passing remark or greeting. Who are these visitors to my mother's bedside that keep her chattering all through the night? She must be happier in this half-dream state because she falls asleep earlier and earlier and willingly goes to bed.

At nights, Mum's home is a busy place. One helper sleeps in her room each night, and every morning, there's a story to tell. Beth speaks some Bahasa Malay and recognizes that Mum is speaking in the similar sounds of Indonesian. Sometimes, she still speaks in English, perhaps sometimes in Cantonese as well, but we can never be sure. Often her speech is garbled and slurred, but it's clearly an attempt at speech. Both Lily and Juvie, the other helper and the nurse, verify this.

Less than a year earlier, when our previous helper Vivien decided to go home for good, Lily returned from the Philippines to work for us again. It has been a convoluted arrangement of more than a decade of musical chairs. The first two we employed fought; the helper who cooked and cleaned stole and was fired; and we retained Lourdes, a nurse. Lily arrived to work with her and assisted in caring for Mum. Lourdes had to leave abruptly because her aunt was killed in an auto accident, the aunt who had been looking after her children, so she now needed to go home and be a mother again. Vivien arrived next, and she and Lily stayed for a good long while. After Mum broke her hip, Juvie became the second nurse to join the team because we needed a third person. Then Lily went home because her mother also did, the mother who has worked for a family in Hong Kong for years, originally at a building down the road until they moved. Beth was a nurse who replaced Lily; she had been working for an abusively ridiculous employer and was only too glad to quit and come work for us. About a year later, Vivien decided it was time to go home, having saved enough money to start her business, and Lily returned. More than ten years, time passing in a blink, and then it's over.

The day Lily returned was a grand homecoming. She has worked for us the longest, the one all the security guards and residents in our building call the pretty one. When Lourdes left, Lily took over her job of caring for Mum. Unlike Lourdes, she wasn't a nurse, one trained in elder care and who regarded her charge as a patient. My mother liked Lily and was still far more cognizant and mobile then. Plus Vivien was an excellent cook who made meals Mum liked. But as the reality of caring for an Alzheimer's patient manifested itself, the constant worry and responsibility proved too overwhelming for Lily. The girls proposed their own solution, to share the elder care and domestic duties. Vivien proved a quick study who handled both duties efficiently and well, and Lily had some relief, and all was well for a time.

But Lily was the good girl, the pretty one, the gentlest soul, the most obedient. She was patient, the one who liked to give Mum manicures and pedicures, the girl who always smiled at Mum, talking to her lovingly like a mother to her child. The day she returned, she came to my mother and gave her a hug. *Do you know who I am*, she asked. My mother gazed at her through the haze of cataracts, held her hand and croaked, *Lily, you're Lily!* It was a rare moment, a brief respite from her empty daytime mind because in that instant, she remembered, and a heartbeat melted stone.

Now, we wait. My sisters and I and the three women in our home. We go through the motion of our days while Mum retreats to the rhythm of her nights.

That night, Auntie Caroline summoned me. Caroline, my mother's older sister, died over two decades ago and is the sibling who looks the most like Mum. I am surprised to see her after all this time because it's the first time she's come to me, and I had wondered for years why she never had. Why she was so silent, this talkative aunt who nagged and cared for all of us in life, a surrogate mother when Mum couldn't be around? Her companion, Christine, who outlived her by several years, visited me shortly after her death. Christine was ninety when she died, and in my dream she smiled and beckoned me to follow her down a verdant path toward a large tree with a spread of leafy branches. We were in Bandung, Indonesia. She didn't speak at all, this auntie who used to tell stories and sing to me in Dutch. Where was she taking me? But her expression, that familiar, naughty grin I loved, told me I needn't ask. And suddenly, as time shifts in dreams, I knew. We were at the gravesite. Christine was going home to Caroline, and what she was trying to show me was that they could be together again. This love that once had dared not speak its name had finally found her way home.

That night, Caroline, whom we've always called Auyin, tells me she wants to see Mum and that I have to fetch her. Obediently, I head automatically in the right direction. The scene cuts to my mother, in the corner bed of a hospital ward, waiting for me. *There you are at last*, she says, and stands up, gripping her handbag. *Auyin wants to see you*, I say, but she barely hears me. Impatient to leave, she heads quickly for the door, and we exit the building together toward a hilly path. We are somewhere in Hong Kong, in the New Territories, where some rural countryside remains. She races ahead and I run after her, saying, *Mum, wait a minute, please wait*, because I can see her going in the wrong direction. *It's this way*, I call, trying to direct her downhill along the paved footpath. Just as I catch up to her, she abruptly turns right away from me and rushes down a steep, unpaved side path. Immediately, she falls, and I know her body is tumbling a long way down into the subtropical undergrowth. I yell after her *Mum! Mum!*, but she disappears from view. I run down the path and circle back round toward where my mother is tumbling down and see some people immediately below. I shout at them that my mother's fallen, pointing toward the path, saying *quick, quick, call 999*. Two strangers, a Chinese woman and a man, join me as we try to search for her. The unpaved path diverges and does not appear to go straight down the slope; there are structures and obstacles blocking the way toward where I'm positive she must have fallen. *Mum!* I shout again, *Mum!* My voice ricochets in echo. I wake up, still calling for her.

Two weeks later, my mother is dead, almost exactly one year after my brother died, minus one day. We, the women, now we no longer wait.

# FOR AS LONG AS WE BOTH SHALL LIVE

The afternoon Mum died, I had checked in for the flight and packed a new bag for my trip to Myanmar. Sister number two was going to drive me to the airport where we planned to have dinner before I headed for the Irrawaddy Literary Festival. I had to spend a transit night in Bangkok, as there was no direct flight from Hong Kong to Yangon that evening.

It was All Saints' Day and one of my more organized moments after weeks of uneasy disorganization.

Less than two weeks prior, Mount Agung rumbled, threatening to erupt in Indonesia, and I was vacillating. The Asia Pacific Writers and Translators annual conference was in Bali, out of the volcano's range. On the conference schedule, my latest book was featured for a book launch reading, and I was also on a couple of panels. Friends and writers I looked forward to seeing would be there. But there was that volcano. A blaring news cycle of experts had pronounced on the likelihood of eruption, only to be refuted by others. Travelers were canceling their trips; others didn't see what the fuss was about. Indonesia knows how to handle emergency management of the constant volcanic activity that is second nature for this archipelago nation. Besides, the saga of Pompeii's last days, one that erupted and replayed in my childhood's imagination, terrorizing me, was ancient history.

Still, I vacillated.

The conference organizer was sanguine. She had arrived early in Singajara, and the volcano was a distant menace. *The airport will close if it erupts*, I worried over email, *and my subsequent travel will all be disrupted.* My excuse for unease was an ungodly number of travel disruptions suffered in the past year. Long delays, nights spent at airport hotels in Hong Kong, Detroit, Newark, losing time in a constantly collapsing and changing schedule, juggling work and life travel in between shifting household goods from my former full-time life in Hong Kong to a life split between my home in New York and Mum's city. My brother's sudden death a year ago on All Souls' Day remained a chronic ache, erupting when I least expected it, making me howl.

I had spent the better part of two glorious months with my partner in our rural home in northern New York State just before returning to Hong Kong at the beginning of October. It is strange to call housecleaning glorious—because that was most of what I did—an attack on the accumulation in a home that had been empty for the better part of seven-plus years while I lived in Hong Kong. During those years, I would land, dump books and files, and try to enjoy the peace and space for the short time I had in between vacation and business trips before returning "home" to Mum. My full-time job having ended, this half-time life back in my real home was glorious, luxurious, extravagantly comforting. But then my brother died almost as soon as that life began, and for the first time in years, Christmas was spent with all my family in Hong Kong to celebrate a memorial Mass for him instead of with Bill in New York. Visiting my sister-in-law and niece in Ohio this past summer shaped the sad new reality of life without my only male sibling.

Of course I did not say all this to the conference organizer. She only needed to know whether or not I would cancel. I canceled. The volcano did not erupt until several weeks later, long after it could disrupt my travel schedule. And Mum died.

Unlike the death of my brother, Felix, my mother's was not a public affair. Felix's position as a music director and liturgist at a Catholic church that served a sprawling suburban community in Ohio meant hundreds of folks knew him, attended masses of his liturgies, heard the choral performances he directed. He presided at baptisms, first holy communions, confirmations, weddings, and funerals and contributed a joyous memory to many lives. Likewise, when Dad had died some twenty years earlier at the age of seventy-five, he was still relatively young in our Asian world of rampant longevity. He even predeceased his own father, who made it to a hundred. We published an obituary. We informed the worldwide network of relatives and friends; only a handful predeceased him. At my father's wake, people tumbled into Hong Kong from Indonesia, Canada, the United States, Australia. The phone rang, telegrams and cards arrived from further afield. Even for us, the children, Dad's sudden, unexpected passing meant we mourned openly, publicly, and our friends called or emailed, offering condolences.

My mother was just shy of ninety-eight when she took her last breath. When the paramedics rushed into her bedroom, I was clutching her shoulders, saying, *no, no, Mum, not yet, please, not yet.* She gasped, groaned; that eerie rattle sounded as I leaned in close, willing her to stay. The paramedics shunted me aside, and the first man declared, *heart's stopped.* Emergency protocols kicked into gear, I rode with her in the ambulance to Kwong Wah Hospital, we paced the waiting room, Juvie and Beth and I. A young medic emerged, solemnly pulled me aside, told me they were still trying to revive her but that I should have 心理準備, "psychological preparation." But his warning was unnecessary because I already knew. Mum was gone, and she wasn't coming back.

It is this literal mistranslation of 心理準備—*to prepare the texture of your heart*—that I prefer. The heart may want what it wants but also knows what it knows to be true. This was two weeks after I dreamed Mum ran away from me, and I should have known that was her way of saying goodbye. Dramatized portrayals of deathbed agonies and conversations do not sufficiently account for the lost Alzheimer's mind. It isn't a coma or a paralyzed patient who cannot move, cannot speak, cannot physically feel even if her mind is still alive. It is not the one who knows she's dying and tries to make the desperately important final utterance. It wasn't even like Felix as he lay in the ICU, half of him paralyzed by a stroke, dying of cancer. My brother squeezed my hand several times in the days and nights before he left us, even tried to tap out a message on my laptop that I brought to his bedside one night. It was a futile attempt on my part; by then we couldn't be sure how cognizant he was of anything that was happening around him.

My mother's last two weeks alive were relatively normal. Dr. Pei saw her for the regular checkup and pronounced her well, cleared of the most recent urinary tract infection. She still was bathed each morning and walked, ate, occasionally took communion, slept. Having skipped the conference in Bali, I had more time at home and could still hug her, talk at her, sit with her over a cup of tea. That she chattered away night after night with mysterious visitors was as real or unreal as I chose to believe. Juvie, Lily, and Beth, the three helpers who were in our employ at the end, will swear to the nocturnal presence of a gaggle of invisible folks in our home. That home is quiet now. Beth, who stayed on to help us after the other two left, says she's not afraid anymore.

It's possible to consider our Filipino helpers merely superstitious, just as my dream can be dismissed as merely a dream, evidence of a subconscious *what if* in the overactive imagination of a fiction writer. I am not partial to the paranormal any more than I believe in ghosts. But what essays its way into my wakefulness now, what persists despite everything I know or don't know about Alzheimer's and Mum is the texture of my heart. It is difficult to define, impossible to ignore for as long as she and I are in conversation, as we have been for so long, as we likely will continue to be. The texture of this mysterious muscle puzzles me more than the coincidence (or not) of the timing of her departure. Naturally, I canceled my appearance at the Irrawady Festival and scaled back my appearances the following week at both the Singapore and Hong Kong ones, only informing the handful who needed to know of my mother's passing. But life for me did not stop, even while my sister and I organized the wake and funeral Mass or obtained approval for a cremation, a feat that required early arrival at the mortuary to meet "our policeman," the one who would verify the circumstance of the death. We juggled schedules around the few relatives who came from abroad and the priests and family in Hong Kong. Even as I went from one government office to the next, submitting photocopies in triplicate, managed interviews by the police at home, grief murmured, refusing to erupt, biding its time like the volcano. Somehow I managed those public appearances to pontificate on writing and the creative life, debate the question of memoir versus fiction, read from my new book in which I bade Hong Kong farewell. In Singapore I hid out in between sessions at the writer's festival, only seeing a handful of friends and contacts, took advantage of the privacy of the five-star hotel room. In Hong Kong it was possible to confine myself to drinks and dinner with only those who knew.

Because when it comes to "Mum and Me," this heart of mine needs to be read over and over, all over again. It wasn't just about the ceremony of death, my having to write and deliver the eulogy, the gratitude expressed for condolences. Nor was it the inconvenience of death for all our busy lives, a cliché heartless in its veracity. Nor was it even about grief because in my mother's case, we all had been grieving for years. Instead it was the nagging sensation that she and I, we would never be done, that we too would be subject to the duration of the promise in New York's civil marriage ceremony—*for as long as we both shall live*. It simply wasn't about life and death. Let's face it: we will always see dead people.

My mother's funeral was not a public affair. We did not publish an obituary in the local papers as we did for Dad. Informing family and close friends was readily accomplished, much more swiftly than for either Felix or Dad. Her church was told, but even there, younger congregants who knew her had already passed away, as had the priest who knew her best. Was she blessed or damned to have outlived virtually everyone who mattered?

It was an eternity ago that I first discovered "Mum and Me." We are all twinned, physically, viscerally, emotionally, with our maternal other. Those who have no mother once did, even if only for a short time, even if it's nothing they can recall. This will continue to be our state of being until we develop a viably universal, freestanding womb outside the mother's body.

We the sibs each have our Mum and Me. I cannot say exactly when mine began, but I like to think it was with "Little Red Riding Hood." Family lore has it that I memorized the picture-book version of this fairy tale around the age of three or so. Mum would laugh whenever she recounted this, saying that because I recited this and turned the page at exactly the right moment, everyone thought I could read. She used to read the book aloud to me, and I connected the auditory and visual clues to imitate Mum perfectly.

Yet I doubt I've ever really identified with the tale's hapless protagonist, a girl so clueless she couldn't tell her grandmother apart from a wolf. Neither the Perrault nor Grimm versions are instructive. The former concludes with the girl's ultimate fate as the wolf's fecal matter and the latter employs a deus ex machina of the woodcutter's extraordinary appearance, just in digestive time to liberate her and the grandmother from the belly of the beast. Neither tale maps either my life or my relationship with Mum. Also, regardless of the story's numerous possible origins (a magical cape of immense powers or ritual of blood and puberty) or the later revisionist retellings (the girl infused with feminist agency while others dramatize her as a rape victim), all these reveal are simply the multiple meanings of being a girl. In the end, "Little Red Riding Hood" remains for me a fundamentally simplistic tale.

Instead, what I like to recall is my mother's voice, the way she added high drama to the dialog between girl and wolf: *the better to EAT you with, my dear!* which made my heart miss that beat. She read this to me at the beginning of my life, a life spent absorbing, forgetting, recalling, imitating, deconstructing books, so that I could recreate the shape, sound, sight, taste, and feel for words on the page.

Instead, what I know is that my mother's terrible condition, the Alzheimer's that imprisoned her mind, destroying its very essence, forced me to love her all over again. In the fifteen or so years that she and I danced around this unwelcome, hovering guest, this still-inexplicable disease that made longevity less the blessing it should have been, I found it possible to vanquish the devil that had become Mum and Me in favor of the angel we once were. The role reversal, a daughter becoming mother to woman, has been less the anguish I thought it would be, just as my mother's death with Alzheimer's proved less awful than it might have been had I refused my filial responsibility.

Mum's death does, however, leave me with a mystery to solve. Who will be my filial "child" since I chose to remain childless? What happens if I end up with Alzheimer's? Will I simply have to consign my care to the horrors of that old-age home we her children refused to subject Mum to? I have already told my third (and, I am determined, my last) husband that if I do end up with dementia or Alzheimer's, he must not try care for me at home; all I ask is that he ensures I am reasonably well cared for somewhere. No one should have to take on that kind of elder-care responsibility without the luxury we had of hiring two and later three full-time live-in helpers. I will likely not be nearly as financially well-off as my mother, who, because she remained in Hong Kong and had children who did not covet either her home or her money, was afforded this privilege. Unless we hit the lottery, my husband and I will not be able to afford anything close to what she had. Nor do I expect him to live out his life with a partner who no longer knows who he is, as the odds of him contracting Alzheimer's, if we go by family history, are less than for me. For now though, this remains the mystery I must contemplate through my sixties. If history does in fact repeat itself, then I have perhaps fifteen to twenty years to solve the problem. Despite being vanquished by calculus and the mysteries of probability in my youth, I'm betting on science, research, and common sense to take care of my aging years.

But my mother's death gave me a wonderfully unexpected gift, that of witnessing her end. It was the first time I had seen a human being die. Once upon a time, when she was still Mum, she taught me not to be afraid of anyone or anything life dealt me, because *you can overcome anything if you try hard enough*. Her final lesson, unspoken, is kinder, gentler, less demanding: *it's okay, my darling, it's only death*.

So about Mum and Me? I think we're good.

# WO/MAN ROARS

# FEMINISM AND FAITH

My brother's funeral Mass at Saint Michael's the Archangel in Findlay, Ohio, was held on election day. His unexpected demise meant rerouting flight plans and scrambling schedules on short notice. Consequently, I could not cast my vote in my northern New York State district, either in person or abstention, during this controversial year. It was the first time I did not vote in a presidential election since becoming a U.S. citizen twenty-nine years earlier.

My baby brother, the youngest sibling, the one boy after three girls, was only fifty-five and predeceased my mother with Alzheimer's, at home in Hong Kong with three live-in helpers and where I now lived with her part time to help supervise her care.

My brother, Felix, was a man of faith. A liturgist and music director at his Catholic church for the past twenty-one years, he was also a noted composer of religious music. We were all raised in that same faith by our devoutly religious mother and attended Catholic schools in Hong Kong for most of our primary and secondary schooling. I am severely lapsed. These days, it's rare for me to make a sign of the cross. I will not genuflect or kneel in church and no longer attend Sunday Mass.

Instead, I misplaced faith in feminism and proudly anticipated my adopted country's first woman president.

Felix's death happened at a savage speed. Several months of an ongoing complaint about migraine-like headaches led to a diagnosis of possible lymphoma. Within a week, lymphoma transformed, shockingly, into stage four lung cancer that had already spread to his liver, lymph nodes, and bones. The oncologist immediately scheduled a first chemo treatment. And then, within days, a text from my sister-in-law—*can you come?* My brother had suffered a massive stroke and was in the ICU on a ventilator, his left side paralyzed. We three sisters dropped out of our lives, mine in New York and the two younger ones in Hong Kong and Washington DC respectively, and came to his side. In the remaining days, hours, and minutes before hospice at home, we rotated sleeping in his hospital room, squeezed his right hand, and spoke our hearts to him. The hospice counselor cautioned: cancer patients can, unpredictably, live longer than expected or die tomorrow. But tomorrow arrived, and he was gone, with only his wife, daughter, and our youngest sister at his side. Both my second sister and I learned the news of his demise en route home to Hong Kong and New York.

Six days later, the funeral brought me back to Ohio, and I attended Mass for the first time in years.

Since breaking her hip a few years ago, Mum no longer climbs the stairs to the third-floor Dominican chapel in her neighborhood to attend daily Mass. The priests take turns coming down to the foyer on good weather days to administer communion and bless her. Her unwavering faith has astonished everyone for years. Although she no longer speaks much, she can still mouth lines of prayers and occasionally moves her own hand to make the sign of the cross.

My brother's funeral Mass was well attended. The church seats 1,500 and was over 90 percent filled. His work and music touched many, many lives, and I, the ex-Catholic, made the sign of the cross, mouthed the familiar prayers, and sparingly uttered the language of the faithful because grief surpassed my lack of belief. What mattered more was honoring Felix's life and faith in a manner that was appropriately dignified. I sang. My late father, brother, and I are the three musical ones. I sang the songs Felix composed. As the family's writer, it was my job to deliver the eulogy. But when the Mass was ended, I did not go in peace.

*Dear Hillary Rodham Clinton,*

*Thank you for your candidacy. You gave my citizenship great meaning. Right after I pledged allegiance in '87, I immediately registered to vote. And then I applied for a U.S. passport. Since then, I have twice lived as an American abroad and voted each election, by absentee ballot if I couldn't get back. Your dedication to public service is admirable.*

*It is unfashionable today to be a feminist, but I have never cared about fashion. Instead, I believe in the necessity of women's lives writ large. Until women are truly equal to men, female leaders in all endeavors are the role models we need. Those younger women with little faith in feminism need not be "good wives" because they have the choice to be or not to be. They also may choose to be a public servant or trophy wife, or at least they can in this country right now. Walk back Roe vs. Wade and one less choice for women will mean one more "privilege" for men.*

*Dear Mrs. Clinton, you were never merely just about women vs. men. You made choices, and for you, I believe, the political was the personal. You raised a remarkable daughter. You were a courageously tough First Lady. As you were my former State Senator and Secretary of State, I am grateful you were not a polarizing feminist. But a part of me wishes you were— radically, noisily, stubbornly feminist—because I suspect many of us would have supported you, regardless. Female culture in this nation could use an overhaul. For all our privileges, we are a handicapped womanhood here, quick to give up our hard-won rights in favor of having a man decide for us. To keep things simple. To pretend we used to be a greater nation back in the age of the Stepford Wives. To dumb down our female instincts and insist greater importance be placed on baking cookies and babying our men than negotiating with world leaders and shepherding the nation's well-being.*

*Dear Ms. Rodham Clinton, keep the faith. After all, you won the popular vote, the* only *presidential vote ever to be won by such an unprecedented landslide. Some four million citizens and I signed the petition to the electoral college, asking that the election result be overturned. Whatever you do from here on out, know that you gave us a glimpse of what we should be, what we could be, what we must never stop wanting to be, if only we dared trust our minds more than the transitory yearnings of our hearts.*

*Sincerely, etc.*

I had returned home to New York State in October this year, having completed my six-year contract at the university. Those years of living in Hong Kong had begun as a nightmare and ended as an awakening from a prolonged bad dream. Although I knew I'd still have to go back regularly as long as Mum was alive, it was time, I told my siblings, to get on with my own life. My partner of some twenty years awaited my homecoming, and I wanted more than the stolen moments we'd had of our overly long-distance relationship. I anticipated visiting Felix and his family in their new home of two years, which I had yet to see. He and his wife had adopted a daughter from China; she was now eleven, and the last time I'd seen her was three years earlier. Although I did manage to meet Felix briefly whenever he came to visit Mum, it had been a while since we spent prolonged quality time together.

My other great hope was to vote, in person, for America's first female leader.

My sister-in-law asked if it would be okay to have donations in lieu of flowers sent to a women's center Felix supported. *Of course,* I replied immediately, even though I knew they were pro-life. My brother advocated against abortion and had been quite vocal in recent years. It was not an argument I chose to have with him. Besides, the women's center he supported did help many young, vulnerable women in crisis and provided a valuable community service. There was little to oppose in the face of his demise.

Yet I could not help believing his faith was misplaced. It is not the sanctity of life about which I quarrel but the disregard of the living, pregnant woman who is judged, often demeaned, while the man goes off scot-free. My brother was a man who understood women—how could he not with three older sisters?—but I did not always believe he fully understood men. Felix was incapable of abusing or mistreating a woman, and he treated intimacy with the respect and love it deserves. When it came to relationships, he was extremely mature, even as a young man. Which is why he made an excellent first and only marriage because he trusted in love, understood commitment, and chose an independent, intelligent woman as his wife. I am twice divorced, have suffered far too many immature lovers, and have endured tediously sexist (and racist) corporate and institutional environments run mostly by men and their supporting cast of too many women who prefer to succumb to men. But I prevailed and still have faith in feminism and try to live out that faith. I will always support a woman's right to exercise choice over her own body and know the fight for gender equality is far from over. The Catholic Church world that was my brother's life is supported by women with faith and ruled by male priests who pronounce on the practices of that faith; my mother's religiosity is dauntingly similar. If I am faithless, it is in part because the Catholic worldview is lopsided and downright superstitious when it comes to the meaning of life. A living mother trumps a fetus most of the time. King Solomon's judgment should be the parable for understanding what is reasonable and fair.

*Dear Hillary Rodham,*

*Are you too political and not sufficiently personal? By all accounts, you are personable in private and friendlier. Should public persona count for such a lot? I mean, seriously, Nixon was hardly a barrel of laughs. Too many of my male friends and acquaintances were quick to disparage you from the start, were quick to give Bernie the nod. These same men exerted influence over women—daughters, students, employees, lovers—who saw them as role models for manhood, these men who loved strong women, who supported women's rights, who treated women with respect and shared in childcare and domestic work. Or were gay. And what I couldn't help feeling, each time conversation turned to the election, was that deep down, the fear of a woman in power trumped most other agendas.*

*Even after you won your party's nomination, the rumblings of discontent among both men and women remained. You can argue policies and practices till you're blue in the face; "not to be trusted" was bounced around as if the minutiae of party politics mattered more than the weight of your record of public service. Or common sense. You prevaricated too much, they said, and in the end, so did they.*

*But somehow, I couldn't help feeling it was the "good wife" who was not winning their full support.*

*I was amused to learn you watched that show. It made you more like one of us—smart but confused, in love yet also frustrated, sometimes overconfident and at other times insecure, ambitious and exhaustingly (even painfully) challenged by the glare of glass above us. TV is fiction though, and reality, like a commitment to public service, is about compromises with fewer happy or melodramatic endings. Real progress is slow, often ambiguous or uncertain. Not always pretty. Absolutist certitude and grandiosely claimed Pyrrhic victories are the delusions of those who believe their own lies.*

*I don't imagine you believed your lies, let me rephrase that, your questionable assertions; instead, you countenanced the demeanor of a seasoned, intelligent, and overly cautious politico. Do we love our political animals? Not generally. As a rule, they're all rather too close in nature to the Underwoods, a case where fiction trumps reality. But you are not so different from those thousands of political men who live their public lives under far less scrutiny than you do and are more readily (even too readily) forgiven. I mean, seriously, if groping pussy or other body parts and ridiculing influential female newscasters, entertainers, and political rivals in inchoate, adolescent language is the measure of a president, we of the feminist faith have miles, no, leagues to go. Let's face it: women still have significantly more to prove. Life is unfair in our postfeminist era.*

*Dear Ms. Rodham, this election put me in mind of an earlier era, when the media noise was all about impeaching your husband, our then-president whom I voted for, although I had to be persuaded to do so the first time. By a feminist, no less, who was one of only three woman bosses in my long professional life of working for many, many more men. Maureen Dowd, the* New York Times *columnist, summed it up best—your husband's sexual missteps were not grounds for impeachment but were indeed grounds for divorce. But hey, he left our nation solvent, and as a result, we got you.*

*Dear Miss Rodham (surely you too were a Miss once upon a younger time), I would have supported you if you had divorced Bill, but a divorcée could not have as easily run for the Senate, would not have been as readily appointed Secretary of State, and could not, unlike Reagan the divorcé, have run for president. At least, not yet. In the end, my mind said as much, even though I rooted, even yearned, for that divorce.*

*Sincerely, etc.*

The faith I witnessed in my brother's community was humbling. The words of the gospel and the consolation of Catholic philosophy felt genuine, even uplifting, though it did not shake my fundamental disbelief. Felix's most well-known contribution to the hymnal is his "Psalm of Hope" which adapts and reimagines "Amazing Grace." The music and lyrics made me cry the first time I heard it, and over the years, I would play it on the piano, occasionally sing it, and it never failed to move me or dispel despair. The song captures the dark night of the soul and the shaken faith of a believer. It asks: *My God, my God / Why have you abandoned me?*

Back in the late seventies, when my brother was still an undergrad music major at the University of Iowa, he and I once made a trip to Chicago. I was working in Hong Kong at an airline and could get standby tickets to visit. It was rare for just the two of us to travel together. The seven-year age difference, the gap in where our lives were at, all contributed to the distance. But our bond in childhood remained from when I used to sit him on my knee and make up stories to tell, and we were the two creatives among the sibs.

That summer, we bunked at the empty graduate dorm of the University of Chicago and cornered the piano. We played for each other, he told me about his dreams for a future as a singer and musician, and I shared my desire to leave a business career in favor of my writing. That trip was the beginning of a lifelong ongoing conversation we shared about faith in our creative arts. Some years later, I sang him a song I'd composed during a trip to Moscow about my mother's white orchid. *It's so sad*, he said, *a minor key*, as he scribbled out a harmonic chord arrangement for me. We have always talked music and commiserated with each other over the angst of our creative lives.

As our lives, and more significantly our faiths, diverged along radically different paths, he was still my brother, someone to love. In the end, despite our minds, we are mostly led by our hearts. He and I, we never even bothered to agree to disagree. You can't, not really. That kind of intellectual stance guides decisions we make that are beyond love—about electing a president, taking a new job, accepting familial responsibility for elder care, dealing with medical issues (about which my brother proved as rationally calm as was possible when handed his death sentence, the bigger picture of family and other responsibilities always in sight)—when the rational should trump the emotional if we truly have evolved beyond the ape. Which is why I rarely shout about religion, politics, or sports as played out on the world's stage and refuse to engage in that most deplorably misguided racist or sexist mudslinging fostered by a far-from-model minority, one that was whipped into a frenzy by an irresponsibly egotistical man who only cared about winning, not governing. In the end, frenzy will not prevail long beyond the latest sputtering tweet, not as long as we the people have faith in the soundness of our democracy.

*Dear Hillary,*

*The feminist convention of using only a famous woman's first name colored your campaign, and it was heartening. Language matters, whether it's the use of* they *instead of* he *or* grrrlllls *instead of* girls. *Even though linguistic political correctness exhausts me, as an educator, I have learned to pay attention. After all, teaching writers is a responsibility, even though literary work doesn't change the world. But the raising of consciousness that is the feminist's quest is a coalescence of language and action. For me the personal is still the political, even when the personal compromises my politics. We are not so one-dimensional, though, are we? Isn't that* the lesson of feminism?

*The emotionally charged language of hatred that prevailed in this presidential campaign did, I admit, stop me cold. The first amendment matters, but so does intelligence, truth, and civility. If there was one thing I learned through this horrifying race, it was that words really do matter. Sticks and stones, we say. But in our twenty-first-century virtual reality—and let's face it, technology does a new humanity make—this peculiar combination of visual images coupled with tweets or soundbites become our sticks and stones. "Alt-right" whitewashes "evil"; "immigrant" equals "un-American"; the right to bear arms is the reason to shoot the innocent; woman is created solely for the pleasure of and dominance by man. If we read it on the internet or heard or saw it on our preferred media channel, it must be real. An election that is "historic" for its controversy—and the result will undoubtedly prove our national, even global, future grief—is not history that honors this nation. Slavery is also our dishonorable history, as is the Japanese internment. A woman's right to an abortion should forever be a moment in history, marking an important turning point when society evolved beyond its traditional patriarchy in favor of commonsensical change, alongside a woman's right to vote. Misnaming, misreading, misspeaking will break our bones and, if we do not push back, eventually break our hearts.*

Was it faith that persuaded my brother to become a parent?

For the longest time, Felix could not imagine himself a father. He shared his doubts in our ongoing conversation and I played devil's advocate and questioned his true motivations and desire. I reminded him that he was fundamentally selfish when it came to how he needed to live for his music. For the longest time, our mother did not approve of the idea of adoption and later persisted in misspeaking the existence of my niece, saying "adopted" to imply that she could not truly be a part of the family. As if blood trumps all.

The stories of parents returning "unsatisfactory" adoptees from other nations are appalling to witness. Likewise, Chinese girl babies were for a time much in demand—all the rage, you might say, if you choose to misspeak the meaning of such responsibility.

But this too is our human condition, to harbor such distinctions of blood or lineage, as if abandoned innocents are somehow to blame. To treat adoptees as the latest fashionable must-have. In my mind, I knew my mother was wrong, dead wrong, as misguided as those adoptive parents who treated their children as if they were goods to be bought and returned. Is it not our mental enslavement to value blood above all, to believe that adoption somehow lessens the value we need to assign to the child? To abandon responsibility when the going gets tough in favor of an easier answer?

Ours is not a procreating family. My siblings and I survived the problems of our parents' incompatible marriage just as we managed the challenge of our movable, emigrant lives, where your footing in the next new world is never entirely assured. Despite my brother's long service as a liturgist at his church, where he clearly proved fluent in English, I was asked, in English, by more than one congregant at his funeral whether or not I knew English. Some commented on my niece's "resemblance" to our family. Do we all see only what we want to see? Know only what suits us to know? Must we hold onto beliefs despite the truth that confronts us?

Is humanity really so deplorable in its ignorance?

When Felix finally did decide, he immersed himself in the adoption process, one that was long and grueling. And yet as he updated us on that progress, I knew my own uncertainty, even though I argued with Mum, wanting to prove her wrong. Even though I understood the artist in him— the self-centered ego that demands as much space as my own does—and wondered if he would really be up to the sacrifice and responsibility. The girl he and his wife adopted was an abandoned baby; there is no record of her parents. She is and always will be the mystery for our family. When I look at my niece now and see this wonderful girl they raised, it is my brother's faith that haunts me.

Which brings me back to our divergence of faiths. If abortion had been readily available to the birth mother, my niece might never have been born. I like to think Felix must have felt that deeply, the more he came to know and love his daughter. Which is probably why he advocated so strongly against abortion. I could argue, readily, that China's one-child policy is really to blame for the proliferation of unwanted girl babies, as is the culture that overvalues the superiority of the male. But Felix is gone,

and our divergent views are trapped in eternity. In the end, his faith is
the mystery that allowed the miracle of his daughter.

*Hillary!*

"*Feminist" is a dirty word. In particular,* Roe v. Wade *is as bad as it
gets to those who would deny us our rights. These same opponents might have
sisters, daughters, mothers, cousins, or friends whose lives were upended by an
unwanted pregnancy. Or worse yet, were raped. I have known those women,
have trembled myself at what were signs of an unwanted pregnancy, mercifully
a false alarm. After that, I made my choice—tubular ligation—extreme to
some for a twenty-five-year-old. But it was a decision I never regretted, and
one my brother never criticized, though he probably wouldn't have approved it.*

*Dear, dear Hillary, feminism gets a bad rap. Yet I persist in believing
that your candidacy was one giant, feminist leap for wo/man-kind. I also
persist in believing that our democracy was well served because you won the
popular vote by that huge margin. Let's face it, the gerrymandered electoral
college is the other national phenomenon long overdue for an overhaul,
founding fathers be damned. The election was indeed rigged, as it has been for
decades, by a relic of a system that now coddles an angry and yes, increasingly*
deplorable *minority despite the will of the majority.*

*But I do not feel my faith in Democracy is misplaced.*

*Years ago, I voted with my feet to migrate because the United States was
The Nation that welcomed immigrants as national policy and enshrined
a belief in the equality of all "men," which we can read now as "people." It
was the country that gave my gender a chance, thanks to legislation and a
tolerant, humanitarian, fair-minded citizenry. It was also where truth and
reconciliation mattered, because we track and measure women's earnings to
men, just as we try, though not always successfully, to protect victims of sexual
assault and rape. We can debate the equal considerations women still are
not granted, in sports, the military, the arts, in myriad professions. We even*

*discuss men's rights in this postfeminist time because all people really* are *created equal. This was the democratic space where a civil society prevailed and feminism had a future. This was where I could choose to be childless because no one would stop me from making a surgical choice, one that made all the difference for my life.*

*Dear Hillary, please tell me my faith in feminism is also not misplaced. Women's lives, women's success, women's worlds matter, and men will change because they must. In the end, winning isn't everything. In the end, it really is how you play the game.*

*Sincerely,*

*Still With You.*

# ON BEING FOWL

## Notes on Some Explorations in Home Economics

It does raise the question: why not the fish side of this equation? Perhaps because fowl feels feminine. Not female, frantic, futile, or even feathery, but *feminine*. Fowl embraces the contradictions of femininity: both game bird and poultry, simultaneously wild and domestic. Fish requires an evolutionary transubstantiation that might be one step too far. So I would rather be fowl, a pheasant or hen ruling the roost. And frankly, the wild pheasant holds significantly less appeal than a domesticated chicken.

Which brings me to the existential reason for being fowl, that of domesticity.

My British colonial education included that quaintly named subject, domestic science, for secondary-level students. Inclusive of the study of cooking, sewing, knitting, how to be a hostess and run a household, this was the one academic subject my mother considered pointless. At my school, streaming in form 4 split all us girls into arts, science, and domestic science. For Mum, it was bad enough that I had been streamed into arts but, *Lord have mercy*, at least I wasn't in domestic science! Donning her woman warrior face, Mum marched into the principal's office and demanded I be rerouted into science. A complicated battle, but in the end Sister Rose was no match for my mother and I suffered my secondary education as a science student.

Now, while essaying on gender roles and how they have affected my life, it's something of a surprise to me that Mum is, in fact, astrologically feminine, a Capricorn, while I, Aquarius, am considered masculine. A greater truth likely lurks in this transgendered view of my existence, at least in astrological terms.

Domestic science eventually became known by its American equivalent, home economics, even in British schools. This academic discipline in the United States originated more than 150 years ago, championed by one Catherine Beecher, sister of Harriet Beecher Stowe. In 1909 the American Home Economics Association was established, and its first president, Ellen Swallow Richards, was a scientist who promoted opportunities for women to pursue scientific education. It was nearly a century later, in 1993, that the association was renamed the American Association of Family and Consumer Science, which more accurately reflects the breadth of what this "feminine science" truly comprises.

Ellen Swallow Richards was the first female graduate of MIT, where she achieved a bachelor of science in chemistry; she died in 1911. At the 1893 Chicago World's Columbian Exhibition, she was put in charge of an exhibit space known as the Rumford Kitchen. This initiative occurred under the auspices of the Department of Hygiene and Sanitation to showcase the "application of the principles of chemistry to the science of cooking." Prior to that, Richards had refused to participate in a demonstration kitchen set up in "The Women's Building." Nutrition, she insisted, was not only women's work because the knowledge involved was important for all people, not just women.

I proved a lousy science student, temperamentally suited as I was to the arts, which is where my life ended up. My maternally engineered secondary education is slightly puzzling in retrospect. Mum was extremely domestic, and she taught me to sew, knit, lay a table correctly, iron, cook, even launder and clean house. All this despite the three domestic help-ers employed in my childhood home prior to Dad's bankruptcy. It was necessary, she claimed, for girls to know how to fend for themselves in case their husbands couldn't take care of them properly, which meant, presumably, couldn't afford to provide a life of relative luxury. Mum said more or less the same of professional careers for women, which was one reason she wanted me in the sciences, in order to assure me a well-paid job; the arts, according to her worldview, did not require or offer real work. Yet she scoffed at domestic science as an academic subject, deeming it the refuge of the academically stunted. In fairness to Mum, there was a general snobbery about education in Hong Kong, especially with respect to the superiority of science over the arts. The domestic science stream was, I suppose, a way to provide girls who were less academically inclined with a secondary education. Those girls still had to study math, history, or geography and other academic subjects, so they were hardly uneducated. Besides, girls in Hong Kong who were not domestically skilled grew up to be women who were considered socially stunted. After all, what man in his right mind would choose a woman without abilities in domestic sciences for a wife?

Isn't this conundrum of Hong Kong womanhood just plain foul?

However, I soon discovered things weren't all that different in the United States either. My college girlfriends vied on the domestic front to bake the best chocolate chip cookies. The most ambitious wielded mastery over household consumer products—cleaners, detergents, house-hold appliances, sheets, towels, the dizzying array of foods on sale at the typical American supermarket—with opinions about which brands were best in order to keep house that kept up with the Joneses. They cooed maternally around infants, even while they took the pill to avoid the child before its time. This was the early seventies, and a remarkable number of college-educated women wanted marriage or at least an engagement ring by the time they got their degrees. Whether this rush to domesticity had to do with maternal urges wasn't entirely clear. But after college, when I returned home to Hong Kong, it soon became apparent that several secondary schoolmates had elected a kind of domesticity through marriage and motherhood, even though a significant number pursued professional careers as well. At our class reunions over the years, what struck me was that the most contented appeared to be the girls from the domestic science stream, whose own careers outside the home were secondary or nonexistent compared to their husbands', while the so-called smart girls, especially from the sciences, the ones who pursued demanding careers in addition to courting that same domesticity, contended with fouler existentialist dilemmas. It wasn't even a question of which spouse had greater earning power or status. When it came to raising the children and running the household, that simply was a wife's responsibility, this unpaid labor around the domestic sciences.

Of course, seemingly happy domesticities are not all alike, not once you peek under the sheets. My worldview is undoubtedly skewered by my own two divorces, an uncompromising unwillingness to bear children, and my willingness to risk material well-being in pursuit of the writer's life. So why is it, as I cross life's threshold from sunlight into eventide, I am feeling femininely fowl, desirous of courting domestic bliss?

A confession. At fourteen, I would have been horrified had I been streamed into domestic science. My strong subjects were English, literature, and French, and I could handle history and geography despite my attention deficit around the remembering of facts. Math was required of everyone in the public exam, and I could be competent enough when I wasn't daydreaming. Domestic science, however, I probably would have failed, mostly because the science of anything was simply not my strong suit. It took me years to figure that one out, though, because teenage me craved

Mum's approval that was meted out for academic excellence and professional ambition. At fourteen it was easier to scoff at what my mother considered the "pretend" science of domesticity.

And yet.

I used to sew and embroider. In primary 4, when I was around nine, we had a class assignment to learn a number of different stitches, which I sewed along parallel lines as a pattern for an apron. I privately harbored great pride over that apron. It was an unremarkable achievement, one that received neither a high grade nor praise from my mother. But I held on to that apron for years, in love with this pattern of stitches—cross, back, running, chain, tack, tent, hem—amazed that I had actually managed to create it. Later, in college, I would embroider butterflies on my young American cousin's blue jeans in bright and beautiful colors. She remembers this fondly, and even now she and her mother remark on this shared memory.

Similarly, I loved the dresses I sewed as a young teen on Mum's Singer. Selecting the fabric, matching and contrasting colors, searching out the right Butterick or Simplicity pattern, such work never felt onerous. My handiwork was never all that neat or precise, so I stuck to uncomplicated patterns that even a monkey could get right—the straight sheath, the A-line without a waistband, the empire line that was easier to fit around the darts, zippers instead of buttons, plain sleeves or no sleeves, plain cotton that didn't crinkle, bunch or otherwise slide out of my grasp. By adulthood this simplified approach applied to all other domestic tasks as well. My cooking is basic, and I don't use recipes, mostly because that requires marshaling facts in the correct order, sorting out British versus American measures, and remembering to turn the oven off or on in sequence at the right temperatures. But I pride myself on being able to whip up a meal with anything that happens to be in the larder and fridge. I also excel at what I know are the easier domestic sciences, namely, the laundry, ironing, and housecleaning, all of which I actually quite enjoy and find a therapeutic and welcome distraction from the art of filling the blank page. Two marriages to men who wore suits and one who wore tuxedoes made me reasonably competent at ironing shirts. In another life, I would probably have been a pretty decent maid or washerwoman.

Because Ellen Swallow Richards wasn't wrong. The higher domestic sciences such as nutrition, food preparation, and child rearing, along with the attendant knowledge around health and wellness, demand rigorous attention and require far more discipline than I could possibly muster. Motherhood terrifies me. Mothers need to know a shitload about pretty much everything and must multitask a daily roster of duties that would be way beyond most Fortune 500 CEOs. Yet they suffer the mockery of children who quickly become too cool for school and for Mom, are taken for granted by husbands who only have to be the good cop parent, and are assumed to have found their "natural" role in life, regardless of whatever educational or professional accomplishments they may have achieved— rocket scientist, concert pianist, commercial airline pilot, lawyer. Such achievements are merely, as Mum said, *in case your husband doesn't make enough and you need to go back to work.*

It's hell being a feminist. Much of my earlier professional life in business was spent mentally shooting angry birds at glass ceilings. You know the ones, those tiny little blue birds created by Rovio for its wildly popular electronic game, the ones best employed for smashing glass? There were many more men than women in my workplace milieu who competed to rise through the ranks of management. Even though I avoided the indignity of lesser pay, a boys' club ruled the hierarchy, and whatever rise I accomplished was destined to be a solo performance of luck, persistence, and a stubborn refusal to cry "uncle." Fortunately, I had a parallel career as a writer, an "indulgence" that kept my ego intact. What contributed to steeling me sufficiently to survive this reality imbalance had roots in Ellen Swallow Richards's discipline, one that more appropriately should be named the science and art of home economics.

As an MFA grad student at the University of Massachusetts, Amherst, I was assigned one semester to teach advanced expository writing in the Home Economics Department. It was an odd moment. I was in the last year of my degree program, had wanted some relief from teaching freshman writing, and asked the Writing Center to assign me an advanced course. My teaching evaluations were good, so I knew I probably would get priority. But home ec? I didn't know whether to be pleased or repulsed.

I was in my late twenties, recently married for the second time to an American jazz musician, overall rather non-domestically inclined in favor of being "the writer and artist," and not entirely happy with life on the MFA track. I had given up a promising business career in Hong Kong, along with its corporate international travel perks and excellent benefits, and gambled on the Writing Life in the United States, only to find I was now competing for a financially unlucrative career where the odds of success were about as good as winning at roulette. For a time, later in my fishy-fowl existence, I haunted roulette tables at casinos around the world. Auckland, Amsterdam, Macau, Lisbon, Dunedin, Atlantic City were a few I visited. The spinning wheel was mesmerizing, as were the multiply layered odds a player could stake, and I chose to ignore the lousy probability that math and common sense dictated. I was simply a sucker for the long-shot one-in-thirty-six win, and if I hedged bets around the table and left when I had lost my limit, things usually balanced out. This ex-habit was my nod to flunking calculus in school.

But I was recalling a semester of home economics before roulette interrupted.

It was in an ambiguously uncertain mood that I wandered through the hallways of home ec, a department I had not known even existed at the university, to meet the person in charge of the course.

She was undomestic, this supervisory professor, which was the first surprise. What exactly had expected? A housewifely matron, perhaps, her apron pocket lined with recipes on index cards for angel food cake and pot roast? Instead, my supervisor more closely resembled my idealized image of a real academic, certainly much more so than the disheveled and forgetful, unprepared and underwhelming, cold and distant, intellectually snobbish, or, worse, predatory male professors who inhabited academe, all the ones encountered both as an undergrad and grad student. This professor was sharp, intellectual, professional, and her entire appearance and demeanor exuded subtly excellent taste. More significantly, she immediately commanded my respect and, I later came to understand, was one of the rare older professional women I encountered who proved a role model for my own life.

My second surprise was what comprised the student body. On the first day of class, I faced approximately thirty-five to forty students, all female, 95 percent fashion marketing and 5 percent "real" home ec majors. It was revelatory. Here was modern womanhood of the early eighties in all her glory. A couple of decades later, I was reminded of this time when *Sex and the City* recast that glory.

That semester was my introduction to being fowl, as I attempted to enact a kind of rule of law as the graduate assistant of the henhouse. It also forced me to rethink the true value and meaning of domesticity.

Of the many writing classes I've taught, this was the one that most tested my sense of a feminine self. Teaching freshman writing, which had been my main experience at the time, was a rite of passage for the MFA student to determine if a teaching job was her best option after graduation. I found that work entertaining. Where else would you get to read, out of the same pile of papers, a smart-alecky essay titled "How to Open a Bottle of Beer," followed by an articulate philosophical meditation on the meaning of death, capped by the story of a national hero in a foreign student's country, a story he never thought anyone would care to read. My student conferences proved an education in human desire and motivation. Here was the good girl who smiled too brightly, in agony over her lack of straight A's during her transit from high school to college. Here was the mature student fighting to balance an unexpected single motherhood with deadlines for papers, and your heart melted as you handed out an extension. And that giant boy, the basketball player terrified of writing, who finally realized that yes, he did have something to say if he wrote about what he knew. It was easy being the teacher and grown-up for these eager, frightened, cocky, desperate, clever young things. As a rule, they really didn't care who or what you were because all they wanted was to get through this course, this requirement that began for many with a groan but ended, at least for some, with a little more enlightenment about the meaning of their existence.

The juniors in home ec were another story.

Admittedly, my supervisor did roll her eyes when we discussed the fashionistas. It was a concession, she said, to surviving academia, as the enrollment numbers of fashion marketing majors kept the department alive. Besides, these graduates potentially would place in really desirable jobs that led to lucrative careers. At least this was true if you *loved* fashion, and what girl didn't? Her practical take on the realities of college education was eye opening. In the English department where my MFA was housed, it was evident that creative writing was the lifeblood of the department, especially at the graduate level. As the masters and PhD students often told us, we MFA writers threw the best parties, where the booze always flowed. Yet it was also clear that not all the literature professors welcomed us. I had accepted the funded offer to do my MFA at UMASS, a three-year program with a curriculum that required graduate literature credits, because I was still partly interested in the possibility of a PhD. But the unwelcome response from some of the literature professors, who looked askance at my presence in their academically superior seminars, was off-putting. Clearly the writing of fiction was not, in their opinion, worthy of a degree. In fact, by the time my semester of teaching in home economics ended, I actually found that discipline more appealing than literature for a doctorate. Today, as a published nonfiction and fiction writer, I know a background in home economics would have provided excellent material for literary nonfiction, much the way the serious study of any academic discipline will yield knowledge for a writer.

Because the most challenging and exciting students I taught in that class were the home economics majors.

My own background in marketing and advertising did serve for teaching the hens of fashion marketing. When confronted by an attractively chic bunch of twenty-year-olds who read all those fashion magazines I never read, my one hope of sustaining their attention in class was to entertain with my real-world experience. As sophisticated as they strove to be, I did have one up on them, having worked for an international airline and traveled to some of the great cities of the world, including Paris, London, New York. I'd even known women who worked in fashion and could talk knowledgeably about how New York designers traveled to Hong Kong and Taiwan to reproduce Parisian knockoffs for department stores in the United States. Truthfully, I had met exactly one woman who did that, but a good fiction writer doesn't let facts get in the way of a good story. But I did hang out in New York regularly, thanks to my jazz musician husband, and knew my way around Manhattan. Somehow, I managed to eke out a reasonable amount of critical thinking from essay assignments as long as I could keep these girls awake. They were all generally sweet, earnest, and pretty girls; at worst there were airheads and at best ambitiously savvy ones who understood the value of researching the world they craved to enter and who therefore wrote decent research papers. I directed some of these latter students toward the MBA, a useful degree if money and power are desirable goals. None of those students are memorable. But from among the former, the earnest airheads, one girl still speaks to me through memory's mists, even now. She was at best a C-plus or B-minus student, but she came to class, turned in work on time, showed up to student conferences, and always thanked me profusely for whatever help I tried to give her. At the end of our last conference, she spoke about her desire to go to New York, excited that I had actually been to the city of her dreams. "I *so* want to be in Soho," she confided, "and be where all the yuppies are." She was dead serious, but her enthusiasm was infectious. I wished her well in her quest for yuppie-dom.

However, it was the home economics major, the A-plus student headed for grad school, who became my favorite. My task was primarily to help improve the students' writing skills, as I was not expected to be conversant in their academic discipline. The course supervisor oversaw the critical rigor of their research. In our early conference sessions, she expressed irritation at her fashion marketing classmates. I allowed her to vent but also played devil's advocate, challenging her opinions and ideas, even though I privately agreed with her critique of their materialistic, wasteful world of fashion and its anorexic view of womanhood. Her own passions centered around a domestic feminist worldview, one that I had not at the time fully considered. She spoke about the undervaluing of the domestic sciences and the role of women as we progressed, postfeminism. Our conferences evolved into a Socratic conversation where we taught each other. I could be forgiving of the fashion business world because it offered more opportunity than most other professions for women to rise in power and take charge. She could articulate power for domesticity, this largely feminine condition, through her research and critical work.

Perhaps in time, we agreed, the gender imbalance could correct itself, and the relevance of home economics had many contributions to make in this regard.

These days, when I retreat to my rural homestead, it is domesticity that gives me the greatest joy. Although I no longer sew dresses or embroider butterflies, I still launder and iron, grateful for the science of washing machines and dryers. I have lived in more than one home where it was possible to hang laundry on a clothesline in the garden and to inhale the fresh scent of sheets air-dried in the sun. Such memories ease the inevitable process of aging, certainly more so than the glass ceilings that persist, that deserve all the angriest blue birds of feminist outrage.

I work better in a clean and orderly home, where meals are nutritionally balanced and the food is prepared with fresh ingredients from neighboring farms. My professional life still demands that I travel here, there, and everywhere, appearing in fashion choices to make just the right statement as "The Writer," hoping to impress the yuppies of the literary world as well as those who wield power. But the older I get, the less that really matters.

In 1873 Ellen Swallow Richards, then Ellen H. Swallow, submitted a thesis for her BS to the Department of Chemistry at MIT. It was titled "Notes on Some Supharsenites and Sulphantimonites from Colorado." The handwritten manuscript opens with a statement about specimens of "silver bearing minerals" that were obtained in Colorado mines. "They were called by the miners," she writes, "brittle silver or grey copper, but as they had never been analyzed, nothing definite was known as to their composition." The rest of the paper is a scientific analysis of the presence and compositions of other minerals in the mines and is more science than I can fully appreciate. I think of it as a kind of giant recipe, one that shows us what these mines comprise should we ever wish to reproduce or understand their composition. I think of it as a record of intellectual curiosity, one that required hours in a laboratory, patiently testing and measuring these substances to understand more about their existence. I think of it as the early work of an unusual and very special young woman, who later applied her knowledge toward matters that would have a major impact on modern life. Her paper ends with a modestly cautious conclusion: "I have begun a series of investigations on the behavior of the other metals with hyposulphite with a view to employing hyposulphite in qualitative analysis, in some instances at least, instead of sulphuric acid. I think it might be used as a preliminary test and save much time."

It is high time I became that feminine fowl, as this foray into the domestic sciences or home economics might suggest. Call it a preliminary step in my path toward old age as a more contented hen than the younger, angrier blue bird, flinging myself endlessly against glass. There are ceilings and ceilings. It isn't only about the shattering.

# CONCUBINE LOVE

No one knew him as my lover. No one, among the very few people who were aware we knew each other, thought we were anything more than merely acquaintances. And no one guessed he virtually lived with me for almost a year before I finally ended things.

A concubine, or 小太太, Cantonese slang meaning the "little wife," was no longer legally recognized by the early seventies in Hong Kong. Prior to that, polygamy for men was legal, and multiple wives or concubines were a sign of wealth. I took up with my male "concubine" in the midnineties. I was divorcing my second husband, and the notion of "dating" in my early forties after a twelve-year marriage felt uncomfortably foreign. Besides, the city was a lousy one for older single women, given the surplus of younger women who would hook up with any older man with a wallet. I had a full-time job with business travel, an unhappy ex-husband-to-be in Singapore to placate, and a novel to finish, which would be released as my third book in '97. There was more than enough to juggle without courting the uncertainty of a new relationship.

It was in such a state of being that I tumbled into this concubine love.

We say that narratives need a beginning, middle, and end, but when I recall this time, it's all about an endless middle. I have written fiction about extramarital love, about mistresses and concubines, about transgressive sex, but my own real story has defied recorded remembrance. It was a surreal time. I went down two whole dress sizes because I ran, swam rigorously, walked several miles each day (often uphill), ate little, and did not drink alcohol daily, only occasionally binging with colleagues at the ad agency where I worked. At 94.5 pounds, I weighed the least I'd ever weighed since age sixteen and was underweight for my height at five feet two. For the first time, I even had a waist, measuring around 24.5 inches. For my short-waisted physique, which even in my teens was best suited to empire line dresses or low-slung jeans, this was like becoming a whole other person in midlife. I sometimes gaze at before and after weight loss images, exhibited for the selling of diet pills, food substitutes, or culinary regimens that are horrible for health, and think, *was that me too?* But I've never been and still am not overweight, have never resorted to dieting, have never really cared much about my weight or appearance, not even after I became "the author" and found myself endlessly photographed and videotaped by news photographers, photojournalists, and just about anyone who can point and click for newspapers, magazines, posters, television, all kinds of websites, university archives, YouTube, even live visual-radio broadcasts, and Facebook, Facebook, and more Facebook until I have finally agreed with my broker that yes, perhaps I too should own Facebook stock. Even now, I keep hardly any photographs of myself, except for publicity shots, and rely on my sister, the family historian-archivist, for images of family. I've become marginally better at posing for photos in this era of cell phone cameras, but I am still as invisible to myself as I was as a child, convinced that no one really saw me because even when I looked in the mirror, I did not really know who it was looking back at me. To date, none of my books sport my photograph. Somehow I've managed to get that past all my publishers.

Then, though, with an almost-real waist, I was for the first time in my life conscious of and pleased by the way I looked. He absolutely loved my slender self. He was relatively small and slim as well, and we fit together remarkably well. I do not possess a single photograph of him.

A few years ago, while sorting through things at my home in northern New York, I finally deleted the size zero dresses in my wardrobe. My hips have surrendered to the sixty-plus spread, which no amount of diet and exercise will curtail, and my breasts post-menopause decided to bloom into a real décolletage that my third and final husband confirms as real and not imaginary. When I was younger, my mother used to joke that I was as flat as an ironing board, which was more or less true. Nothing about the me of now could fit into those remaining dresses that were even slightly loose on the me of back then.

My concubine love was, I suppose, partly about the sex of thin.

Feminist me still has trouble believing I desired to be so thin, or a concubine. Both states simply happened. Concubinage was our private fantasy, this strange 二人世界 we inhabited, an isolationist love universe of two. Our families, our friends, our respective professional worlds had no idea we were dating and virtually cohabitated. He was on a prolonged but temporary sojourn in Asia and could pretend that he was bunking here, there, or anywhere to the wife back in France; I would in time learn he actually lived with a girlfriend and her daughter in London. Meanwhile, his mother in Singapore was just happy he had taken time off from Occidental life to engage his Southeast Asian self—he was part Asian, part Caucasian, a complex deracination. His children by his ex- and current wives loved to visit him at Grandma's spacious home in Singapore, owned by her family from a long-ago colonial era. The teenage son by his then-wife even came to Hong Kong and stayed at my—our—home when I was out of town on business and was told the apartment belonged to a friend. Did the boy look inside my closets, see the hanging dresses, wonder who this lady friend was his father knew well enough to have the key to her home? Will this boy one day seek me out, ask me to tell him about the father he rarely saw and barely knew, now that my concubine lover is dead? Or was he not told who I was? I could never be certain my lover kept our secret the way I did, the way I have, until now.

For many years beginning in the early sixties, my father shared an office on Ice House Street with T, a Shanghainese businessman. When this man died, suddenly and prematurely, the older of his two daughters came to my father in a panic. A second family had appeared out of nowhere—a 小太太 and children—a family he had secretly supported. Dad was shocked. He had known T for years, *years*, saw him almost daily in that tiny office space they occupied, even moved together to a second building on Ice House when the first one became too expensive. T had been a fixture of my childhood. His wife often sent us the most scrumptious homemade turnip cake at Chinese New Year. We knew his family well. How was this possible? The daughter was distraught and wanted my father's help to deal with this other family because her mother was now not just grief-stricken but horrified, unable to believe this was happening. Dad took charge, sorted out financial matters, made the second family disappear sufficiently for T's wife not to be publicly humiliated. But that was the end only of my father's role in this situation. For T's family, this betrayal must be never-endingly indelible.

When Dad died, suddenly and unexpectedly in '98, I as eldest child was dispatched by my siblings, without Mum's knowledge, to interrogate Dad's younger cousin and our favorite Hong Kong uncle as to whether or not we should brace ourselves for a repeat of T's drama. If anyone would know, Uncle would. We spoke, as we always do, at his regular bar of the moment in Tsimshatsui. He paused, swallowed more beer, and declared,

*No, I really don't think so.* It was not lost on me that he could not say, as a large part of me wanted him to, *No, absolutely not. No.*

So this propensity for concubinage is in my DNA. Since I was quite young, I was aware there were always other women in Dad's life. At his funeral wake, to our relief, no second family showed up. But I must admit it would not have completely surprised me if a mysterious woman had appeared, paid her respects, and left, never to be seen again. A woman no one recognized. Dad's funeral drew many mourners, so it's possible she slipped in and out unnoticed. We were all in shock at Dad's untimely demise and might not have noticed even if she had been there.

Feminist me still does not know the "correct" attitude to adopt about the men women choose to love and how women choose to love the men they do, if indeed such ways of loving can truly be called "love."

How did we begin? I don't recall exactly when we met, except that it was in Singapore, an unremarkable circumstance. Someone said, *you two should know each other,* because we both were creatives hovering between Asia and the West. The conversation was pleasant enough: I said I was moving back to Hong Kong soon for a new job, and he mentioned he would probably be there soon as well for a project, and that was that. We exchanged cards as everyone does in Asia. We weren't even flirting, as we later agreed. Although my marriage was rocky, divorce was not yet a given. The plan was for me to move first, rent us a place, and then my husband would close down our Singapore home and join me. I did find us a large, beautiful, ground-floor, two-bedroom flat in a low-rise, prewar building off a main road up a sloped driveway hidden behind trees. The separation confirmed my feelings that I needed to end my marriage, and for a few months I shuttled this turmoil between two cities. In the end, my husband stayed in Singapore and never lived in that flat.

That flat. It was my emptiest abode. My husband and I owned minimal furniture, and our rental house in Singapore was furnished. I bought two tatami mats and slept on those for a time before eventually acquiring a futon; the second bedroom became my writing space. The main room—a long and wide rectangular space for the living-dining area—was bare except for my three floor-to-ceiling bookshelves and large floor cushions, although I did eventually acquire some chairs and a small dining table. My jazz guitarist husband had occupied all the living rooms of our various homes as a music studio to house a drum set, keyboard, and multiple amplifiers for gigs and band practice. But in this home I was the soloist. Eventually, I did buy an acoustic piano, something I had not owned and missed playing during many years of moving around the United States and Asia, although when we first married in Amherst, Massachusetts, I did possess one.

That flat. It was my loneliest address until he moved in.

Let me name him by at least an initial, R.

The first time R and I crashed down together on those tatami mats, we were violently sober. We were both simply starved for sex. That's how these things begin, two lonesome, horny beings, reasonably compatible, doomed to a magnetic, sexually irresistible, hopelessly wrong affair once we bothered to take a closer look at each other.

All it took was that first look. We had run into each other several times in the claustrophobically small, foreign-but-not-quite-expatriate world of creative types we inhabited. He hung out where everyone I cared to know did, at Visage, the Jazz Club, the Fringe, the Arts Center, and would occasionally waltz into the Foreign Correspondents Club, this venue I sometimes haunted because my advertising and media work worlds meant many professional acquaintances were members. Plus my then-publisher Mike practically lived there and hosted lunches or bought drinks for his authors and media types who interviewed us. But it was at

Visage, the movable feast barber shop that transformed into a semilegal club after dark, where we first sat together, late one night, talking. He was a commercial filmmaker and chef-restaurateur who really wanted to be a jazz musician if he had the choice, trumpet being his axe; I was a corporate cog who really wanted to write, just write. He read. Voraciously. I rarely saw him without a book curled in his pocket, its pages underlined, the corners bent with notes scribbled in the margins. But he read mostly philosophy and poetry, and my library of novels and short fiction, plus a few poetry and political books, did not have enough to interest him.

And at the end of that night we looked at each other, after talking for more than two hours nonstop, our wine glasses long empty. The staff were closing up, and it was well past three in the morning. A piano jazz rendition of Ray Noble's "The Touch of Your Lips" was improvising around the line *And now, at last*, when we simultaneously leaned forward and kissed each other. This would never happen in fiction, which is why you don't bother making up real life. When I resurfaced, Sonny the bartender was grinning and said to me in Cantonese, *hurry up then, go on home*. He liked R, approved of him I guess. He was the only witness to our one instance of public intimacy, and after all these years, I doubt he remembers. Besides, the original Visage, like R, is long gone.

At first, it had all the makings of a brief, torrid affair—with all that cliché implied—that would be over when he had to return home in a couple of months. He was crashing at a friend's place on the outlying island of Cheung Chau and often stayed over at my flat because we were up long after the last ferry sailed. Neither of us slept much. Then he moved to another friend's place on Lamma Island, which he called an expat ghetto, and preferred to stay with me because my Mid-Levels place was the height of luxury by comparison. I never minded because he cooked delicious, healthy meals, which after my long hours at work were better than sex.

He even did dishes. And his small and wiry physique—he was only about five feet seven or eight—meant he had no trouble sleeping on the hard tatami surface. It was like the early days of my marriage, when my husband and I slept on a sheet over our carpeted bedroom floor, and the furniture we cared most about was my writing desk and his musical equipment. My husband used to earn a living as a sous chef in a fancy restaurant in Amherst and performed in his free time until he abandoned the promise he had as a chef for the music life. He later sold commercial real estate in Brooklyn and was financially successful, but our move to Asia meant he could abandon that also for music because my salary was enough to float us till he could establish himself, which he eventually did, quite well.

*Why did you leave him?* R said, *that is my perfect life.*

In fiction, that would be the foreshadowing of things to come. After some thirteen years of an obsessive intimacy with my husband, one that eventually collapsed from the sheer weight of it all, R was a repeat of more of the same. Except that, unlike my husband, he wasn't a real musician. I heard him play a couple of times when he sat in with the local jazz musicians, and he was competent but unremarkable, a much lesser Chet Baker but sexier and better looking. By then, after years of *jazz, jazz, more jazz* all the time, twenty-four-seven, my ear was trained to screen out bad and indifferent performers. But that was before R and I had fallen in love, if in fact that was what happened. Cocooned as I was in the creation myth we narrated to each other of our concubine love, he could have sung to me off key and it wouldn't have mattered.

I became his concubine because his girlfriend no longer wanted to be.

The Saturday evening she called, we had just sat down to supper. Steamed shrimp, shelled and flayed in an artistically wrought presentation, accompanied by a salad of mâche and thinly sliced radishes, with the promise of his signature flaky apple tart for dessert. I had splurged on an expensive white since Saturday night meant no conference calls with

New York, and Sunday morning allowed me to rise later than my workday 5 a.m., oftentimes earlier. I *loved* mâche ever since I first discovered it in Paris and mistakenly sautéed it, thinking it similar to Chinese snow pea leaves. But I rarely had it since it was expensive and difficult to find in Hong Kong. R had acquired some for us through a friend who was a chef at one of the top French restaurants.

This was pre-cell-phone existence, and I was surprised when my land-line rang. She asked for him, and I handed him the phone, a question mark on my visage. By the time he returned to the table, supper may as well have ended. The conversation had been heated and, to my surprise, in English; he always spoke to his wife in French. It was how I learned about the girlfriend in England, the one he had been living with for years without divorcing his wife, the girlfriend with the four-year-old daughter who might be his, although, he was quick to add, she had not insisted on this because she admitted she had been screwing someone else at the time. Apparently, their affair began shortly after his son's second birthday, and he had moved in with her that year. His son was now sixteen. I stared at him, slightly shocked but unwilling to judge. We had been together for about a month, and I still thought our relationship would soon end. A very private and increasingly desirable relationship, but temporary, and I had prepared myself for the predictable farewell scene.

*I'm sorry* was the first thing he said when he sat back down at the table. In the year—actually, nine months, twelve days, and thirteen hours—we were together, he repeated that apology often, usually after his then-second-wife or girlfriend called. The first wife—that marriage resulted in two daughters and ended in divorce when he took up with the second wife—did not call because she communicated only via their adult children, who did call, although he sometimes called her. My own love life of two marriages and one former fiancé whom I didn't marry was, by comparison, simplicity itself, since there were neither children nor lingering liaisons to juggle. I think that was what finally ended it for me, all those calls, all those demands of family swirling around him in an eternal vortex.

We barely touched supper. I drank most of the wine while he only had, at most, a glass. R did not really care much for booze, a failing, I would later think, because even though I appreciate that constant days of wine and roses hardly constitute a better way of living, I cannot bear reality without intoxication. He was too sober, too sensitive, too, too, too perpetually involved with the women in his life, and would probably always be.

Except for me.

The secrecy was mutual and instinctive. At first, my desire for discretion stemmed from the continuous versus past tense of my state of divorcing. My husband was still trying to understand why, even though I had stated categorically that as far as I was concerned, the marriage was over. His insistence on asking all our friends rather loudly and publicly why the hell this was happening made me want to run and hide. My cousin who was living in Hong Kong at the time broached the subject, saying that my husband was hurting, and was I being fair? Another writer and musician friend, which meant we both could lay claim to his friendship, tried to stay neutral, but I think even he wondered at my seeming callousness. The truth was, I had taken the coward's way out and literally run away. But our lives had become so separate. I worked days, he worked nights, we rarely saw each other, and the last time we went on vacation to Langkawi, it had been an unmitigated disaster. Most of all, we were unable to talk to each other anymore, where previously we had screamed to high heaven in our earliest years, followed by a mellowing out via our respective therapists, and eventually we found a kind of comfortable truce. The truth was, we had fallen out of love with each other, even if he would not admit it, and, having been divorced once before, I no longer thought marriage was for-ever. Unfortunately, he thought it was or at least had a principled belief in preserving the marital state of being, as did my mother-in-law, despite her three divorces. It is a truth universally upheld that the institution of marriage, despite its resounding failure in our times, is still the most sacred rite of humankind, regardless of race, religion, or gender.

His secrecy, I suppose, was due to the fact of his second marriage, even though it was a nonmarriage, but there was his current girlfriend-concubine and daughter, the one that was still not his. I don't know if he ever acknowledged her because he hadn't by the time I broke things off. The girlfriend was yelling RFLP (pronounced *riff-lip*) and PCR, meaning DNA testing for paternity, and he was yelling *fuck that, it's not foolproof,* and she was saying, *99.99 percent is good enough for me.* And he was demanding, *why the hell now, why now all of a sudden?*

When he returned to the table, his countenance black, he told me all about this woman, and I began to understand why he wanted this time away. She was insisting he leave his wife to make her legal and adopt her daughter.

How does a mistress, or concubine for that matter, get the right to demand that supreme wife status? Zhang Yimou's 1991 film *Raise the Red Lantern* offers a visual symbol in the form of the lantern hung outside the door of one of the four wives, signaling which would be the man's choice as lover for the night, the home in which he would sleep. It has always struck me as a truly universal film because rarely are women in any culture afforded the equal right to occupy this man's role. Whenever I consider R and his girlfriend, I suppose her perceived right to ascension had something to do with longevity and her ability to "earn" it. His then-wife was reasonably well-heeled, a lawyer with her own career and practice. Being French, she simply refused to divorce him, and R, having at least some French DNA, saw no reason to complain. The girlfriend, on the other hand, was English, a stay-at-home mother and lady of leisure, well educated but uninclined toward work or a profession. To be his much younger concubine, as she was, being even younger than me, she was granting him beauty and youth for the price of being kept in the manner she expected. Or so he claimed. Much of R's real life is lost to me because I never met any of his people. Nor was I certain, after this incident, that he was telling me all the truth of who he really was or what his life was about.

What quickly became apparent was that he was financially stretched. His small restaurant in London did okay, and he picked up sizable contracts for the commercial films he shot for corporate clients. But I saw his address once on correspondence forwarded by his girlfriend, and it was in a tony district in London. Although his wife paid for her own life and their son's education, R contributed and paid for skiing and beach vacations in Europe and America. He also forked over regular gifts of money to his daughters by the first wife; I suspected he also paid her a form of alimony. The girlfriend and daughter, however, were entirely his financial responsibility. He couldn't possibly afford me as well.

Feminist me has never expected a man to afford me. One tried by offering me his apartment in Athens to crash for a time, but I moved out after two days once I understood his true intentions. In both my marriages, I earned more than my husbands. A relationship is not just about money but about sharing lives. Money, however, complicates love, especially if the balance is tipped toward the woman with greater earning power or resources.

R and I, we were *never* about money, until we were.

We had been seeing each other almost daily for about two months when R told me he would be going back to London.

*I'll miss you*, were the first words out of my mouth.

He gripped my arms so roughly I froze, unable to respond to his wildly passionate kiss as he pulled me toward him. What *was* this? We had not yet constructed our fantasy narrative of concubinage at that point, so in my mind he was still dispensable. But his strange embrace still returns to me, viscerally, after all these years. It was more than just a tiresome and clingy or a too-rough lover. He *needed* me, and that certainty rushed through me right then. There are very few actual moments I can recall of the past, but this one remains.

He whispered so softly I could barely hear him—*I love you.*

*Then don't go away*, I said. *Come live with me.*

That was how we really began. All he needed was to afford a place in this expensive city, and the rest—the pretense of work (although he did in fact take on a few contracts), the need to be near his mother (whom he *obviously* couldn't live with), the reason to hold off marrying his girlfriend for now (I think he eventually did but am not absolutely sure)—the rest of his absence could be readily explained away. His two daughters from his first marriage could come visit, even stay (they did, he paid for me to stay in a hotel that week and created a temporary film set out of my apartment to make it look more like one he would be living in), his *girlfriend* could visit (she *almost* did, but I put my foot down on that one), and his mother was delighted he was close by, in Asia, finally.

And what I needed, at least for a brief time, was the comforting illusion of love.

For the next seven months, I had what every overworked woman in the midst of a divorce needed—a "little wife" who didn't complicate my life. He shopped for groceries, prepared all my meals, took care of the laundry, cleaned house, regularly made love to me, and disappeared whenever I wanted to entertain friends or had family visiting.

Many years earlier, long before my second marriage to the jazz guitarist, I dated an Australian man in Hong Kong who kept a Thai woman. It was not immediately obvious the first time I stayed over because she appeared to be a domestic helper and acted like one. He introduced her, she served us dinner, and then we sat in the living room while she cleaned up and disappeared into the maid's room. It took a couple more visits before I realized she was furious at me and that I was likely usurping her place in her own home. Perhaps if I had been a Caucasian woman she would have minded less, but to watch him fuck another Asian woman was probably more than she could stand. I finally asked him if he was living with her, as in, *was she his lover*. He didn't deny it, and that ended our relationship.

Is it my Chinese city that makes such lives possible? Is it Asia? My father's business took him to Japan and Indonesia frequently when I was a child, and Mum's excuse about his philandering was that *this is how business is done in Asia*. In Seoul on my business trips back in the seventies, women wondered aloud to me, *how is it you can travel alone, a woman without your husband?* One woman was a masseuse who was surprised I was not a man when she arrived at my hotel room, the other a university graduate whose role was clerical and mainly involved serving tea at meetings for the Korean male executives and the foreign visitors, me included.

The subservient Asian female role is one I do not readily occupy. Although a respect for your elders is dinned into you if you grow up Asian in Asia, the willingness to serve my elders feels unnatural. I can and will host parties and know how to make people feel welcome and do not stint on the food and booze I serve my friends and family. But the need to give in to a man simply because of his gender is foreign to me. Around me in Asia, women put up with a remarkable amount of patriarchal behavior with surprisingly little complaint, even now. What I chose to live is someplace else, a subterranean demimonde existence of sexuality and secrecy, one that is not easily resolved, and one that I was no longer willing to perpetuate after R and I ended.

In Hong Kong it is perhaps our interminably colonial state that allows us to perpetuate such states of being. Since the return to China, we have become neocolonials of the mainland, running dogs who lust after their money and resources as long as our Nero-fiddling party life goes on. When I consider how my concubine love was spent, it is apparent that the luxury of amorality was an indulgence made possible by both the colonial and mercantile life of my city. It is partly about the economy, *stupid*, I remind myself. I dragged my ex-husband "home" to Asia in the early nineties because jobs were better there for returnee pseudo-Asians like myself. It was easier to be globally soulless, well fed, clothed, and pleasured than to confront the smash-up of what we once held dear. Marriage, for example. In essaying on marriage it is easy to be cynical but not so easy to know truth. Why after all does marriage persist if mortals like us persist in perverting its central morality—*to love, honor, and obey* (each other, since women are no longer chattel, we hope), *till death do we part*? An even longer time ago, when I was somewhere between a tween and a teen, I came to the conclusion that having children really was for the birds. Yet mine was not that unhappy a household, nor were the financial setbacks my father experienced so terrible as to engender such extreme views. Because it is still "extreme" for a woman to declare, *I do not believe in marriage or motherhood*. In my life, for better or worse, it is the men who cared more about children or marriage than I. My first husband eventually remarried and fathered a son, the child I would not give him; my second husband remarried, was widowed, and remarried a third time and continues his life as a jazz man.

Was I R's concubine or he mine? Even now I do not really know. Our love was about being sexy and thin, secretive and healthy, sensually fulfilled without fuss. Our life was luxuriously Spartan: the flat was in an expensive neighborhood afforded by my corporate salary but was void of all but the barest necessities. I did eventually move to a smaller place once my husband and I began legal divorce proceedings, and R visited me for a while in that space, but only for a very short while because I had pretty much broken things off before my move. What strange love we were able to nurture happened only in that empty transit home, one with neither a future nor a past.

I don't miss R. There are lovers I've dated for shorter periods whom I recall fondly. Not R. He was solace and comfort, but I'm not sure it was love. For one thing, it was far too easy to cheat on him when I was away on business trips, which I did twice, the second being fatal to our relationship because I really did fall in love with the man, who is still my man today. For reasons I can't explain, I cannot cheat on someone I'm in love with. My love life is peculiarly marked by my origins, by the two Asian cultures that shaped me and the tolerance for a man's "right" to have all the women he wants, regardless of love or marriage. This is further complicated by a postcolonial and globalized Asia in which Western men hold out the promise of a better life to Asian women who might only have a young body to trade.

My solution was simply to live the life of an Asian man with female characteristics.

It is hellish being an educated, professional Asian female in Asia. You are marked a harpy for being too feminist, denigrated by governments for choosing not to marry and have children, excoriated by other women for living off a financially well-off husband, looked at a little askance by both Asian and Western women if you marry or date a Westerner, and simply dismissed by women of lower socioeconomic classes whose problems far surpass your own. There are really no good choices for carving out an independent life in a so-called globalized world where ethics and morality are the slipperiest hillsides.

With R, it was one way to duck and hide from all that for a while, at a moment of personal chaos and uncertainty. More desirable than trying to date, less expensive than therapy. For my brand of womanhood, it was resorting to the cowardly lioness without responsibility for a pride. Did I leave him because I saw the light? Hardly. I fell in love and took up with another man is the truth of the matter, but it doesn't seem either wrong or despicable, even though by some measures it is. I did not throw him out of house and home because he hung out till he sorted out an alternative space, and soon afterward, he returned home to London and his English girlfriend and daughter and did not witness the handover of Hong Kong to China as he originally planned. I remained in Hong Kong at my last corporate job through that time, and the man I eventually married visited shortly after the handover.

Three years later, I saw R again. He was in transit in Hong Kong on his way to Singapore, and we ran into each other at the airport. By then I was living with my man in New York and spent only part of my time in Hong Kong. His mother had just died, and he was about to inherit her very valuable real estate. Meanwhile, my father had already passed away, and I was in the throes of working out how to look after Mum as her Alzheimer's progressed. We looked at each other, exchanged pleasantries. And then we kissed Euro style and went our separate ways. Some years later, I heard he had been killed in a skiing accident in Switzerland. It was something heard in passing from someone who didn't know him well and could not furnish further details. I considered researching his demise, and him, but gave up the idea.

# ORIGINS

# A LEDGE, A NUN

Along the slope between the front gate and the primary school playground, a ledge. She climbed up and sat there all through recess, watching earthworms curl into balls, embracing solitude. She was nine. In her head, Sister Miriam Xavier's voice: *mixed fractions are a nuisance, so you must get rid of them.* Sometimes, people, noise, the clamor of the city were a nuisance as well. Once she sat so long on the ledge she was late returning for class. The teacher frowned but did not scold.

In time, she would discover the reason for silence. To think, to reflect, to meditate. To write. You cannot write in the middle of a playground. But the mix of people and voices, that was life. You cannot turn your back on life. *Mixed fractions are a nuisance, but if you transform them into whole fractions, you can add, subtract, multiply, divide.* Transformation. Sister Miriam made math, her least favorite subject, easy and, dare she say it, fun. In time, she would learn to divide life between noise and silence, between humanity's buzz and solitude. In time she would be the writer she didn't know she could be when, at the age of nine, recess and life sometimes meant the need to retreat.

It began on a ledge, a nun's voice in her head. Learning to transform messy life into words, later into stories and essays, even later into books. Nothing is a nuisance if you embrace its mystery and give it life.

# THE ENGLISH OF MY STORY

It began with a coin. The year was either 1960 or '61, and I was a primary 2 or 3 student in a Hong Kong public school run by American Catholic nuns. The class was English composition. Once a week, we were asked to write approximately a page and a half in class. I would often write three pages, and by the time the bell rang could easily have kept going. Most of the time, we wrote essays. That day, however, I wrote the story of a journey. A coin was my protagonist. It fell out of someone's purse and rolled into the gutter. Someone else picked it up. From there it traveled from person to person. I do not recall what its ultimate fate was or if there was a climax or denouement. It was neither a tragedy nor a comedy, but it was the first piece of fiction, in English, that I remember writing.

In the eighties when I was an MFA student in the United States and could not, or would not, only write fiction á la Freitag, I would think about this coin and its journey. Traditional Chinese novels were often episodic and did not fit Shakespeare's dramatic structures of tragedy and comedy. Was that because, I wondered, we Chinese simply experienced life differently? Yet how Chinese (or Asian, since I am part Indonesian) am I as a writer if my literary language is and always will be only English?

When I stumbled onto the linguistic discipline of World Englishes in the midnineties, I had returned to Hong Kong to work, and my first books had been published. My writer's life, post-MFA, was to continue writing alongside my corporate marketing career, and I had virtually no connection to academic life. My initial reaction to the idea of this discipline was that it seemed rather quaint. In university, I had avoided linguistics. At the English department in my undergraduate American alma mater, there had only been one such course, and this was rumored to be a grammarian's masturbatory heaven. That definitely *had* to be avoided. Upon entering the workforce in 1974 Hong Kong, armed with my BA in English, I turned down the one academic job offered me by what was then Baptist College (now Baptist University). The American professor who wanted to hire me for what was more or less a graduate teaching assistant position was impressed by my native English-language fluency and literature education. His Hong Kong Chinese boss, in a subsequent interview, expressed skepticism that I, a Hong Kong–born, more or less Chinese girl could really be a native speaker of English. He clearly wasn't and spoke what some in World Englishes describe as "Hong Kong English." But I was an arrogant young fiction writer in English (never mind World or Hong Kong English) who hated having to go home after three, gloriously liberating American collegiate years. His skepticism felt like unfair and, more significantly, ignorant criticism of my very existence. Why, I wondered, should I kowtow to a boss whose English was "lesser" than mine in what was supposedly an English medium academic institution? Besides, did I *really* want to spend half my time correcting second language errors? There was nothing offered that remotely resembled the creative writing workshop I had taken in the United States, which boded ill for teaching assignments. When I declined the job offer, it was my fuck-you to Hong Kong academia in favor of the international English-language world where I would take my chances as a writer.

The rest, you might say, is my kind of mongrel history because I did become a Hong Kong writer in English. At least, that is one of the identities I am willing to own today, alongside my mixed-race Asian, American, Asian American, global writer identities. In what Aristotle might consider a reversal of fortune, I did end up at the academy I once eschewed, back "home" again in Hong Kong. In fact, City University of Hong Kong is just up the road from Baptist University and my mission there, since I chose to accept it, was to try to position the university on some kind of literary map. Which is how an "Asian MFA in English creative writing," as the program I founded and directed is sometimes referred to, came into being.

Yet when I'm asked to describe myself, the default answer is: *I'm a writer. I happen to write in English.*

What does it really mean to be a writer in English today, especially in the literary sphere, if Asia and Hong Kong color almost all your work and life? Despite the quaintness I once ascribed to World Englishes, the notion of English as a plural forced me to consider my life's work in a new light.

As a child, I despaired at my linguistic fate of being born in Hong Kong to wah kiu Indonesian parents who made English our (the children's) mother tongue. On the one hand, this early, near-native English fluency assisted an entrée to the elite world of our British colony. It also eased my passage into a later American life, allowing me to abandon an Indonesian nationality that seemed at odds with who I was (my parents purposely did not teach us Indonesian, believing that English and Cantonese were more than enough). On the other hand, despite a near-native Cantonese fluency, I am only semiliterate in Chinese and, more significantly, only semi-acculturated into local Hong Kong culture. I never watched Cantonese television or movies as a child, did not have much of an extended family with whom to celebrate major Chinese holidays, seldom even ate Cantonese food until I was an adult, and, by primary 5, had flunked out of Chinese. It was hellish sitting in Chinese class and only half under-standing what the teacher said. My parents were not fluent in Cantonese (my mother is virtually illiterate in Chinese, and while my father was very literate, his dialect was Mandarin, which he preferred over Cantonese), but my classmates were mostly native Cantonese speakers, and we were taught Chinese based on that assumption and reality. Meanwhile, I aced English, while many of my classmates struggled, but was studying it as a second language. I had more in common with and mostly befriended the other "foreign" locals—the Portuguese, Indian, Eurasian, or odd British, American, or European girl who ended up at my school. They all spoke English or some version of it. It was a relief to abandon Chinese in primary 5 and join the non-Chinese study group for advanced English classes and later, in secondary school, to take French as our second language. Yet when I finally arrived in the United States as an undergraduate, I realized I knew less English than I thought I did and did not fully appreciate the distinction between British and American English or literatures (or grammar, spelling, and syntax for that matter).

For years I believed that the only way I could be a writer successfully was to remain in the United States, and specifically, New York City, to where I moved in 1986 and where I felt, and still feel, very much at home. By then, I had obtained an MFA from a good program, mastered or at least was sufficiently conversant in American English—its literature, grammar, syntax, and punctuation, as well as American slang, baseball English, and copyediting and publishing conventions—had published a few short stories, and landed a literary agent on Fifth Avenue. Asian American fiction was making its way into mainstream literature, and my prospects looked good. Besides, New York felt like THE city to live in as a writer of mongrel origins.

I had even studied Mandarin-Putonghua in recognition of China's growing importance and improved my Chinese literacy enough to read contemporary Chinese fiction and newspapers slowly, with a dictionary close by. It was a no-brainer doing this in the United States—all the other students were native English speakers in contrast to my Chinese education as a child. I had found a way to flip around my linguistic dilemma: no longer was I surrounded by non-English speakers, and I could now learn Chinese angst-free. This was as close to paradise as it got. The problem with Eden, however, if you are in the West, is that you're predestined to lose it. Had Milton been Chinese, *Paradise Regained* might have been hailed as the masterpiece instead of his other book, but that's a different tragicomedy. Mine was economic. In the early nineties, New York was crashing while Asia was rising. A writer still must eat until her royalties catch up with her life, and the jobs to be had were more lucrative in Hong Kong. So I ended up, once again, back "home" and became that "Hong Kong English writer."

This created new complications. Even though I drew upon my Hong Kong and Asian world for my fiction, when I lived in America, distance allowed a perspective that disappeared as soon as I returned. Now I was no longer reliant on memory or primarily inclined to an investigation of the past. Instead I was thrust back into a present tense mode of observation, most of all, linguistically. When I returned to Hong Kong in '92, I had lived away for eleven years and only visited briefly twice, mainly to see my parents. Yet my Cantonese returned with a vengeance, in part because my corporate marketing job required constant use and also because it is a close second as my mother tongue. Eventually it eclipsed my Putonghua entirely, and the more or less "correct" accent my Beijing language instructor once praised gave way to one that immediately identifies me as Hong Kong the moment I open my mouth on the mainland (Taiwan is a tad more forgiving). Yet what I was prized for, as a U.S. multinational corporate employee, was my fluency in American English. It didn't hurt that I also understood and liked baseball.

When my first book was published in 1994, it was reasonably well reviewed and sold out quickly, mostly because, I suspect, it was a curiosity in Asia—this Hong Kong family story that was not just another potboiler thriller by an expatriate writer—and because of its controversial sexual content, about an incest between a brother and sister. There were no Hong Kong writers in English who could claim (or wanted to claim) to be local; admittedly even I did not always call myself a local writer. The few other Chinese English writers I met whose experience somewhat paralleled mine were all poets, most notably Louise Ho and Agnes Lam. The fiction writers were mostly expatriates, albeit some longtime ones, but many spoke little or virtually no Cantonese, although some were fluent in Mandarin. The identity conferred upon me as a "Hong Kong Chinese writer" felt odd at first because it did not seem real. This was further complicated by my English byline and name, which, at the time, was my married surname Chakó, a made-up name my ex and I legally adopted by combining the first syllables of both our last names. In the United States, I had used it as a byline for all my published work, and it never once raised an eyebrow. In Hong Kong, more than eyebrows were raised. Blood pressures soared over this "Indian" author who had the temerity to write a Chinese story, the subtext being "what gives *her* that right?" There is a Keralan surname that is similar, which I've seen rendered as "Chakho" or "Chako." I even received fan mail from Keralans wondering if I were a distant relative.

In addition, whenever I gave readings in Hong Kong or elsewhere in Asia, the inevitable-to-the-point-of-*ad-nauseum* question from some Chinese member of the audience always was *why* won't *you write in Chinese?* The tone was accusatory and sometimes quite hostile. Even when I answered, truthfully, that my Chinese was simply not good enough for me to do so, this was met with further skepticism and, in a few extreme cases, further questioning of my origins and "right" to pen a local Hong

Kong story. In the West the same question was mostly curious, as there was already a growing Asian hyphenated literature in English by the diaspora. The answer about the "who of me" would usually satisfy the questioner, especially in the United States, which is after all a country of immigrants.

This identity-centric audience response was what prompted my then-publisher to suggest I adopt my Chinese name as a byline, and thus, with my second book, Xu Xi was born (or rather, reborn), a shortened form of the Mandarin Chinese name (Xu Su Xi—許 素 細) conferred on me at birth by my father. It is not, however, my legal name, which creates other complications, but that problem of identity for a writer who must function in the nonliterary world is another story.

Initially, it astonished me that name, race, and language could create such an issue for me as a writer in Asia. The Hong Kong I grew up in was, admittedly, a rather parochial, insular, even Cantonese-xenophobic culture, but surely, I thought, these English speakers-readers of fiction were more cosmopolitan than that? Yet I am reminded of the Chinese American woman I met in New York in the mideighties at a management training seminar. We were the only two Asians there and struck up a conversation. She was originally from Taiwan and had lived in the United States for more than thirty years. I had recently immigrated and spent my earlier adult life in the seventies living and working in Hong Kong and Asia and had only just become a U.S. citizen. In myriad ways, I was still far more connected to Chinese Asia than she was, at least in terms of recent life experience. She spoke fluent English with what was clearly a Taiwan Chinese accent and was surprised that I spoke with such American English fluency. I spoke of my mixed background, said that I was married to a Caucasian American. Her startling conclusion, leveled at me with an unbecoming hostility: *well, you're not a* real *Chinese after all*. Such a disturbing example of my ethnic tribe! Here was a relatively successful executive living and working in the United States, her adopted country where she obviously "belonged," who was no longer Taiwanese, never mind Chinese, if passport and country of residence are determiners of identity. Yet upon meeting a fellow Chinese, or at least a part Chinese, her first instinct was to judge my Chinese-ness harshly because of my lack of racial purity and American English-language fluency. I avoided her unenlightened superiority for the rest of the two-day seminar.

What did it mean to be a "Hong Kong Chinese writer in English"? Could such a being really exist?

World Englishes, with its theory of the expanding circles of English, describes a linguistic phenomenon that is a reality today. The term *lingua franca* is applicable to English in the international business and professional world, whether you're in Asia or Europe. Even the European Union adopts English, rather than French, the former lingua franca of Europe, for its proceedings. And ASEAN probably couldn't function if its members couldn't default to English. Certainly, in academic disciplines, most recognized scholarship is written and published in English. In 2013 in Hong Kong, mainland Chinese sometimes resort to English to communicate with Hong Kong Chinese who are less comfortable in Putonghua than in English.

But literary work is another matter.

Wang Ping, a U.S.-based English-language fiction writer who is originally from the mainland and who writes poetry in Chinese and English, describes the dismissive attitude of a prominent American literary critic who believed that poetry could only be written in one's mother tongue (fiction or essays, apparently, could be written in "English as a second language," or so she pronounced). In her provocative and thoughtful essay "Writing in Two Tongues," Wang says of writing in her adopted tongue:

I write in English, and Chinese always runs as the undercurrent in the process. The two tongues gnash and tear, often at each other's throat, but they feed on each other, expand, intensify and promote each other. They keep me on my toes, opening new doors and taking me to places I'd never have imagined otherwise. . . . After twenty years in America, my English is still broken, full of holes, and I have fallen through them many times. But I've learned to fall with grace, and turned each fall into an adventure. One never knows what lies at the bottom, what world awaits us when we come through the other end. That's the beauty of language and poetry: to see the invisible, to reach the unknown through our gracious fumble and tumble.

Further in the same essay, she goes on to say that "a poem must tear away from the mother tongue's zealous cling" and that "a second language gives us new eyes and tools." She concludes with this thought: "Poetry may indeed belong to the mother tongue, but it also belongs to the heart that no logic or rules can bind, to the myth of life that sings with multiple voices." Her belief that literary expression can and does have "multiple voices" resonates for a mongrel writer like myself and gives credence to this very idea of World Englishes. Strictly speaking, I do not write (or speak) Hong Kong English or even Chinese English, nor do I think at all in scholarly linguistic terms about the language when I write. But in trying to find the right voice for my kind of fiction, the notion that multiple Englishes exist as legitimate (or at least recognized) forms of the language is useful. Writing, after all, truly is a series of fumbles through a maze, and language the means to bumble our way through.

Some of this search for the right literary voice was informed by my peculiar auditory, rather than linguistic, sensitivity. As a rule, I do not learn foreign languages easily. I struggle with pronunciation, cannot remember enough vocabulary, hate the study of grammar and rules, and have a hard time learning to hear any foreign language (this was marginally true for Putonghua and French, my only two other languages). My two sisters, whose linguistic and Hong Kong educational backgrounds mirror mine, have a much easier time. One can learn to read almost any language with relative ease (Sanskrit, French, and German are among her languages, and she is fluent in French) while the other can learn to speak pretty much any language she has to (Bahasa, Putonghua, German, and French are among her other languages, and she can learn tourist catchphrases easily in any language). My only brother (who had the same Hong Kong upbringing) and I are the language duds and are relieved we can handle English and just enough Cantonese. My brother is, however, a composer and professional singer and musician, and when it comes to librettos and lyrics, he can mimic anything he must (Italian, French, or German for opera or Latin for religious hymns). I am an amateur pianist and avid jazz fan. Over the years, my ear has become attuned to chord changes, and I can readily hear the melody behind jazz improvisations. I also have an absurd memory recall for lyrics, especially from the American Songbook of the twenties to the sixties, far better than for poetry of the same era. Likewise, I can hear and comprehend most Englishes, regardless of the speaker's accent, mother tongue, or in whatever position it belongs on the World Englishes' linguistic circle. In Hong Kong this is further compounded by my knowledge of Cantonese, as I can hear Cantonese phrases in English (and, oftentimes, the absurdity of a literal translation) as well as the oddly non-Chinese perspective of standard English as it functions in a predominantly Chinese society. The code switching that many Hong Kong Chinese engage in, with both English and Putonghua, falls into the range of my auditory sensitivity. As a result, I instinctively eavesdrop on conversations in this city that are carried on in English, Chinese, and Canto-lish.

Which is a reason why, I've realized, dialogue in fiction was never much of a problem for me. However, what I *didn't* realize, until an editor pointed it out, was how *much* I wrote in between the silence of communication, as, for example, when two people are speaking on the phone or by email or in person in terms of what they leave unsaid. Hong Kong became the petri dish for my study of the global culture that most interested me for fiction. Here was a city where two languages must coexist but where cultural and linguistic confluence did not necessarily occur; Hong Kong is significantly *less* bilingual (or trilingual) than the government pretends it is. Hence the need to tell the story of the life in between, in that "crack in space," as I have elsewhere deliberately mistranslated the "gap" of the subway announcement in Cantonese (空 隙). In particular, when my characters are speaking in English but thinking in Chinese, or speaking in Chinese that I represent in English on the page, I discovered that word choice or syntax can often embrace Chinese expressions, grammar, or syntax. It was a bumbling along, fumbling through the dark at first, with few literary examples to draw upon. Maxine Hong Kingston had given us that wonderful Chinese English term *talk-story* (講 故 事), turning the noun into a complex verb form, and Timothy Mo that *sour sweet* to echo the Cantonese dish, while Hong Kong offered Canto-lish words such as *dimsum*. Yet all this was still something of a curiosity, almost a kind of pidgin. For one thing, Kingston only speaks rudimentary Cantonese, and the Eurasian Mo hardly any Chinese at all, as is the case for many of the early Chinese hyphenated writers in the West. Even Mo, who did spend part of his childhood in Hong Kong, does not necessarily identify himself as a Hong Kong writer.

In fact, not till I began a search backward in time, partially as research for an anthology of Hong Kong writing in English, did I begin to identify with and learn from an earlier diaspora of Chinese and Hong Kong writers in the West who consciously asserted an English Chinese or Chinese

English language and, more usefully, a translingual or transcultural sensibility. Two of the more notable examples include Lin Yutang (*The Importance of Living*) and C. Y. Lee (*The Flower Drum Song*). While Lin remains an influential thinker today, mostly because of his scholarship, philosophical writings, and work in translation, as opposed to his fiction, much of Lee's work is out of print. *The Flower Drum Song* was reissued when playwright David Henry Hwang revived the musical based on that novel, but Lee's other novels are virtually unknown. What intrigued me about both these writers, but especially Lee, was how naturally they were able to render an entirely Chinese world in English. By contrast, Pearl Buck rendered China's rural world in English (she knew Mandarin), but she does use a kind of formality in her English that is meant to represent Chinese speech and thought patterns. While Buck was honored, rightfully in my opinion, for opening up the then-closed world of China to the West through literature, she was also mercilessly lampooned by American critics and writers, including the Algonquin Round Table writer Robert Benchley, who began one of his satiric pieces with the line *It was the birthday of Wang the Gong*. The point is, both Lin and Lee were completely bilingual, and their very fluent English literary works seem linguistically and culturally prescient in retrospect. Today, Buck has benefited from the growing interest in China, as new editions of her work have appeared in recent years. Today, it is not that unusual to encounter TCKs of multiple mixtures, writing in English, simultaneously thinking in Chinese (and other languages), living between Hong Kong and everywhere else in the Anglophone and non-Anglophone world. These creative writers were among my MFA students in Hong Kong. One hailed from Venezuela, his Spanish on par with his Cantonese and English, another was an American in Taiwan who learned Chinese well enough to write young adult fiction in Chinese, yet another in China found voice about lesbian life in near-native English. Their accents are equally as diverse.

Which perhaps means that this "world's English" (as opposed to World Englishes) that we writers share might be turning into a kind of global literary language that will "feed on[,] . . . expand and promote" a host of other languages, including Chinese. But even as recently as the mid to late nineties, when I was trying to find a literary language that would serve both what I could hear and observe in Hong Kong for fiction, it proved to be an isolating experience.

Hong Kong English does not really exist, according to some in this discipline of World Englishes. Moreover (a word I find a curious hangover from colonial Hong Kong, articulated with a pronounced and distinctive attitude), it certainly wasn't enough of a language to justify anything that might be termed "literature." Writing out of Hong Kong in English was not comparable to doing so in India and the Philippines, nor for that matter in Malaysia and Singapore. There simply wasn't a sufficient body of evidence, meaning published literature. Furthermore (also uttered with a distinctive, colonial Hong Kong Chinese flair, perhaps under a horsehair wig), it was implied, how good could such writing be if it wasn't published in London or—and this somewhat grudgingly acknowledged since we were still in colonial times back then—New York? What was left unsaid in Hong Kong was just as noisy as what was suggested with a polite sneer, especially in the academy. Over the years, this made my ongoing presence as a writer around the city problematic. I could be acknowledged as a writer because I came with credentials from the United States and had published work abroad. My English was mother tongue enough to make me "foreign" and therefore acceptable as an English-language writer. Yet here I was, wandering around the city, being this thing, a *local* writer who cared about making the languages and experiences of the world I came from and lived in an integral part of my work. I could not be accused of parachuting in for my fiction as yet another foreign writer (thereby opening my novel with that dramatic but cliché landing at the old Kai Tak airport that every travel writer knows). At the same time, I had been perched at Kai Tak since I was a child, sending my father off on business trips and later sending myself off on numerous trips to here, there, and everywhere. Hence my uncertainty at believing I could possibly be, for real, a "Hong Kong writer in English." Perhaps I was a fictional character, escaped from one of my own novels, pretending to be an author. Perhaps even my royalty checks were like the fake money burned in Hong Kong for the dead and would disappear in smoke when my back was turned. Perhaps I was really still a writer living in New York, and my monkey avatar had journeyed to the East in search of these secular manuscripts that were being passed off as my fiction.

Perhaps even publishing under Xu Xi as a byline was more of a fiction than even I knew. An Hong Kong Cantonese, Anglophone literature professor at one of the local universities asked me why I chose to use such a "strange pen name" (referring to, I suspect, its odd Cantonese sound and feeling). She was rather too startled for comfort when I told her it was my actual name. If even such an eminent intellectual was confounded by my writerly self, perhaps the problem was with that very self? Likewise, I've lost count of the number of times that Hong Kong belongers assume (or misremember) that I am from the city—*aren't you born in Indonesia*, they ask—despite the fact that most of the publicly available biographical information about me (including the information these same people ask me to supply) states this clearly (remarkably, they have no problem recalling that I attended Maryknoll, an elite girl's school). This has occurred so many times, especially in the local academy when I'm introduced as a speaker, or when a bio to be printed is sent to me for a final review, or when I'm interviewed by a local Hong Kong Chinese journalist, that it can't be merely coincidence. The same error hardly ever occurs when I speak to university audiences or the media elsewhere. In Indonesia or Singapore, for example, my Southeast Asian heritage is of interest to journalists, but they make no mistake about my being from Hong Kong. In fact, one scholar who has written about my work was asked not to include me in a locally published book about Chinese Americans in Hong Kong as I was "not really Chinese," which is emblematic of the problem of my role as a writer from these shores. It puzzles me because there are more people like me than not from Hong Kong, with passports of Western nations, lives and homes in one or more countries, with fluency in English and Chinese that is significantly more bilingual than mine. Some even have mixed Asian backgrounds. Yet in Hong Kong, despite my long association with the city, my writer's "face" can feel more mask than real.

My novel *Hong Kong Rose* would have been quite a different book if I had remained in the United States. Released in 1997, it was begun in New York shortly before I moved back to Hong Kong in '92. The story of two sisters, Rose and Regina Kho, who go to the United States for college, is set mostly in Hong Kong with the protagonist Rose as the one who returns home to live. An earlier draft was titled *Red Glare* (echoing the lyrics of the American national anthem), and the protagonist was Regina, who remains illegally in the United States. The published novel details Rose's marriage to her Eurasian high school boyfriend, a marriage that gives her access to upper-class Hong Kong society. It turns into a highly compromised situation, however, when she realizes her husband is gay, or at least bisexual, and she ends up in an affair with an American lover. Yet she chooses in the end to remain in this curious marriage of convenience, which seems to fit Rose's sense of who she is fated to be.

This remains my best-selling and most popular book, especially in Hong Kong; certainly, it is the one that is most widely taught and written about by local scholars. Yet it is the book I identify with the least, and despite a superficial similarity to my background (a Chinese Indonesian family, college in the United States, Rose working for a Hong Kong airline), it is not really autobiographical (the way most of my fiction is not, to a greater or lesser degree). Part of my detachment from this book has to do with what I think of as a Hong Kong sensibility of compromise, one that masquerades as courage or the right way to live. When the book was first published, I described it as a novel about courage, cowardice, and compromise. Yet what I suspect, rightly or wrongly, is that its popularity in Hong Kong has something to do with a local cultural desire to read compromise as a virtue, ignoring the cowardice of the protagonist's character and choices in life.

I do not think Hong Kong is necessarily only about compromise, but it is a dominant sensibility in the way the city functions and is a noticeable characteristic of local Cantonese social interaction, in particular the interaction with Westerners. This latter condition is often what I write about. But just as some scholars continue to insist that Hong Kong English does not (or perhaps they mean *should* not) exist, some of my local readers are comforted by and drawn to a protagonist fated to make a compromise that might appear untenable or even completely ridiculous and laughable from other perspectives. Like all authors, I of course have no control over how any reader responds to my work. What I do know is that the English of my story is all about *not* exerting too much control, in order that my literary language may flow naturally in and out of the worlds it must render in fiction.

Hong Kong writing in English is still only a minor literature and most probably always will be. In fact, now that we are geographically back in China again, as opposed to hovering on our precarious perch as an outpost of Britain, the probability is low that local literature in English will grow significantly. This is neither good nor bad and falls right in the middle of answers to survey questions in the multiple choice spectrum—that too is a very Hong Kong thing, and during my advertising and marketing days, we learned to force respondents out of that comfortable middle by tailoring questions to elicit either a slightly more good or more bad choice (Hong Kong English, at least in my books, for better or worse). Which is likely why the most robust and sustainable "world's English" for literary work is one that is not necessarily rooted in any one country's or society's use of English but will be drawn from the linguistic, cultural, and life experience of the writer herself.

I am that writer, and I happen to write in English. The End.

# AMBITION GAME

Is ambition a game? I hadn't thought so until I was invited to speak at a writers' conference panel of "Smart Girls," women who have sustained careers as literary authors. My corporate life—an eighteen-year parallel existence to my writing life—was a kind of career game, and half-selling your soul was often the menu for ambition. But writing was not the same. That was my soul, never to be sullied, despite my desire for literary success. To unpack the ambition game for myself as a writer, the question I must address is this: what happens to ambition if literary success doesn't come early in your career, as it did not for me?

Here's the problem. I'm Chinese Indonesian from Hong Kong. Quick, name the contribution Hong Kong Chinese Indonesian culture has made to contemporary literature in English. If you drew a blank, that is no surprise because my city is not exactly the literary center in any language. To discover, at age eleven or so, that you're not bad as a writer in English— the lesser language of your city—was my early entry into marginalia. This might not have mattered if I hadn't been born with that ambition gene as well. Because ambition is a gene, an undeniable force of nature that pushes you to play the game, to go for broke, regardless.

Here's the problem. We all come from somewhere, and that somewhere informs who you become, how you look at the world, and ultimately what you write about. Early on, despite a love for literature in English, I realized I would never be an entirely American or British writer, the two largest literary spaces where English-language writing occurs and has currency. Had I moved to the United States or Britain at the age of two with a family that had the fill-in-the-blank Chinese immigrant life—laundry, restaurant, *kung fu* school—I too could write the Chinese American family story that fits neatly under the rubric of "immigrant" or "identity" lit, both of which are recognized and acclaimed in contemporary Anglo-American literature. Given my Indonesian nationality, I could even step in and fill the next identity lit niche—the accidental Muslim perhaps—when the Chinese hyphenated story became passé.

Contemporary life in Hong Kong, however, was not exactly exotic enough, unless you threw in, say, a British colonial East-West transgressive affair, which, to those of us who have real lives in Hong Kong, is as tedious as dragons, bound feet, Suzie Wong, or flying through the air like some martial arts heroine, none of which defines the city of today. However, exotica is what sells in a Western publishing world that cannot yet move beyond its Orientalist romance. Yet the more I wrote, right through my American MFA and beyond, the more I discovered that what I needed to write had everything to do with unpacking my odd city-space—globalized, fashionably consumerist, weirdly postmodern and off-kilter, apolitical, linguistically confused, postnational if you will, since Hong Kong has never been and will never be a nation-state. Instead, my city owes its precarious existence to a very successful "commercial soul"—an oxymoron to say the least—which is not what you'd imagine would decide you down the road less traveled on some woodland stroll with Frost (in my city the phrase would likely be attributed to M. Scott Peck, just as the film *Clueless* has nothing to do with Austen). However, if you're willing to embrace the notion that, as a Hong Kong person, your soul might be similarly shaped, only then will you allow this peculiar brand of "the writer's path" to lead you, uncompromised, where it will.

> *The soul selects her own society*
> *Then shuts the door*
>
> EMILY DICKINSON

Sometime in my midtwenties, despite encouragement from editors and publishers in London and New York, I figured out that the novel about the Hong Kong I knew was not high on anyone's radar. What I also learned was that unless I paid attention to the likes of AWP and what MFA students cared about—i.e., getting into Yaddo or Breadloaf, teaching creative writing at prestigious MFA programs, publishing in the "right" journals—I wasn't going to satisfy my ambition gene as a writer in the Western World. The problem was I didn't really care about any of that, not even the MFA, because the real reason I applied to and enrolled in a program was to get a foreign student visa, which would allow me to quit my business career in Hong Kong, hang out legally in an English-speaking space for a while, and learn how to write what I needed to write without completely pissing off my parents. A master's degree in English sounded legitimate. I neglected to mention the MFA didn't necessarily equate to becoming an English professor at some university back home, which is what my mother hoped.

To get the MFA in creative writing, an unheard-of degree (or ambition) in Hong Kong of the eighties—and even today would still be obscure (and to many, obtuse)—meant a hiatus from a good career in business. That was the life to fuel ambition—well paid, extensive international travel, prestige working for an airline. Infinitely more important in Hong Kong, it gave my family face, which translated into my parents telling friends and family—*ah yes, our daughter's come home with her expensive BA from*

*America and now contributes to family and society.* This Confucian acceptance of duty, especially for an eldest child like myself, is the done thing
for the educated classes. Meanwhile, my peers and colleagues wondered
why I wasn't doing the MBA at Harvard, the degree and university of
which everyone had heard.

It's a bitch, isn't it, being true to thine own self? How can you be
ambitious in a literary space where Shakespeare matters more than Confucius if you can't completely forsake your Confucian world? Life as an
English-language writer with (by this time) an American accent would
have been much easier if I'd just hung out in New York as an illegal alien
in some Chinatown restaurant, done the bohemian thing, and tried to
meet editors in bars in the East Village. That was what I would have
done if I really were a "smart girl." Instead I wrote a version of that life
for a character in my second novel *Hong Kong Rose*. Many books later, I
recognize I have been ambitious or I wouldn't still be publishing fiction
and essays or editing anthologies of Hong Kong writing. Whether or not
the way I did it was smart is something I still don't quite know.

The problem with lurking around the margins is the enforced digestion
of unsavory life lessons.

Life Lesson 1: *You do not belong.* Back in '81 my application for a student visa to study the MFA was denied—U.S. Immigration doubted my
"sincerity," especially as I was a single female (and of dubious migratory
ambitions) and the officer hadn't heard of the MFA. (Besides, we all know
Asian students only study business or science, right?) This so shocked and
angered me I had a public meltdown at the American consulate.

Life Lesson 2: Do not have meltdowns in any place guarded by the
Marine Corps because these towering, hulking, uniformed guys will come
at you, guns and all. Eventually, I begged my way back into the United
States for this dubious degree through a friend of a friend at the consulate.

*Guanxi*, or the Chinese art of leveraging your two and a half degrees of separation, was alive and well in expatriate America.

But the real life lesson was that the American literary MFA world, the one that had come to define my writer's path, held absolutely no meaning in the world I came from. Here was my real problem: How would I balance living that world with my ambition of succeeding as an English-language writer?

Then, life interrupted, as it conveniently does in fact and fiction when we do not know the answers to problems. While studying for my MFA, I met and married an American jazz musician. He taught me everything about jazz and how to be an artist in America. Marriage also meant citizenship that let me work legally in the United States, and I was saved from going home for a while. As in a novel, I willingly suspended disbelief and time, lived in my new home, and wrote in the largesse of an American space where writing in English, or at least one form of English, reigned.

If ambition really is a game, I was a lousy player. Post-MFA, instead of doing everything possible to get published, I instead set about finding a job that paid more than the pittance a graduate teaching assistant made to get free tuition. Where I came from, you simply didn't waste time or money getting any kind of degree to live a downwardly mobile life. In China you could at least invoke the Tang poets, who, despite the Cultural Revolution, are sacred in the nation's literary memory; they may continue to imbibe forgetfulness under willowy branches in permissible penury. Hong Kong, however, is not quite China, and dead poets (of any complexion) are not convincing as role models. My Chinese terra firma was this British colony that never sought independence and was ultimately "handed over," like some wayward child, back to the motherland.

Which means that to be Hong-Kong-ese is a kind of balancing act, and our security, to put it bluntly, is money.

Our citizens buy property in and outside Hong Kong to ensure a home somewhere. We play the stock market, get well-paid jobs, become wealthy entrepreneurs, and acquire foreign passports. We nurse an undue respect for the rule of law in force at the moment since our history is all about a ping-pong match where we don't call the shots and must submit to laws we did not necessarily make. Only after you've retired comfortably do you become generous toward all your overlords because life has treated you well, despite them, and then you indulge, if you wish, in arts and leisure to paint pretty landscapes, play an instrument (these days, a Chinese one), perhaps even publish a book about how fabulous life is in Hong Kong (thus implying how fabulous you too must be), which all your friends and family can buy and then proclaim you a literary genius.

But not if you're ambitious, really ambitious, to write for real, without compromise or self-delusion, the balance be damned.

It's a conflict, this ambition thing. I had to earn a good living to prove I wasn't entirely crazy to get this MFA, which meant playing catch-up to get back on a career track in marketing, the one I rudely interrupted with my other troublesome ambition. I scrambled, got a relatively good starter job in Cincinnati, the first rung on the ladder to the better job in New York City. In the process, I almost went insane.

And here we pause.

In that process, I almost destroyed my marriage, my sanity, and my writing life because ambition overtook common sense. It's like a drug, ambition. It keeps you high, but you become needy, insecure, and eventually, unable to see straight. The problem was thinking I didn't have a choice, that I had to do it all, whatever "all" was (to any feminist, and I claim to be one, this has a despairingly familiar ring) because nothing was ever good enough, safe enough, successful enough. Ambition fueled an unnecessary desperation. Having interrupted my marketing career, I was not as far along as my former peers in Hong Kong who had gotten the MBA or otherwise paid their dues. Similarly, my MFA classmates who stuck to their writing guns were establishing their lives and careers. I didn't just *want* to weep, as characters in novels tend to do. I wept, copious tears and finally, when exhaustion set in, decided to be smart for a change and learn from my mistakes.

Ambition is not a life. This was a strange realization to arrive at given how blatantly obvious it is. But ambition was an unhealthy obsession that blurred the obvious. Instead of going for broke and borderline insanity, I accepted a compromised ambition in order not to compromise the self I had to live. I concentrated on doing my chosen marketing profession well and spent lunchtime buying books to read on the daily New York subway commute. I joined writer's groups, eventually published a little, won the odd literary award or fellowship, found an agent, the one who is still my agent and still faithfully reads everything I send him and gives me, still, the best advice about how to survive in publishing. In '92, Hong Kong beckoned again because the U.S. economy was on a downswing, and I accepted a job offer that brought me home.

It was a good time to be back. Asia was rising, work traveled me all over the Australasia region and Middle East. In Hong Kong a cultural surge was happening in cinema, art, literature, and yes, there even were a few writers in English. And there I was, at the start of it, and at least in Hong Kong and Asia, there was a hunger for our stories told from within and not just Hollywood-style narratives to suit Anglo-American tastes.

The good thing about living life, as opposed to playing the ambition game, is that a space for destiny unfolds. This was to be my feast before the next famine, whenever that might be. My parents are happy because I have a good job in Hong Kong, my marriage is in better shape because I'm not going nuts, I'm reading and writing and forming a writer's group in my home city and introducing others to "workshops" and telling would-be writers about that MFA degree. I'm hanging out at jazz bars where my husband plays with Filipino and Chinese musicians, and one night I meet an editor of an Asian publishing house and one thing leads to another and before I know it, I've sold my first book, a novel in connected stories about a contemporary Hong Kong Chinese Indonesian family. That novel *Chinese Walls* launched my brand of a literary career. The rest is a kind of history I could never have foretold.

Aristotle and Freitag say there must be denouement. Since I haven't entirely given up on their ideology yet, my story needs its post-epiphany quiet. In 1998 I gave up my corporate marketing career. It had been a good run, and the only thing ahead was an even more grueling schedule of work and travel to balance with writing. *Okay*, I told myself, *you've published three books, so maybe it's time to say goodbye to all that and take a chance on the writing life?*

Frost's poem is titled "The Road *Not* Taken." It is easy to forget the "not" because his path down the road less traveled is the one he says "made all the difference." We don't reflect too long and hard over the other road. When I arrived at the fork in mine, I too "could not travel both / And be one traveler." It isn't easy to give up a life you know, one that has been dependable, challenging, provided medical (and even dental) benefits, made you friends, taught you how the world works, lives, and loves, and above all shown you the world in all its splendor and horror. I know now that I would not be the writer I am if not for that parallel existence. But the other road did indeed have "the better claim" on me and, having regretted other decisions in life, this one I doubt I will ever regret.

The moment of decision remains remarkably clear in memory. I was on the forty-seventh floor of Central Plaza, to where my office was moving, staring out at Hong Kong's harbor. My career path ahead was either in that corporation or elsewhere in Asia. I was making more money than I ever dreamed possible and still writing. But now I was also living like a bohemian in my own city, renting a relatively inexpensive place in a marginal neighborhood where a local cultural and arts scene was blooming. My parents still didn't quite get this writing thing, but at least they saw my photograph in familiar newspapers under headlines that read, "Local writer publishes new novel." Even though they never read novels, they saw these books with my name, and knew that universities sometimes invited me to speak. The thing I had tried to explain before now needed no explanation.

Was I still on the literary margins of the English writing world? Well, perhaps, if you view the world from an immovable "center," but now I was shifting the center to where I wrote and helping to make it real.

So there I was, gazing at the Hong Kong harbor, which had been my front yard and muse as a child, staring at this city that worried all my novels, stories, and essays, even those set in Greece, Singapore, or New York, because Hong Kong scatters people all over the world, in some constantly movable diaspora, sparking our restless transcultural and postnational lives. Someone has to tell their stories and collect their work, I decided, and it might as well be me. So this city some Brit once dismissed as a "barren rock," this city that once so amused Queen Victoria with its peculiar reality, this city of skyscrapers and suicide jumpers and some 7 million densely packed people who are still as apolitical, pragmatic, money minded, fashion conscious, and uninterested in things literary as they always were, this city is my literary home, and it was time I owned up to it.

And that, at least for now, is all she wrote.

# THE BOOK THAT SAVED
# MY WRITING LIFE

In 1988, the year Evan S. Connell's novel *The Diary of a Rapist* reappeared from North Point Press, my American Dream life was seriously awry. In October of the previous year, I had just become a U.S. citizen. Shortly after that, I was laid off from the well-paying job that afforded me New York City. Freelancing paid only half my former salary; also, my marriage was in bad shape. I had originally gone to the United States to be a writer. Now, having finished an MFA and having written two novels no one would publish, my writing life no longer felt real.

It was in such a mood that I first read *The Diary of a Rapist*. This is the story of Earl Summerfield, a lowly clerk in San Francisco's unemployment bureau who rails against life in the pages of a daily diary that begins on New Year's day. His disintegrating marriage to a domineering wife Bianca, a schoolteacher seven years his senior, enrages him against all women. Cursed with a certain intelligence, Summerfield despairs at the violence he sees daily around him but cannot control his own violent desires. The novel chronicles one dark year of the soul as he descends deeper into his obsessions and rage, manifest in his raping a local beauty queen on the Fourth of July, a crime for which he does not get caught. He deludes himself into believing that his victim would love him had she the opportunity to know him. His only escape from his private hell is suicide or insanity; the novel leaves his actual fate to the reader's imagination.

The book enthralled me. In the frustration expressed at his existence, and in his desire for vengeance against the world, Connell's protagonist mirrored my own feelings. But what struck me most, at the end of this difficult and painful read, was the uncompromising clarity of Connell's craft and vision. My own private anger and despair seemed trivial by contrast.

Reading this book saved my writing life. It continues to do so even now, this book I still return to, this book with a title you almost want to hide from view.

Evan S. Connell is a writer everyone should read. Born in 1924 in Kansas City, Missouri, his oeuvre to date comprises some eighteen books of fiction and nonfiction. Two companion novels *Mrs. Bridge* (1959) and *Mr. Bridge* (1969) were adapted into a Merchant Ivory film, and yes, the books are far superior. In 2000 he received the Lannan Literary Award for lifetime achievement. Despite a fairly illustrious career, he remains surprisingly unknown. Ironically, one reason is this: Connell writes books for a living. He doesn't give readings or many interviews or teach creative writing or globe-trot the literary circuit like some media monkey. Except for a few odd jobs back in the fifties, including a stint as an interviewer at San Francisco's unemployment bureau, Connell has earned his keep writing literary work in his precise, exacting, obsessive, but stunning prose and has done so steadily since the late 1940s.

*The Diary of a Rapist* was first published in 1966 and was Connell's third novel and sixth book. It has aged well, and today seems remarkably postmodern. The New York Review of Books Press reissued it in 2004. But it was not a book that easily found critical acceptance. In 1966 reviewer Eliot Fremont-Smith, despite praising what he called its "great imagination and impressive skill," panned the book because it was a novel: "Without the diarist's crucial reality," he writes, "the diary is a fraud—fitfully inter-esting, very occasionally slightly moving, not titillating, and mostly a depressing chore." How prescient of this *New York Times* reviewer, long before the titillations of reality T V! How depressing, though, his limited notions of fiction.

A later review, also in the *Times*, by Conrad Knickerbocker, took a different view of "this horrifying, almost intolerable novel" with a pro-tagonist "so beyond the pale of ordinary experience, that he ceases to be a man and instead becomes a case history." Yet he recognized it as "a bold and original piece of writing [that] further emphasizes the importance of Mr. Connell's talent. He knows all the colors of darkness and the full sound of the heart's anguish." But even this reviewer misses the point because the protagonist never "ceases to be a man" because humanity, however intolerable, is not so easily denied.

What kind of writer takes on such a horrifying, almost intolerable subject for a novel? In a 1987 *Ploughshares* profile, Gerald Shapiro quotes from a letter Connell wrote him three years earlier: "My own experience [as a writer] indicates that it is mostly a career of rejection and lost illu-sions." Many writers can identify with this sentiment, which is perhaps why Connell is a "writer's writer." He brings some of that same perspective into this novel. Here is a paragraph from *Diary* on August 8, which is after Summerfield has committed the rape: "Perhaps it is true that Man must close his eyes to see. Changing light & color, we must be prisms. Who can describe us who hasn't seen us from every side? Hmm. Well, as somebody once remarked, there are plays that can't be performed. Yes, and a good many lines already memorized won't be spoken. At least, that's the way I look at it."

Isn't the writer's impulse to observe the human condition and see ourselves from every side? Shouldn't fiction writers be such observers to fully flesh out character, the most fundamental demand of our craft?

The novel's success resides in its authorial challenge, a bold declaration that this rapist, Earl Summerfield, is a man we cannot ignore because his tragic darkness resides somewhere in all humanity, and the sooner we recognize, understand, and transcend it, the better. Summerfield's depravity aside, he does demonstrate a chilling logic and self-awareness in his losing battle against the violence within. To recognize the potential for this same violence in ourselves allows transcendence and moves us beyond despair to hope. Connell understood this important human reality, and for his literary gift to the world, I will be forever indebted.

# TO LOAF, OR HOW NOT TO WRITE A CV

To loaf. Perchance to write?

Life is much ado about Aspiration, or so the brand-marketing image-makers would have us believe. We aspire to fame (and living forever) and wealth, stardom for a second or so on YouTube because *America's Got Talent* enough for the individual to rise as the Top Cat. Of course it's not just America but the whole world that's got talent, as the brand reality of singing, dancing, magicianing, contorting, acrobating, coercing animals and children into little apps of horror has gone viral round the globe in multiple tongues. Babel revisited.

But me? My aspiration, like Larry of *The Razor's Edge*, has long been to loaf (and write a little fiction).

Growing up in Asia as an aspiring writer in English, you had to read the British author Somerset Maugham. He wrote *The Razor's Edge* and traveled around Empire that became the setting of much of his fiction. Later, R. K. Narayan expanded my reading. He was an early Indian author in English who achieved international recognition. Both these chroniclers of the human condition understood the importance of loafing. After all, colonizing was all about marshaling the natives into service for a master or mistress who loafed. Being colonized was all about village life (both rural and urban), where idle minds found solace in mischief instead of loafing. Which is why colonial desires fell off the cliff, all that govern-ing out of sync, and there we go, another country on the independence warpath again.

Loafing entered my life via Larry when I was thirteen or so in Hong Kong, circa the 1960s. The BCC, or British Crown Colony—our city's then-official suffix—was a Valley of Darkness not unlike fourth-century Christianity's conception of BC as a demarcated era until Christ's birth, after which Time awoke, transformed as AD. Of course, PC has since trans-formed BC into BCE, but that's another alphabet soup of our shrunken language. Like heads in some tribes.

But the BCC, now that was the place to aspire to loafing. My teenage life was weighted down by the School Cert, our public school-leaving exam. You had to pass that Cert if you wanted a hope in hell of a life without penury—this was repeatedly dinned into you. When Larry loafed into my life, I was transformed. Finally, a *sensible* adult aspiration. If I too could one day traverse the globe as Maugham had—sexually active and fraught, famous and egotistical, financially successful, an intrepid mind-traveler who lived in luxury—I was indeed willing to buckle down into that hope in hell of a life to loaf in comfort, even if it meant studying for and passing that Cert.

Time, in the way that it will, passed. I got my BA, fell off a few cliffs, and forgot about Maugham but not Narayan. Both were prolific, but the former wrote too much that was forgettable, while the latter offered a tentatively viable model for the writer in English from Asia. Loafing, however, acquired Maugham-ish characteristics in the seventies due to my day job at an airline's marketing department. Hong Kong's airline, a profitable plaything of the Brits. Colonial privilege in this last outpost of a sun-setting empire, surrounded by a world that was fast becoming Post. This was my daily rice bowl, which deserved serious consideration if I didn't want to further provoke parents over my already wayward life. (*Twenty-four, already divorced, should we* really *have allowed her to go alone to the U.S. for university?*) At least now they could brag that I was away on business trips because of a well-paid job for a prestigious employer.

Singapore Slings at the Raffles. Gin and tonics at Penang's E&O. Pimm's Number One at Bangkok's Mandarin Oriental in the shadow of its authors' lounge. I loved the liquor, cities, and hotels Maugham flitted through. After all, my British bosses loafed daily in pubs long after lunchtime (except when their boss called) while their Chinese minions (me included) held fort at the office. My sojourns into decadence down in the southeast were tame by comparison, and the trips were, after all, Business. Up north, loafing acquired a certain formality. Seoul under curfew lockdown after midnight meant my South Korean colleagues loafed till four in the morning over whiskey at the Hyatt's bar. Business meetings, you know, they told their wives. When the moon was high, we glimpsed north beyond the thirty-eighth parallel from our hilltop perch, that invisible divide across which reigned another Valley of Darkness. In Tokyo salary men perfected loafing to a high art—push papers around and attend meetings where you nod at whatever the bosses say all day and then converge around sake and whiskey in the evenings till just before the last train. The next morning, start all over again. Getting drunk in Tokyo was the daily grind, after meetings that accomplished what one phone call could have done. Business decisions, like life, were predestined, this being the Asian way.

Loafing, I realized, was Serious Business.

Then I moved, for a long, long while, to the United States of America.

The trouble with countries with long names is that its citizens are afraid to loaf. *Republic of* plus *Country* is about as long an official name a nation should adopt, and ideally a short form, preferably one syllable—France,

Greece, Spain—is easier on the tongue and puts its citizens in mind to loaf. Multiple syllables are trickier, because loafing must be performed in the guise of work—Japan, Korea, Portugal, Indonesia—although that is at least attainable.

The trouble with countries with long names is that they resort to acronyms—USA, UK, PRC, USSR—which complicate identity and the right to loaf. Which is what happened to me when I moved to the U.S. of A. and eventually pledged allegiance to the longer name and its republic. Perhaps things would have been different if I, like the pioneers, had gone west. But I went east toward the coast that was the longer trek from Asia, to pay homage to all those immovable mountains—Emily Dickinson, for instance, who, unlike Mohammed became the mountain toward which her pilgrims (myself included) flocked. Which is how I ended up in Amherst, Massachusetts.

Baker Street dead-ends in Amherst. 221B was not, unfortunately, an available address (homage must also be paid to heroes like Sherlock who defy detection), so I settled for a lower number. A room of one's own was all I asked, to loaf and write a little while completing my MFA in fiction.

But the Japanese bamboo in the yard had other ideas.

In my truth, universally acknowledged or otherwise, even plant life could not loaf in this republic in which it grew. I arrived in autumn, when mellow fruitfulness soon gave way to winter's wind and a desolate landscape. By spring the dead greenery showed signs of life at the property's border. How pleasant, I mused, while sipping beer on Pioneer Valley Sundays, the irritation of that week's MFA writing workshop critiques already forgotten. By summer, however, humid fecundity erupted into bamboo madness. Roots and shoots marched forth, encroaching the house. *Yep*, said my Farmer Brown neighbor, *Japanese bamboo does that*. According to *GreenShare*, a fact sheet at the University of Rhode Island's Landscape

Horticulture Program, Japanese bamboo (a.k.a. *Polygonum cuspidatum*) first arrived in the Northeast as an ornamental, but "it escaped from cultivation and became an obnoxious weed." You would think, wouldn't you, that the good citizens of the Northeast might think twice about harboring this anti-loafing ornamental that was supposed to just sit still and look pretty? But the gilded cage is still a cage: its inhabitants harbor only one aspiration, escape. To where may fugitive plants go? To "waste places and old neglected garden areas," apparently, where this particular plant is found. Nature not nurture, its rapid spread is achieved by underground rhizomes and offshoots, what horticulturists call "suckers." One born every minute in this fecund land of the free. *GreenShare* is polite (being staffed by New Englanders) and notes that regardless of its being an "obnoxious weed" Japanese bamboo is still found in some nurseries.

So instead of loafing (and writing a little), I was forced to engage in vigorous gardening. Being at least part Chinese, a Japanese foe was de rigueur.

After that, time sped past. First there was The Job in Cincinnati, where I thought loafing would be de rigueur. Wasn't Twain famously misquoted about that city, the one where he'd rather be when the world came to an end, because everything in Cincinnati happened twenty years too late? Not if you're Cincinnatian, apparently. My car, advised my ambitious employer, said everything about me, which was why I should work hard, scrimp and save, and go into debt for the fanciest car I couldn't afford. A year later, I asked to go part-time because the job did not offer enough time to loaf. He was not amused.

Which was why, like Huck, I eventually lit out.

Being American, Huck did not get suckered into traveling in the wrong direction. For one thing, he understood the importance of a river for loafing. The current does most of the work, leaving you free to seek out the moral high ground at leisure. Also, the Mississippi is long, more than

2,500 miles, while the Hudson is a mere 315. Being not yet American at the time, I failed to appreciate this geographical reality. To loaf effectively in the U.S. of A., you need time and a river that goes on forever. What you do not need is New York, New York.

Those "vagabond shoes" tripped me up. Sinatra's breezy voice made the city sound positively upbeat for loafing. There were large companies with structural hierarchies in New York. Surely there was a slot for me to engage in the business of loafing (and writing a little), as there had been in Hong Kong? I was determined to find my way there.

Which meant a brief reprieve from loafing.

It took hours, days, weeks poring over gigantic tomes of business directories in the Cincinnati Public Library to create The List. Two-hundred-plus resumes went by snail to every prospective employer in Manhattan that seemed like an intriguing place to loaf. How Woolworth's got on that list I'm not sure, but I got an almost-interview inside that historical building. But the interviewer never showed up, loafing, undoubtedly. After that mail campaign, followed by scores of interviews at advertising and public relations agencies and companies with cool-sounding names in locations you wouldn't send a pet flea to, one employer finally said, *when can you start?*

The year was 1986.

Here's the spin for parents back home. Top marketing position for America's first detective agency: how *positively* cool is that? And in Manhattan. This was Pinkerton's, the same company that saved Abe Lincoln from the first assassination attempt, and the folks who tracked down Jesse James and his gang. Entrée into my imagined Americana, marrying my youthful literary fascination with the Private Eye (their original logo was a drawing of an eye)—Sherlock, Ellery Queen, et cetera, et cetera—with the Wild West. Both had once sparked excitement and romance in my Hong Kong childhood, when I dreamed of escape with the Lone Ranger.

Here's the real deal. A company that pays peanuts to (mostly) guys to sleep at their security guard posts. A history of strike breaking and union busting by the agents who worked for the Pinkerton National Detective Agency during the 1892 Homestead Strike. A subsidiary of a Connecticut-based parent who were making one last gasp at leveraging the brand but who dumped it a little over a year later, at which time my pink slip arrived and I knew the joys of loafing on unemployment.

Here's the persistence of memory. I was flown to Manhattan, Kansas, for my final job interview because all the top brass were there at a national sales meeting. For a moment, I panicked. Perhaps I had gotten the company's address wrong and the job really was in Kansas?

After I was offered the job and relocation package to the correct Manhattan, it dawned on me that I was working for a MVP basketball team. Now this was attempted loafing on a grand scale. The VPs and their bosses lined up thus. Marketing (my boss) had played for North Carolina; nuclear security, Indiana; chief operating officer, Rutgers; the chairman, Saint John's. The chief financial officer and my director-level counterparts in investigations, administration, sales, all the people I worked most closely with, also had the height for the game. At five foot two, even my three-inch heels didn't raise me sufficiently. You really *cannot* make this stuff up.

Loafing proved difficult, if not impossible, when you're constantly craning upward to the stars.

Pinkerton's was the start of over a decade-long, international, American-businesses-rice-bowl life, one that offered rooms of my own to write without starving but somewhat less space to loaf. There were other benefits. The layoff sent me to a temporary nightshift traffic manager position at a graphic arts and design agency, leaving me mornings to write. Milbank, Tweed, Hadley & McCloy, a Wall Street law firm that became my next employer, had excellent photocopiers at which I could park and produce multiple submissions for literary journals. A few years later, Federal Express Asia Pacific were obsessed with sending managers to meetings all over the world, which meant hotel nights in Memphis, Dubai, Singapore, Hong Kong, Kuala Lumpur, Manila, Subic Bay, to the point where the Conrad Hotel in Hong Kong used to welcome me back by name every time I checked in. Room service means never having to change out of jammies to write. At Leo Burnett Asia Pacific, they were courting the Chinese, which meant short meetings and long dinners (I also met my muse there which every writer needs) and indulging in Mad wo/Men life, the stuff of fiction. Dow Jones was still publishing the *Asian Wall Street Journal* as a weekday daily when I ended up there managing their paper route. I spent dawn at print sites and distribution centers in several major Asian cities, so my workday sometimes ended early. There is a strange calm just before dawn on the streets of Taipei, as the trucks unload bundles of newsprints for vendors, hotels, and businesses.

The paper route was my last corporate job. By then I had published my first three books. In 1998 I abandoned that life to write full time. And loaf.

The trouble with the writing life is that your rice bowl may be filled by the teaching of creative writing. My initial inclination was to pursue the loafing life, so I applied to and was rewarded by several residencies. Eventually, however, I too was suckered into becoming a faculty member at that great American invention—the low-residency MFA—to teach aspiring writers with full-time lives and the inability to loaf.

For anyone who's ever attended one of these residencies as either student or teacher, you know there is no time to loaf, never mind breathe. Ten years of this life in the high-minded state of Vermont meant I had to loaf while teaching by distance. Worse yet, I fell in love with that life, immersed as I was with all those writers for confabs about Everything A Writer Thinks About. Loafing almost fell off the grid.

Until Hong Kong beckoned.

The trouble with going home again is that you know you really can't. Why we do not pay attention to our literary foreparents I'm sure I do not know. Hong Kong beckoned with an enticement—*why don't you head up Asia's first low-residency MFA? Yes-no-maybe*, I replied, because wasn't the point to get out of Hong Kong in the first place and loaf around the world? But I was tempted and succumbed.

The City University of Hong Kong's Department of English was post-colonial with Chinese characteristics, which meant everyone worked in a perpetual frenzy. The real work—teaching—was the least frenzied, but the make-work that filled up hours, days, and weeks comprised mountainous reports that had to be compiled. At first glance, this seemed a barrier to loafing. But the full circle that is life soon reared its dragon's tail—this *wasn't* postcolonial, despite Britain's relinquishing of sovereignty. Hong Kong's natives had never trekked that independence warpath, having been suckered instead into a postcolonial, *colonial* state as the SAR of the People's Republic of China.

Being an SAR or Special Administrative Region has some distinctive advantages. Work is all about keeping your head down, obeying the Supreme Leader, and thereby never having to say you're sorry. It's ideal for loafing if you remain under the radar. Despite our sovereign ruler's long name (and our own similarly long one hidden in yet another acronym), there actually was space to loaf (and write a little), as long as the *appearance* of work was maintained. After a first year of diligent report writing, I quickly realized that a talent for cut and paste was all that was required by the college dean (our department's Supreme Leader), who never read any of the reports submitted. This was the height of colonial civil service: file reports, suppress dissent, and you will be left alone to collect your salary, do what you want to in peace (teaching and writing a little), and loaf. Perhaps Thomas Wolfe was wrong, after all. Not only could I go home again, but I could do so and even loaf again.

But I am a fiction writer, and we still need beginnings, middles, and ends, and no rising action will last forever without a crisis and denouement. In an echo of an earlier time, a Japanese bamboo appeared in the form of Directives from above. In my three years under four different Supreme Leaders (all but one dean of the college was an acting dean), as well as three different heads of English (all but one was an acting head), this thespian crew proved highly detrimental to loafing. The problem was not the work for which I had been employed, namely directing the new program and teaching (and writing a little as befitted my position as writer-in-residence); the problem was the mental exhaustion of keeping up with constantly changing stage directions. It was difficult if not impossible to understand why the university ever approved this first (and to date only) low-residency MFA in creative writing degree program in Asia at their institution. For one thing, the illogical Directives from above suggested a complete lack of comprehension regarding its requirements. I spent an extraordinary amount of time producing numerous revisions of budgets, curriculum, and even additional proposals for other programs which were approved, then disapproved, and then partially approved and in most cases never fully read. The purpose, I was assured, *was to keep* your *program afloat* (remarkable how quickly *our* became *your*). This on top of all the regular reports and budgets no one read. Near the end of the third year of my three-year contract, I finally said in disgust, *if this program is such a problem for the university to cope with, why don't you just cancel it*, to which they all stared at me in horror and replied, *good heavens, no!* Against my better judgment, I renewed my contract for a second three-year term, only to find a fifth Supreme Leader (for real, not acting) and, in the second to last year of my contract term, a fourth head of English (acting) who told the Department of English that his English was not very good. This was not reassuring, since it defied common sense and eventually cut into all forms of loafing when bad English seemed to imply no English was necessary in our department. Thanks to this revolting leadership, "my" program was eventually closed—abruptly, clumsily—just when it broke even and the students and graduates began to get contracts for books and win literary awards internationally. Surely, the point of a writing program is to turn out successful writers? Apparently not, said this Supreme Leader and acting head as they tap-danced the program into oblivion.

And so the crisis arrived, and my job became damage control, winding down the program, responding to shocked students and faculty and others in the writing world, all the while trying to remain calm and afloat. A proper crisis comes with its share of heartbreak, anger, and disappointments, as this one did. But the denouement, meaning the end of my second contract, now that was another story. It was cathartic, tremendously so, because I realized that life could soon be all about loafing.

Which brings me to the present day.

Aspiration be damned. This has caused more diversions from loafing in my professional life and served mostly to puff up the CV. There is a tide in the affairs of men, as Shakespeare penned, if handled correctly, that can lead to fortune. He was staging the declarations around a civil war at the time in *Julius Caesar*, and the dramatic imperative was "to take the current when it serves / Or lose our ventures." As this meditation on loafing spirals to its end, I recognize that I have failed too often to take that current while afloat on a bloated and swollen CV ocean.

It's time to invoke that other dead white male, M. Descartes himself, and reflect instead on doubt. My central existential problem is this: I have stupidly doubted my right to loaf! Finally, thanks to equally stupid Supreme Leaders and their lackeys, I am finally freed from doubt, as Confucius declared a man should be at fifty, even though it took me a decade longer than a good Chinese should.

Still, better late than . . . *Ergo*, I loaf (and write a little), therefore I am.

# THIS DOOR IS CLOSE

Halfway up the stone staircase to the Pousada de Coloane, there is a door with a sign that reads "This Door is Close" (fig. 11). My English-language mind asks—*adjective or verb?*—and adds the "d" to what must be the verb once the rest of the sign's meaning becomes clear. The Chinese translation brooks no such confusion, tense being happily absent from Chinese grammar. Were there a Portuguese version as well, I imagine it would be accurate, here in this former Portuguese enclave, this Chinese city of Macau. It's a little like the name of this verdant bay, 竹 灣, otherwise known as Cheoc Van in Macanese, where the pousada is located. *Bamboo bay* would be an accurate English translation, but I imagine that Cheoc Van perfectly captures its essence for any Macanese, either Chinese or Portuguese.

Earlier this year, 2012, at Macau's first international literary festival, my mind danced between languages in much the same way. It was not always easy to follow the simultaneous translation of Portuguese into Mandarin, as my primary Chinese dialect is Cantonese. My sense of Macau has always been that of a Canto-Euro space. My late "Portuguese uncle" who lived here in the latter part of his life first introduced me to *vinho verde* and the cuisine of the Clube Militar—he spoke Portuguese, English, Cantonese, and probably a little Thai and Korean and a smattering of other languages as well—and I loved the stories of his life and travels around Asia, his familiarity and ease in both the Asian and European worlds he inhabited. At the festival, I was struck by a similar feeling of entering a truly global experience, unlike those of other "international" literary festivals around Asia. The difference, of course, is that English was not the dominant language.

For an English-language author, globalization can be advantageous. English has become the lingua franca of commerce and diplomacy, and the spillover into what passes as "global literature" favors those who write in English. The Anglo-American publishing centers of London and New York are dominant financial powerhouses, and when their best-selling authors trot the globe, everyone pays attention. It's no different in Asia. Since 2001, when an international literary festival first established itself in Hong Kong, the race to bring best-selling authors, especially those with Asian faces or backgrounds or who write about Asia, has mushroomed

11. "This door is close": Sign on the door halfway up the steps to the main entrance of the Pousada de Coloane in Macau, summer of 2012. Photo courtesy of the author.

around the region. As an author from and often in Asia who gets to attend such festivals, this mingling with the stars can be heady fun and a great way to win new readers and sell books. But I must confess I have grown a little fatigued by and impatient with the Anglo-American dominance at the expense of authors from elsewhere on the globe in terms of what gets publicized, translated, read, or taught as "significant" literature.

Which was what made the Macau Literary Festival, and what makes Macau, a space that ignites surprising possibilities.

Which brings me back to doors.

Literature is exciting when there is a collision of sensibilities, when you can open doors that were previously closed to you. My entry into Portuguese literature was like that. More than a dozen years earlier, a Colombian painter who was at the same artists' residency I attended introduced me to Jose Saramago's *The Year of the Death of Ricardo Reis*. This was before Saramago won the Nobel, and his work was new to me. An English translation of that novel was in the residency library; he, the painter, had read the book in Spanish. This was to be the beginning of my ongoing love affair with Saramago, and Portuguese literature generally, and I eventually found my way to Lisbon in 2006. The advantage of the Nobel was, naturally, that Saramago's novels suddenly became readily and widely available in English. In fact, if not for the Nobel, I would probably never have read Kawabata, Mahfouz, Canetti, Jelinek, Gao, or Miłosz. Also, the Columbian painter made me realize how much litera-ture was translated into Spanish that never made it into English. Which was why the Macau Literary Festival excited me with its possibilities of an alternate kind of international literary discourse, one not dominated by the Anglo-Americans.

*Fringe* is an American sci-fi TV series that captured a cult following since its first airing in 2008. In this drama featuring the FBI, a unit called the

Fringe Division investigates unexplained occurrences. There is a parallel universe that can be accessed by a mysterious portal, where a doppelganger of every person on earth exists. Part of the dramatic suspense hinges on the possible collision of these two worlds, especially when timelines are interrupted and destinies fractured.

The door, you see, is extremely *close*, the adjective, not the Chinese English verb.

The notion of parallel universes entrances me because my fish-fowl existence is manifest in parallels. The point of traipsing around the world in search of writers and literature is to prove to myself that yes, this "global literature" I claim as my heritage really does exist. It has been a long and oftentimes frustrating journey as a writer in English who is not situated clearly within a single Anglophone literary tradition, who is constantly on the verge of being fish or fowl or neither. It is too 複雜 to be constantly attuned to the borderlessness of existence, whether in languages, cultures, ethnicities, literatures.

Or even memories. Parallel universes, like the Pousada de Coloane.

I originally booked this Macau trip to hide out for a weekend away from my Hong Kong life. This impulse arose after months—actually, two years—of an intense twenty-four-seven work schedule between Hong Kong and the United States. I had seen the pousada several years earlier when it was closed, just before its refurbishment and renovation. My visit was postponed once, I almost canceled the rescheduled one, and to finally have arrived still startles me. The turbojet ferry ride from Hong Kong was uneventful, check-in relatively easy, and the water in the swimming pool pleasantly cool. So what made me ask myself, with a slight annoyance— *what are you doing in Macau?*

Late yesterday afternoon, I walked along the beach toward the Piscina de Cheoc Van, luxuriating in the sun and sea breeze and fresh air, thinking that perhaps the *why* was simply R&R, nothing else, and that I need not search so hard for meaning in every act. But my walk eventually led me to a parallel world, one arising from memory, from childhood, from when my world was a Canto-Anglo city that readily embraced hybridity because that was just the way things were.

At Dragon Inn, monkeys pranced, a ping-pong ball shot up in a cage on a jet stream, and the swimming pool was fringed by bamboo groves. Once, a green snake fell into the pool, and we screamed as we scrambled out of the water. Down the hill, the nineteen-and-a-half mile beach stretched out across the Rambler Channel toward the horizon. Long summer afternoons were spent on that seashore, climbing rocks, fishing, tasting the salt of the sea when we swam. Afterward, back up the hill, after we had rinsed the sea and sand away, my sister and I would explore the grounds of Dragon Inn, where waiters teased us in Cantonese, where the jukebox played American hits and I first heard Earl Grant sing "House of Bamboo."

Later, dinner was served at the open-air restaurant, where dragonflies and butterflies flitted. Huge bowls of steamed shrimp were shelled and consumed, followed by Cantonese dishes that my extended family and friends feasted on; the noisy chatter across the large, round table was in Javanese, English, Cantonese, Dutch, Mandarin, Japanese, and more, all those languages of my childhood. I don't recall that my Portuguese uncle was ever with us at Dragon Inn, but he might easily have been, along with all the other Europeans, British, Chinese, Indonesians, Japanese, and international people my parents seemed to know. At night I fell asleep to the sound of the waves below.

Dragon Inn Villa used to be an actual inn, a holiday beach motel that offered spare, clean rooms on two floors. The walls were white, the roofs and shutters were a bright Chinese red. The location was often featured in Cantonese films of the fifties and sixties. It was not luxurious, did not have a five-star brand on its logo, and probably had no logo, just a painted sign in Chinese and English at the foot of the hill to indicate you had arrived. Back in the sixties, this inn was rather remote, more than an hour's drive to the countryside where the hills were green, the beaches accessible, and the waters clean enough to swim.

The establishment still exists in 2018 but only as a seafood restaurant. The general area has been developed over the years, transport improved with a new highway, and, in the mid-1990s, all the beaches gracing the old Castle Peak Road—including my childhood seashore—were officially closed by the Hong Kong Government due to the polluted water quality of the Rambler Channel. Four were finally reopened in 2011 with the remaining three scheduled to reopen in 2013. They simply fell victim to the unrelenting pace of progress in Hong Kong, the same progress that assails Macau, which no longer resembles the sleepy village I knew as a child. But you cannot get too sentimental about change in our Chinese-international pinpoint on the globe. New and uncharted territory of twenty-first-century possibilities abound, the way the Macau Literary Festival offered me new mindscapes.

Coloane, 路灣, the district where this pousada sits on a hilltop, is still the *beach road* it once was. There is still a remote feeling to this area. On a partially sunny weekend the beach is relatively empty and the piscina not so crowded as to be unbearable. The Pousada de Coloane itself is a heritage space, and heritage, in our rapidly transforming world, matters, as literature should. A literary festival is not the first thing that comes to mind when you think of Macau, this city where the *golden sands* of 金沙 denote a casino, not a beach. The literary here is fringe, as fringe as my writing in English as a Chinese Indonesian author from Hong Kong is, while I continue to wander and read the world in search of connection and meaning.

At times I wonder, am I trying too hard?

There was a moment in my writing life, back in the heady days of a late eighties and early nineties success streak in New York, when I thought I could shut out these parallel worlds forever. It was exciting to be able to walk up to Don DeLillo in a bookstore, one of my longtime literary heroes, and have him sign my copy of *Mao II*, which had just been released. The *Quarterly* edited by Gordon Lish was a thing at the time, and I attended their readings and met Lish, who was generous with introductions to agents and editors. You could talk to editors at the major houses, and a few actually talked back. And then there was the NYFA, a fellowship for writers resident in New York State, and among my year of fellows, I met Jessica Hagedorn, Kimiko Hahn, Eric Darton, Robin Hirsch. The latter runs the Cornelia Street Café, a legendary space in the Village for readings and other artistic performances, where I got to read as a younger, aspiring author. Some years later, I was privileged to stage a jazz fiction reading there, accompanied by composer David Amram, whom I'd met through the Kerouac House where I was one of their earliest writers-in-residence. And there always was the Asian American Writers Workshop, a home for all of us with Asian faces in the United States who wrote, and the English language was simply the obvious literary one.

Why should I care about Hong Kong or Macau and the multiplicity of the global literary world, on their precarious perches far away from the center of the literary world? Didn't every author still desire translation into English for an "international" readership? What did my parallel realities and memories and echoes of other languages matter?

Wasn't New York good enough?

Once, in the early 2000s, at a reading I gave in the East Village back when it was still hip, a strange encounter gave me pause. I had read a new story set in Hong Kong. One of the reading series organizers, a bookseller and East Village denizen, said to me afterward that Hong Kong was not a city he had ever thought about and added it was not a place he would ever want to visit. Remarkably, he was not being nasty, simply stating a fact of his existence, and that, I by then had begun to suspect, was the truth of many of the literati who swarmed around the provisional village that was the city. Later I told myself that no, New York was not nearly good enough, or at least, not as good as it thought it was when it came to taking the pulse of the world.

Over a decade later, wandering around Macau, I knew the reason to walk the sands of this bamboo bay that is Cheoc Van because it became a doorway to imagination. I know why I came to Macau: to enter this point of an alternate universe, this memory, where Cantonese Portuguese China serves as a portal to a hybrid, transmigratory, international experience unlike any other. Not unlike my life. In the end, you write who you are, fish, fowl, mongrel, or whatever hybrid creature you happen to be, regardless of what supposedly equals "success" for a writer.

It is almost June, the month of the death of Jose Saramago. By now, I have read well beyond this author in Portuguese literature, and thanks to a forward-thinking fringe division in Macau have been introduced to even more Portuguese writers and their literary notions. As Fernando Pessoa—creator of the imaginary poet Ricardo Reis—suggests, we are all heteronyms of ourselves and each other. This is perhaps an even more urgent reality today in our hybrid, complex, multilayered, global twenty-first-century world, regardless of the current reactionary, backward isolationism in some nations. All we must do is locate the right entry point.

As I write this, it's already 2018, and another door is about to close on one parallel track that has been my life. This summer, I will finally leave Hong Kong for good and no longer keep a home in that city. The prospect is both exhilarating and daunting. My mother's death freed me from having to be close by and allows me to live in my rural New York enclave, and also in Manhattan, with Bill. It's a long-imagined dream, exhilarating in its prospects. I will have a road back in time to a parallel piece of my childhood, the sleepy rural world that was Macau, the idyllic summers along the Rambler Channel and at Dragon Inn when the New Territories was truly Hong Kong's "countryside." Both my parents grew up in tiny Javanese villages, and I sometimes think that despite their very urban lives—just as my own has been—a part of them, and me, are really country mice, scurrying out of the city whenever we possibly can.

Yet it's daunting to think I will no longer have a home base in Hong Kong and Asia.

The thing about doors, though, is that they don't stay closed. Late last year, after some two and a half years of pitching proposals to universities around the world, I got the nod from Vermont College of Fine Arts to recreate and expand what the "murdered MFA" (as some of the students named it) envisioned when I first set it up. The program in Hong Kong was a kind of Asian writing MFA; now I codirect a new low-residency program, an international one, offering both creative writing and literary translation. The residencies will simply move around the world, and in each location we'll read the literature, meet the writers of that country, while focusing on the art and craft of becoming a writer, one with international influences and characteristics. One of the residency locations already on the schedule is Lisbon, so that my love for Portuguese literature, albeit in translation, will help shape other writers the way it did me.

As an insomniac child, I used to talk-story to myself in bed about a grown-up life that would place me among peoples from all over the world. The location was immaterial. I made up friends of both sexes, we had no language barriers, and it didn't matter where we came from or what we looked like or where we were in the world. These people became more real to me than those from the provincially insular Cantonese majority in Hong Kong. Yet I had no illusions that they could rescue me from my situation; even then, I was a fiction writer and understood that the imaginary was simply a point of departure. *The Purple Rose of Cairo* was not the rabbit hole I tumbled down because books, unlike movies, are not dominated by sight and sound. Instead, the imagination fills in the blanks around the written word.

I wandered the streets of Lisbon or Istanbul long before I ever arrived in those cities because of Saramago and Pamuk, just as South Africa came alive for me in Lessing's books. Which was probably why, despite the overall insularity of Anglo-American publishing, I decided that there would eventually be readers who would walk the streets of Hong Kong, whether or not they ever landed on these shores, because of Xu. It might take me a little longer, and I wouldn't have the privilege of being yet another New York writer who could simply embrace and write herself into the heritage of American literature, the content and approach to be defined by that tradition. But isn't that the point of writing? Isn't that the reason for parallel worlds? We need them because they offer us alternative imaginaries, those that show us that these are really more like our own worlds than we imagine. Only then may we usefully contribute to broadening Anglophone literature beyond its traditional borders. The door, as some might say, is close, and Macau my unexpected portal.

# BY ANY OTHER NAME

*'Tis but thy name that is my enemy;*
*Thou art thyself...*
*O, be some*
*other name!*
*What's in a name?*

JULIET, IN *ROMEO AND JULIET*, ACT II,

SCENE II, WILLIAM SHAKESPEARE (1597)

The first time my name changed, my father had sat the family down to discuss our choices.

Kolankaling, he proposed.

We guffawed. In Indonesia, you will find tinned and fresh kolang-kaling for consumption, this immature fruit of the feather palm (*Arenga pinnata* or *Arenga saccharifera*). We four siblings had never tasted this in our home city Hong Kong, so all we knew was our parents' description of this hilariously named food from their native land.

However, what intrigued me was the political reason for the proposed change to our surname, one that was *not*, Dad emphasized, a requirement of Indonesian citizens of Chinese ethnicity, as we were. But, Dad also said, *everyone was doing it* under President Suharto's new regime. This was

1967, a year after China's Cultural Revolution began. With Suharto in power, communism was no longer fashionable. So Chinese was out and Indonesian in, including for those of us resident in British Hong Kong which was already too Chinese for Indonesia. Even we *educated fleas*, as Cole Porter would have quipped, did it.

But *Kolongkaling?!* Absolutely not. In the end, we chose Komala.

I was thirteen. The idea of abandoning my Chinese surname at birth, Khouw, was completely, even *insanely* desirable. Khouw was an Anglicized Fujianese or Hokkienese (福建) name—these two terms describe the people and dialect of Fujian, a Chinese southeast coastal province. The former is spelled in pinyin for its Mandarin sound, and the latter is a transliteration of Fujian's dialect. This weird spelling "Khouw" was naturally mispronounced "cow" instead of its correct sound "ko." *Uhh, your grandpop* (paternal), *so complicated*, my mother grumbled, although she may have been wrong, as I've seen the same spelling over the years. Had we used Kho, as our American cousins did, or Koh, as much of Southeast Asia transliterates this Chinese clan name 許 (the eleventh most common surname in today's China, where Mandarin dominates), I would have argued in favor of retaining it. After all, there was no law that said we *had* to do this, and having been raised in Hong Kong, I knew more about being Chinese than being Indonesian, which was merely my nationality. Instead it was my father's business dealings in Indonesia that persuaded him to adopt a new identity. *It's just better to do this*, was his rationale, although it neither bolstered his future opportunities nor reversed his earlier misfortunes due to nationalistic government policies. What he didn't need to say was that an anti-Chinese prejudice prevailed, since any overseas Chinese, or hua qiao, knew this to be our inescapable fate. It was only one of the reasons that my parents separately found their ways out of their Central Java home villages, long before they met, even though they both remained, at heart, deeply Javanese, Chinese, *and* Indonesian.

But any Indonesian who sees us and hears the name Komala knows we're probably Chinese.

From the age of five, upon entering primary 1, I despised my English name. Sussy (rhymes with *fussy* or, worse, *hussy*) Khouw (*moo*) was the most humiliating name to be roll-called publicly in class. *Suzie Ko*, I protested, but with class sizes of forty-plus, I was rarely heard. It was not that many laughed at me. This was a local girls' school of mostly Chinese pupils, so the inelegant English made little impact. But the few "foreign" English speakers—the Portuguese, Eurasians, the odd Indian, European, or English girls—they heard. What mattered most was that I heard that dreadful name and knew it simply wasn't me.

The weird spelling, "Sussy," of my first name was the product of my father's complicated mind. Having been educated in Chinese school in Java and at university in Shanghai, he was taught in Mandarin. To him, the Chinese language *was* Mandarin. The problem was, he left China in 1949 when the Communists took over and ran away to capitalist Hong Kong, where English prevailed in the British colony, but the majority of the population, around 96 to 97 percent in my childhood, were Chinese, mostly Cantonese. And Cantonese was the city's real language. In Mandarin my name is Xu Su Xi by today's standard pinyin romanization (pronounced *Shoo Su See*). But if you reference the Yale romanization (something my father couldn't have known; he was just into creative English), this romanization made for English speakers and taught only at Yale (which the CIA used for years to train its operatives), my name is spelled Shu Su Ssy. I didn't learn this until after my father died, when I was researching Chinese Romanization as background for a novel. *Dad, you got it right*, I wanted to say, but it was too late for him to know how his complex linguistic acrobatics gave me a very right name. Su-su, Dad called me as a child, and when he wrote letters, it was always *Dear Su*. It remains the name of my heart, the name I've always loved, and is not a false rhyme for either *fussy* or *hussy*.

By the time I was six, I hated my Cantonese name as well.

In Hong Kong, my name became Hui So Sai (pronounced more or less as it's spelled) and each Chinese studies teacher, on first calling the roll, would hesitate, frown, look puzzled, and I eventually understood that my name sounded and looked completely wrong in Cantonese. 素 細 means pure and fine, but it is not its meaning but its feeling and sound that poses the problem. *Why isn't it Hui Soo* 蘇 *See* 絲? I'm often asked, because most of the Chinese diaspora worldwide, until recently, spoke Cantonese. This alternative is more feminine, which suits the conservative Cantonese worldview. I'm tempted to reply, *because it isn't and I am* not *some floral mint silk*, but that much transliteration-translation is way too complicated, and I have passed my argumentative state of being. Instead I simply nod in pretend agreement or say, *my father was a Mandarin speaker*, and leave things at that. I would later discover, when I studied Mandarin, that my name in Mandarin raises no eyebrows. It's even considered beautiful. One Beijing opera singer used to delight in intoning my name, his tones and voice perfectly pitched.

Becoming Sussy Komala at the age of thirteen was a heavenly transformation of at least half the clunk of my English name. By then, I had also dropped all use of my Cantonese name.

In my midtwenties, when I published my first story and needed a byline, I chose S. Komala. That struck me as a reasonable compromise. Komala is pronounced the way it's spelled and was a name I embraced. In college in the United States my friends often called me by just my last name, and it was with pleasure that I would hear *Komala!* shouted from across campus by one of my fellow student senators or teammates from forensics or by one of the other English majors. Komala was memorable and, most of all, easy on American tongues. Although that was still many years before I actually became American, when I first arrived in 1971 as an undergraduate foreign student, I already desired to live as a writer in the

United States, this nation where English prevailed but was not England, my colonial overlord.

Komala was also the name that carried me through my early professional career in Hong Kong after college. I worked in advertising and marketing, and when I was promoted into my first private office, I used to answer the phone with just my last name, Komala.

This process that characterized my first legal name change was the most convoluted. As a girl I toyed with different versions of my first name—Suzie, Susie, Sue, Suzanne, Suzanna. I even contemplated taking my middle baptismal name, Mary. My youngest sister had her English name similarly mangled by Dad's creative English into Melee (pronounced *Mer-lee*), but my parents legally changed it to Merly when she was about six or seven, after a European friend explained this Anglo-French word. Today Melee, meaning a fight or struggle, would be perfectly fine as an English name in Hong Kong, since Milk, Chlorophyll, Devil, and Rolex are names people choose for themselves. Forty years earlier, before the language's playful transformation, "proper" English mattered. For reasons I'll never quite understand, my father gave my second sister and only brother real English names, Wilma and Felix. My siblings were all given good Chinese names that passed muster in Cantonese and Mandarin, although my second sister has a masculine one because my parents were convinced she was going to be a boy. Which works now that gender is malleable.

I've been married and divorced twice. The first was uncomplicated because I never changed my name legally, although I did answer to Mrs. Cameron. I was young, somewhat misguided, and in love for a very brief while. The Scotsman lasted a year and a half in this marital misnomer, and after that, I would forever and only answer to *Ms.* The second husband, American, wanted us to have the same last name. For the sake of marital peace—because I refused to take his name and wouldn't accede to his suggestion that he take mine—I agreed to undergo a legal name change for both of us. From the first syllables of our surnames we concocted Chakó and pronounced it *shurko*, vaguely exotic with a linguistically indefensible *accent aigu* on the *ó*. Our creative affectation—he was a jazz guitarist and composer—meant my new byline became S. Chakó (I eventually dropped the accent). Twelve years later, I left him too and wanted my own name back, and I legally reverted to Komala. He, however, kept that name and still performs and records using it. His own name was complicated by his father's Greek American immigrant family background, giving him a supposedly Greek name that isn't, and by the abusive stepfather's name he acquired as a boy after his parents' divorce that he later legally changed.

But becoming Xu Xi, this short form of my Mandarin Chinese name, is my only illegal or non-legal name change. The last. My Chinese name is not a legal name, just one given me at birth, and the only documentation it appears on is our family's genealogical chart, the one Dad compiled in his neat and obsessively tiny handwriting, in ink.

I adopted Xu Xi as my authorial or pen name in 1996 at the suggestion of my ex-publisher. Like husbands, I have multiple publishers, but the latter state is polygamous while the former is not. My first book, a novel titled *Chinese Walls*, was published under Sussy Chakó (I was entirely ignored on my preferred byline S. Chakó and the book's cover design, among the reasons why this is an ex-publisher). The problem was Chakó, or rather the Keralan name Chacko (pronounced as it's spelled), which mine was presumed to be. *But why*, inquiring minds in Asia asked, *is this Indian writing about a Chinese family in Hong Kong?* I was tempted to respond, *because*, no ifs, ands, or buts, just *because*. After all, humanity isn't constrained by borders of race, culture, or ethnicity, so neither is the novelist. Publishing stories under S. Chakó about things Chinese in American literary journals hadn't been a problem. But this was Asia, and

Hong Kong, my home city that pretends to be cosmopolitan, is often shockingly provincial. So I became Xu Xi, because the two X's looked graphically pleasing, and this allowed me to sign the illiterate's X. It also ensured a singularly visible listing in the English alphabet, where few author names begin with an X. It is all in the name.

Today, many only know me as Xu Xi. I suppose that *is* who I am, what my birth name intended me to be once all the convolutions of language, dialect, and identity could be put to rest. It's short, fairly unpronounceable if you don't known pinyin (*just think "sushi,"* I say, *but reverse where the* sh *sound occurs, so* Shu-Si), and confuses English and Chinese speakers alike. However, readers like it. As a byline, it's memorable (*that X-woman*). It's gorgeously complicated, not legal, and vindicates Dad, the parent who helped make me a writer, the author I've always wanted to be.

IN THE AMERICAN LIVES SERIES

To order or obtain more information on these or other University of Nebraska Press titles, visit nebraskapress.unl.edu.